My Kind of Town
Chicago

WEST
SIDE
PUBLISHING

Contributors: Mark W. Anderson, Anthony G. Craine, Mary Fons-Misetic, NM Gamso, Anne Holub, J.K. Kelley, David Morrow, Laura Pearson, Dawn Reiss, Adam Selzer, Troy Taylor, Kelly Wittman
Factual Verification: Kathryn Holcomb
Cover Illustration: Simon Fenton

Interior Illustrations: Linda Howard Bittner, Erin Burke, Dan Grant, iStockphoto, Jupiter Images, Robert Schoolcraft, Shutterstock, Elizabeth Traynor

Louis Weber, CEO
Publications International, Ltd.
7373 North Cicero Avenue
Lincolnwood, Illinois 60712

ISBN-13: 978-1-60553-102-1
ISBN-10: 1-60553-102-2

Manufactured in U.S.A.

8 7 6 5 4 3 2 1

Contents

This City Is Second to None

✳ ✳ ✳ ✳

"The pulse of America." "The most typically American place in America." "City of the Big Shoulders." "Never a city so real." Much has been said about the city of Chicago—the Midwestern metropolis, third largest city in the United States, and hub of commerce and culture rising from the shores of Lake Michigan. That's because when it comes to Chicago, there has always been plenty to talk about: the Great Chicago Fire of 1871, the World's Fair of 1893, "windy" politics, stunning architecture, deep-dish pizza, and Cubs vs. Sox. We explore these topics and much more in *Armchair Reader™: Chicago* to take you on an unforgettable journey through the "big-shouldered" city. Along the way, you'll discover fascinating facts, storied attractions, noteworthy residents, and vibrant neighborhoods.

So sit back, relax, and prepare to get a unique taste—like a dash of celery salt on a Chicago-style hot dog—of the Windy City, past and present. You'll encounter such interesting tidbits as these:

- The legendary Billy Goat Tavern got its name when a goat (that had fallen off a truck) wandered in the door of the bar, inspiring owner William Siannis to rename the dive.
- In winter, many Chicago motorists reserve parking spots they've dug out of the snow by placing lawn chairs or milk crates in the spots, thus announcing "dibs!"
- The taste of Malört, an infamous Chicago schnapps, has been likened to nail polish remover and earwax—oh, and formaldehyde!
- "Resurrection Mary," the city's most famous ghost, is said to linger outside Resurrection Cemetery, looking for a ride.

Enjoy learning about all this and more as you take a tour through a real American city in the heart of the Midwest. Welcome to Chicago!

Freedom of Speech

* * * *

Now a sparkling jewel of the Gold Coast, Washington Square Park was once a haven for great thinkers, poets, and kooks.

Long before we could express ourselves by leaving obnoxious comments on Internet message boards, people sought out "open forums" (parks and cafés) to debate the events of the day. In the 1920s, there were dozens of such "forums" around Chicago. The most famous, however, was Bughouse Square, the park officially known as Washington Square Park that still sits at the corner of Clark and Chestnut. In its prime, some people said it was the most educational place in town. Others likened it to an outdoor mental ward. People of both opinions, however, agreed that it was top-notch entertainment.

According to legend, when Orasmus Bushnell left the patch of land to the city in 1842 for use as a park, he included two stipulations. One was that the city had to build a wall around the park (which, in true Chicago fashion, the city got around by putting up about eight inches of limestone). The other condition was that anyone who wished had to be allowed to make a speech in the park at any time. Making a speech in the park became a popular pastime.

Well into the mid-20th century, one could find several people making speeches on soapboxes in Bughouse Square any night when the weather was decent. Some nights, as many as 3,000 people would crowd into the park to heckle the speakers. In those days, the Near North Side was the bohemian capital of the Midwest, and Bughouse Square was a favorite gathering place.

Drunken Hecklers Didn't Stand a Chance

Some of the great speakers and thinkers of the day made Bughouse Square a regular stop when they came through Chicago, but it was the weirdos and cranks who made the park famous. One regular was Herbert "The Cosmic Kid" Shaw, who was known for taking his audience on "philosophic flights into empyrean realms of thought."

"Weird Mary" was just one of several cranks who often harangued the audience on the subject of religion. "One-Armed Charlie" Wendorf had the Constitution memorized. Since he could—and did—debate such famous lawyers as Clarence Darrow, Wendorf had no problem with drunken hecklers. "If brains were bug juice," he said to one, "you couldn't drown a gnat!"

Daily News columnist Mike Royko believed that the weirdos made the park a perfect stop for suburbanites. After one night there, they could go back to their quiet neighborhoods and tell all their friends they'd seen a crazy man give a speech about free love—right out in public!

Today, the Whole World Is Bughouse Square

By the 1970s, the neighborhood around Bughouse Square had gone badly downhill. Clark Street had always been known for squalor, but it had gotten too dangerous for any but the bravest to venture to Bughouse Square at night. And, anyway, by then everyone had a television set to entertain themselves after dark. Open forums had gone out of style. In 1969, Royko noted that he had just walked by the park and had not seen a single soapbox orator.

But the loss was hardly lamented. When Jack Sheridan, a former regular who had presided over a Druidic funeral in the park when The Cosmic Kid died, was asked in 1971 whether he missed the park, he chuckled and said, "Don't need to. The whole world is Bughouse Square now!"

Today, Bughouse Square is a quiet Gold Coast park. But once every summer, the nearby Newberry Library sponsors the Bughouse Square Debates. On those days, the weirdos, cranks and poets of the city head back to the park, just as they did back in the day.

✳ ✳ ✳ ✳

- *Topics at recent Bughouse Square Debates have ranged from immigration to foie gras to the Family and Medical Leave Act.*

A Mile Is All You Need

✳ ✳ ✳ ✳

Chicago isn't called the City of the Big Shoulders for nothing. Its buildings hulk like steel and glass mountains over the Midwest and have made the city the capital of American industry and architecture. But the skyline could have loomed larger— or at least taller.

Today, Chicago houses the Willis Tower (formerly known as the Sears Tower), which is one of the tallest buildings in the world. At 1,450 feet, however, it's only about a quarter the size of Frank Lloyd Wright's never-built, mile-high skyscraper, the Illinois.

With 528 stories and a 400-foot spire, Wright's building would have stood, literally, a mile high. And that seems to have been the point. Originally depicted in Wright's 1956 design as a soaring edifice along the lake, the building was meant to house hundreds of thousands of people, as well as the entire state government. Indeed, it would have been—and still would be—taller than any other building in history.

Sources say Wright knew that the building would never be funded, but he was committed both to the integrity of his design— confident that the building, to be made of steel, could weather the extreme conditions a mile above the surface of the earth—and to a utopian ideology. In a 1957 interview with Mike Wallace, he defended his design and described a skyscraper "where everybody would have room, peace, comfort, and every establishment would be appropriate to every man."

The design is astounding and different from that of the low, open houses Wright designed throughout his storied career. But it's also quintessentially Chicago and reminiscent of the modern designs cropping up in Europe a few years earlier—those that would, a generation after Wright's design faded into obscurity, begin to dominate Chicago's landscape. The most famous of these, naturally, is the tallest building in town—in the hemisphere, actually—though it remains, by comparison, nothing to write home about.

Timeline

1673
Louis Joliet and Jacques Marquette explore the Chicago area for France. Joliet recognizes that the area could be an integral spot if settlers built a canal between Lake Michigan and the Illinois River.

1770s/early 1780s
Catherine and Jean Baptiste Pointe DuSable, the first recorded Chicago residents, establish a fur trading post north of the river.

1803
Fort Dearborn, the first United States army fort in the Chicago area, is constructed.

August 15, 1812
More than 60 soldiers, women, and children are massacred during a Potawatomi raid on a column of Fort Dearborn settlers on their way to Fort Wayne.

April 1832
The Black Hawk War begins when militia fire shots at a band of Sauk Indians waving a white flag. Three months later, it ends with some 7,000 American army regulars overwhelming Chief Blackhawk and his men, killing most of them and driving the rest from the region that will become the Chicago metropolitan area.

1847
Reaper inventor Cyrus McCormick arrives in Chicago. He establishes a factory that will merge with several other farm equipment manufacturers to form International Harvester in 1902.

1847
The *Chicago Tribune*, the city's most influential paper, is founded as the *Chicago Daily Tribune*. It is one of the only dailies in the nation to be published continuously from the middle of the 19th century up to the present day.

1850
The Pinkerton National Detective Agency is founded in Chicago. Specializing in corporate intelligence, the agency will become well known for its successful strikebreaking activities.

April 21, 1855
Chicago's first riot ensues in response to a power grab by a small group of temperance advocates who raise the city's liquor license fees while shortening their terms. Irish and German saloon owners and patrons strongly object, and the Lager Beer Riot ends with some 60 arrests and one fatality.

1856
Chicago begins to raise the grade of its streets to improve drainage and allow for an underground sewer system. Many existing buildings are raised between four and fourteen feet, and often the buildings are raised with business going on as usual inside!

1860
Chicago hosts the Republican National Convention, the first of many conventions to be held in the city.

(Continued on p. 56)

South Side Pride

★ ★ ★ ★

White folks called it the "Black Belt," but African Americans
ultimately dubbed their Near South Side community "Bronzeville,"
a name that radiated optimism for a better way of life.

In segregated Chicago at the beginning of the 20th century, many
neighborhoods were off-limits to African Americans. Newcomers,
many of whom came from the Deep South in search of employ-
ment, were able to make themselves at home in Bronzeville, a
neighborhood bordered by 31st Street on the north, State Street
on the west, Pershing Road to the south, and Grand Boulevard
(now King Drive) on the east. Little did they know that their
"Black Metropolis" would become a major center of African
American culture.

At the Center of Things

Entrepreneurs such as Jesse Binga and Anthony
Overton settled in Bronzeville and set up businesses. Binga specialized in real estate and
banking, while Overton's areas of expertise
ranged from cosmetics to banking to insurance to publishing. Bronzeville became the
center of black business and cultural life in
the city, boasting America's most important
and widely read black newspapers and one
of the country's largest religious congrega-
tions, which was housed in Pilgrim Baptist
Church, an Adler and Sullivan masterpiece.

Andrew "Rube" Foster

At the neighborhood's peak, its commercial districts were filled
with nightclubs, theaters, and movie palaces, all of which attracted
the cream of America's black entertainers. Such legendary figures as
Sam Cooke, Lou Rawls, and Louis Armstrong performed in the
neighborhood from time to time, and such pioneers and visionaries
as Negro National Baseball League founder Andrew "Rube" Foster,

civil rights activist and NAACP organizer Ida B. Wells, pioneering female pilot Bessie Coleman, and Pulitzer Prize–winning poet Gwendolyn Brooks each called the area home at various times. Gospel music found its roots in the work of Thomas A. Dorsey, music director of the Pilgrim Baptist Church. Jazz and blues also flourished in Bronzeville.

Falling on Hard Times

Like the rest of the nation, Bronzeville took a hit during the Depression, and numerous banks and businesses closed. Several industries did hang on, however, until the 1960s, when turbulence and economic neglect began to ravage the community. The area around Bronzeville began to experience the kinds of poverty rates, abandoned property, and population declines associated with inner-city decay elsewhere in the nation. For more than 30 years, Bronzeville struggled with a lack of jobs and opportunities and a feeling of isolation that stood in stark contrast to its vibrant history.

The Comeback Kid

By the turn of the next century, the neighborhood had begun to show encouraging signs of a comeback. Historians, community organizations, and longtime residents began touting the area's historic importance. In 1998, the city designated the area from 31st to 35th Streets and King Drive to Michigan Avenue (once known as "The Gap") the Black Metropolis–Bronzeville Historic District.

Recent restoration efforts have focused on bringing restaurants, art galleries, and other enterprises to the area. In 2009, Bronzeville was chosen as the site of the first cohousing development in Illinois. Residents will have private condominiums but will share other common spaces, such as hobby rooms and children's play areas. Residents will also eat several meals together each week. These and other new innovations are reshaping the heart of black Chicago.

✶ ✶ ✶ ✶

- *A 2006 fire left Pilgrim Baptist Church in ruins. Community groups are currently working on raising funds to rebuild.*

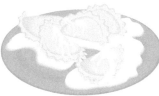 Chicago Cuisine

Chicago is internationally known for its deep-dish pizza and mouthwatering hot dogs, but the pierogi—a subtler contender for the quintessential Chicago food— might one day overtake them both.

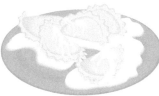

The traditional pierogi is a crescent-shape or semicircular dumpling made of unleavened dough. It can be either boiled or fried, and it is always stuffed. While mashed or shredded potatoes are its most common filler, it might also contain meat, fruit, cheese, onion, cabbage, mushrooms, sauerkraut, or some combination of all of these. Sour cream, melted butter, and applesauce are served as condiments to the pierogi, and garnishes might include bacon, onion, or mushrooms.

Though pierogi lovers consider it unique, many other ethnic groups have their own version of the stuffed dumpling. The Italians have their ravioli, the Jews have their kreplach, and the Chinese have their wont-ons. The pierogi itself is prepared and eaten not only in Poland but also across Eastern Europe and in parts of Russia and Ukraine. The exact roots of the word *pierogi* are not known, but they are clearly Slavic. In Poland, one would call a single dumpling a *pierog,* with *pierogi* being the plural of the word. Here in America, however, even most people of Polish origin would refer to a plate of the dumplings as *pierogies.*

The Pierogi's Home Away from Home

It is certainly no mystery as to why Chicago has become the pierogi's home away from home in the United States. Though in 1860 there were only about 500 Poles living in the Chicago area, that number exploded in the latter half of the 19th century, when many Poles with livestock experience moved to Chicago to work in the burgeoning meatpacking industry. Currently, more than one million people of Polish ancestry live in Chicago, making it the largest Polish community in the world after Warsaw.

Though such cities as Milwaukee, Detroit, and Cleveland also have large Polish populations, Chicago is generally regarded as the capital of

Polish culture and cuisine in America. When the first Polish pope, John Paul II, came to America in 1979, he insisted on visiting Chicago—the first pontiff to do so. The Polish Museum of America is located in Chicago (984 North Milwaukee Avenue), along with such groups as the Polish American Association, the Polish National Alliance, and the Polish Highlander's Alliance of North America. Every Labor Day weekend, Poles celebrate their heritage at the Taste of Polonia Festival in Jefferson Park, their political influence demonstrated by past attendance of such hand-shakers as George H. W. Bush, Dick Cheney, and Tipper Gore.

Traditional or Nouveau, Pierogies Are Always Delicious

Some pierogi fans are hardcore traditionalists, and there are many restaurants and Polish delis in Chicago that suit their time-honored tastes. Szalas Restaurant on the South Side, Halina's Polish Delights in Harwood Heights, and Lutnia on Belmont Avenue all prepare pierogies old-school style. Fans of Smak-Tak!, in Jefferson Park, claim that the garlic filling and extra butter and onion used in their pierogies make them the closest thing to the dumplings of Poland that can be found in the United States.

For those with more adventurous tastes, however, some Chicago chefs at more upscale restaurants are reinventing the pierogi for the 21st century. At Alinea, chef Grant Achatz has experimented with mustard in his pierogies, creating a spicier, more exciting version of the old favorite. Vie's chef Paul Verant's twist is a chicken sausage stuffing for a heartier-than-usual pierogi experience. Chicago chef Michael Baruch, in his book *The New Polish Cuisine,* shakes up both the fillings (spinach, feta cheese) and the dough (a sour cream base).

Old school or upscale, pierogies have finally taken their place as one of the select foods Chicagoans claim as their own.

✳ ✳ ✳ ✳

- *Kosciuszko, Mississippi—birthplace of Oprah Winfrey—was named for Tadeusz Kosciuszko, a Polish hero of the American Revolutionary War. Kosciuszko was a talented engineer who designed fortifications at Saratoga and West Point.*

A Ticket to Ride

* * * *

*For William Rand, the railroad boom
proved to be the ticket to a publishing empire.*

It may be hard to believe that Rand McNally, a company known for its highway maps, actually got its start before the automobile. This publishing giant dates its inception to 1856—a time when the burgeoning rail industry was hailed as the future of the United States. Bostonian William Rand knew opportunity when he saw it; he packed his bags and headed to Chicago, an area destined to become a railroad hub due to its prime location on the shores of Lake Michigan. Rand set up a small printing shop and got to work producing rail tickets.

Two years later, Rand hired Irish immigrant Andrew McNally, an experienced printer. By 1868, the men had become partners, establishing Rand McNally & Company and assuming control over the *Chicago Tribune*'s printing shop. Business increased as the pair began printing railway timetables along with the tickets.

Grace Under Fire

In 1871, disaster struck Chicago as the Great Fire swept the downtown area. With flames racing toward the plant, Rand and McNally had the foresight to bury two printing presses in the sand along Lake Michigan. A mere three days later, the men had the presses up and running in a newly rented shop. This little nugget of company lore remains a source of pride more than a century later.

Mapping Out the Future

By 1872, Rand McNally's future success was on the map—literally. Using an innovative new printing technology that relied on wax engraving, Rand McNally & Company included their very first map in a railroad guide. The wax engraving process allowed the company to mass-produce maps in a cost-effective fashion. By 1880, Rand McNally employed 250 workers and had become the largest producer of maps in the United States. Rand McNally's reputation as a premier mapmaker allowed the company to branch out into the educational publishing market with globes, atlases, and yearly geography textbooks that included pictures, diagrams, and maps.

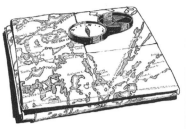

Navigating Success

Rand retired at the turn of the century, and McNally died of pneumonia in 1904. McNally's descendants continued to run the firm successfully. Not surprisingly, Henry Ford's mass-produced automobiles proved to be a boon to the mapmaking business. In 1907, Rand McNally began producing its popular *Photo Auto Guides,* which added arrow overlays to maps to help automobile owners find their way around—perhaps marking the last time in history that American men would actually seek out directions when driving. Renowned aviator Charles Lindbergh boosted sales further when he revealed that he used Rand McNally railroad maps to navigate.

In the 1940s, the company published the work of Thor Heyerdahl, a maverick anthropologist and geographer who believed that the Polynesian people descended from ancient South Americans who had sailed to the distant South Pacific islands. The scientific community largely rejected Heyerdahl's theories, but when Rand McNally published *Kon-Tiki: Across the Pacific by Raft,* the book sold more than a million copies in its first few years. It is still in print today.

Over the years, maps and atlases have remained at the center of the company's business, but the firm has kept pace with the times by offering trip-planning services online. Although the McNally family sold their interest in the company in the 1990s, the firm is still based in the Chicago area and remains one of the world's most respected cartography firms.

✷ ✷ ✷ ✷

- *The Rand McNally* Road Atlas *we all know and love (and have jammed under the front seat of our cars) got its start in 1960. Did someone say road trip?*

Quiz

How well do you know Chicago?

1. The William Wrigley Jr. Company sold what product before switching to chewing gum in 1892?

a) Umbrellas
b) Baseballs
c) Sugar
d) Baking soda

2. Who left nearly 70 Impressionist paintings to the Art Institute when she died in 1918?

a) Juliana Brooks Armour
b) Bertha Palmer
c) Harriet Pullman
d) Mary Shedd

3. On a busy day, nearly 240,000 people pass through this structure.

a) Hubbard's Cave
b) Union Station
c) Navy Pier
d) O'Hare Airport

4. Which famous Chicagoan claims not to watch television?

a) Michael Jordan
b) Oprah Winfrey
c) Bill Murray
d) Vince Vaughn

5. When did the Sears Tower open?

a) 1961
b) 1967
c) 1973
d) 1979

6. Who designed the Auditorium Theatre?

a) Frank Lloyd Wright
b) Burnham and Root
c) Mies van der Rohe
d) Adler and Sullivan

7. Philip Armour, Marshall Field, Potter Palmer, and George Pullman are all buried in which cemetery?

a) Rosehill
b) Graceland
c) Holy Sepulchre
d) Bohemian National

Answers: 1. d, 2. b, 3. d, 4. b, 5. c, 6. d, 7. b

18

Fast Facts

- One of Chicago's earliest pioneers was Jean Baptiste Pointe DuSable, a Haitian who spoke several languages, ran a successful farm, and got on well with the Native Americans in the area. His granddaughter's birth (October 8, 1796) was the first birth officially recorded in Chicago.

- Mother Frances Xavier Cabrini, the first U.S. citizen to become a Catholic saint, worked to help Chicago's poorest Italian immigrants. She founded two local hospitals and a school in Chicago, plus 67 orphanages worldwide.

- Walt Disney attended McKinley High School on the West Side and did cartoons for the school paper. The Disney family later donated a large sum of money to fund the Walt Disney Magnet School, which focuses on art and technology.

- The last Republican mayor of Chicago was William Hale "Big Bill" Thompson, whose last term ended in 1931. As a campaign stunt, he once staged a debate between himself and two live rats (meant to symbolize his adversaries).

- Two Chicago mayors have been assassinated in office: Carter Henry Harrison Sr. (d. 1893) and Anton Cermak (d. 1933).

- Chicago brothers Pops, Butch, and Peanuts Panczko racked up more than 250 arrests in 60 years, for burglary, auto theft, pickpocketing, dognapping, and more. From 1930 to 1990, they stole anything they could move. During each arrest, when asked his occupation, Pops replied: "Thief."

- After World War II, Jack Muller left the Navy and became a Chicago cop. Unlike many of his colleagues, the incorruptible officer would ticket anyone. He ticketed Mayor Richard J. Daley, Governor Stratton, and even mobsters Tony Accardo and Sam Giancana. Muller died of kidney failure in 2005.

Bringin' Down the House

* * * *

*Many Chicagoans must have been mystified when Mayor Daley
declared August 10, 2005, "House Unity Day." But younger
generations were surely grateful for the shout-out.*

What was Daley celebrating? If you have to ask, you've shown your
age! (Don't worry—we won't tell your peeps.) House Unity Day
celebrated Chicago as the birthplace of "house music," a style of
electronic dance music that marked its 21st anniversary in 2005 (also
the 21st anniversary of the founding of Chicago's Trax Records).

That's the Way (I Like It)

In the 1970s, disco ruled supreme on dance floors across America.

But by the early 1980s, the scene was
suffering from backlash, and Chicago DJs
decided to get creative with disco. It happened first in a Chicago nightclub called the
Warehouse. The Warehouse location
bounced around a bit, finally landing on
South Jefferson. The club attracted a largely
African American, Latino, and gay clientele,
and it rivaled such well-known New York
clubs as Paradise Garage when it came to
atmosphere and music. Clubs in Washington, D.C., were still playing
go-go style dance music, and in New York, hip-hop was gaining
ground. But at the Warehouse, Chicago began laying the foundation
for house music—one of the most enduring styles of dance music the
world has seen.

A Man by the Name of Knuckles

House music got its start when DJs began to experiment with disco
records—adding sequencer effects, reverb, and the newly available
sounds of the stand-alone drum machine to create an edgier sound.
If there was a godfather of house music, it was Frankie Knuckles. A

New York–born DJ who was supplanted to the Warehouse in 1977, Knuckles was among the first to spin and mix what is now known as house music. Knuckles's sound—with raw, drum machine–based edits and heavy effects on the vocals—made him a popular producer, remixer, and composer. House music spread to such Chicago record stores as Importes Etc., where the term "house music" allegedly referenced music played at the Warehouse.

Knuckles wasn't the only major DJ on the scene. Ron Hardy spun his house music at the Music Box and Larry Heard (aka "Mr. Fingers") provided healthy competition at the Powerplant. Between these DJs and the throngs of dancers who loved the repetitive, "four-to-the-floor" style of dance music, songs such as Knuckles's "Your Love" became instant club anthems.

The Hot Mix

Detroit got its hands on the trend in the 1980s, with radio station 102.7 FM WBMX featuring "the Hot Mix 5" with local house DJ Ralphi Rosario live at the turntables. The sound of house music began to change, becoming more technologically influenced. Chicago and Detroit shared DJs, ideas, and gigs and played a significant role in popularizing house music. Though DJs across the pond had been experimenting with the house style for some time, the genre took off in a huge way during the late 1980s. American DJs were invited to play huge clubs in the UK throughout the 1990s.

The Culture of the Dance Floor

When clubgoers visited any of the Chicago clubs to hear the early house DJs spin, they crowded the dance floor in a style of dance called "jacking," which meant moving the torso forward and backward in a rippling motion. The freestyle dancers also incorporated salsa and traditional disco moves. Most of the "house-heads" wore T-shirts and sneakers, and some even wore headbands to keep the sweat out of their eyes while grooving to the music all night long.

House music is alive and well—as evidenced by Mayor Daley's commemoration of the musical style through House Unity Day. We imagine the music isn't Mayor Daley's style, but who knows? Maybe he's jacking at a club this very second!

The Voice of Chicago

* * * *

When Mike Royko talked, Chicago listened.

Pulitzer Prize–winning columnist Mike Royko
was a man of the people. Over his 30+ years in
journalism, he worked for the *Daily News,* the
Chicago Sun-Times, and the *Chicago Tribune,*
ultimately penning approximately 7,500
columns. At the time of his death, Royko was
the most widely published columnist in the
country—syndicated in more than 600
newspapers nationwide. He had his finger
on the pulse of Chicago, with column topics
that ranged from art to politics to discrimination to the Cubs. Royko even dedicated a

column to a topic that is near and dear to many a Chicagoan's heart:
the precise recipe for a Chicago-style hot dog. He said, "I won't
condemn anyone for putting ketchup on a hot dog. This is the land
of the free. And if someone wants to put ketchup on a hot dog and
actually eat the awful thing, that is their right." Indeed.

Chicago, Born and Bred

Raised on the Northwest Side by Polish/Ukrainian parents, Royko
came by his blue-collar wit honestly. He grew up loving baseball and
working at various menial teenage jobs. When his parents bought a
tavern and moved the family into the flat above it, his father began
to drink heavily and carouse with other women. Though this was
undoubtedly painful for the young Royko, the quirky patrons who
frequented the bar provided him with a wealth of material for his
future writing career.

Later, Royko took college courses at Wright Junior College, the
University of Illinois, and Northwestern, but he never graduated.
He enlisted in the air force and was sent to Korea for the final
months of the Korean War. After the war he was transferred to

O'Hare Field (then a military base), and it was during his service there that he began writing in earnest. He convinced his superiors to allow him to edit the base newspaper because he did not want to cook or work as a military police officer. He later recalled, "It struck me that any goof could write a newspaper story." Royko continued his journalism career after his service and began working for the *Daily News* in 1959.

No Need to Mince Words

Although he was a liberal, Royko had no patience for political correctness. Following Royko's salty opinions on everything from Mayor Daley to Catholic theology, readers felt as though they were in conversation over a drink at the corner bar. Royko's columns ran the gamut—from humorous ("Complete Apology for Overrating the Irish Thirst," March 15, 1966, and "How to Cure a Hangover: First Try Moaning," December 27, 1974) to sentimental ("Algren's Golden Pen," May 13, 1981, and "Daley Embodied Chicago," December 21, 1976) to enraged ("How This City Really 'Works,'" May 31, 1974, and "Ghetto Burial for a GI Hero," March 19, 1968). Chicagoans trusted Royko's even vision and his love of life, imperfections and all. They looked to his column to laugh during the good times and for wisdom and insight when times got hard.

The More Things Change . . .

As many parts of the city gentrified, Royko invented High-Rise Man, Lakefront Man, Health Club Man, and Singles Bar Man to express his frustration in such "sissy" changes. As long as Mike Royko was alive and writing, a bit of that tough, old Chicago survived. He died of complications from a brain aneurysm in April 1997, and the city hasn't been the same since.

✳ ✳ ✳ ✳

"The subject of criminal rehabilitation was debated recently in City Hall. It's an appropriate place for this kind of discussion because the city has always employed so many ex-cons and future cons."

—Mike Royko, *Chicago Tribune,* March 6, 1985

Local Legends

Chicago's old Water Tower stands more than 150 feet tall along the world-famous Magnificent Mile—one of the city's most popular tourist attractions. However, many visitors don't realize that the site is haunted by a hero who died during the Great Chicago Fire.

On the evening of October 8, 1871, the Great Chicago Fire began behind the home of Patrick O'Leary. Contrary to popular belief, the fire was not started by a cow kicking over a lantern. Nevertheless, the flames did originate in the O'Leary's barn.

When the smoke cleared a couple of days later, charred buildings and ashes littered the city. The fire had cut a path nearly a mile wide and four miles long, leaving more than 100,000 people homeless. Approximately 300 people died in the fire, but the heat was so intense that only 125 bodies were recovered. One of those bodies was a suicide victim found inside the Chicago Water Tower.

A Hero's Last Resort?

According to legend, a lone firefighter remained steadfast at the water-pumping station in Chicago's Streeterville neighborhood, trying to save as many homes as possible. But as the flames closed in around him, he realized it was a losing battle. With his back to the Chicago Water Tower, there was no place to run.

As the fire edged closer, the brave firefighter considered his options. Apparently, a slow death by fire seemed more frightening than a quicker end by his own hand. So the story goes that the firefighter climbed the stairs inside the Water Tower, strung a rope from a beam near the top of the structure, and, in a moment of desperation, looped the rope around his neck and jumped to his death.

The Solitary Ghost

The heat of the fire did not destroy the Chicago Water Tower, but it scorched everything inside. The heroic fireman's identity was never known, but his spirit lingers. Hundreds of people have seen the sad figure of the hanging man and smelled smoke inside the tower, especially on October nights around the anniversary of the tragedy.

From outside the historic structure, some people see a pale man staring down at them from a window near the top of the tower. His expression is sad and resigned, and he seems to look right through those on the ground.

Other visitors have reported an eerie, sorrowful whistling that seems to come from inside the structure. It echoes through the tower, and then it stops abruptly.

However, most people who've seen the Water Tower ghost describe him as having a rope around his neck, swinging and turning slowly. His face is twisted, grotesque, and highlighted as if flames are just beneath him. The ghost appears so real that many witnesses have called police to report a suicide. But most responding officers, who have often seen the apparition themselves, know that he's a ghost . . . and a reminder of valor during a tragic fire more than a century ago.

- *In 1871, just an inch of rain fell in Chicago between July 4 and October 9, setting the stage for Chicago's great conflagration. Shoddy construction and an understaffed and poorly equipped fire department allowed the fire to rage out of control.*

- *Oscar Wilde once famously called Chicago's old Water Tower "a monstrosity with pepper boxes stuck all over it," but Chicagoans revere the tower as a symbol of the city's resilience, spirit, and hope for the future.*

Chicago Chatter

"In the midst of a calamity without parallel in the world's history, looking upon the ashes of thirty years accumulations, the people of this once beautiful city have resolved that CHICAGO SHALL RISE AGAIN."

—Joseph Medill, in the first post-Fire issue of the *Chicago Tribune*

"I have struck a city—a real city—and they call it Chicago. The other places do not count. San Francisco was a pleasure resort as well as a city, and Salt Lake was a phenomenon. This place is the first American city I have encountered."

—Rudyard Kipling, *From Sea to Sea: Letters of Travel*

"Was there ever a name more full of purpose than Chicago's? . . . . Spoken as Chicagoans themselves speak it, with a bit of spit to give heft to its slither, it is gloriously onomatopoeic."

—Jan Morris, *Locations* ("Boss No More")

"A city [that] contains so much, is so much. You can spend a useful life studying a hundred-celled creature. A thousand devoted students have not exhausted Chicago."

—Richard Stern

"Most fantastic and folksy of great cities. . . . She is unruly at heart; more than a little goofy; she will be one of the last to be tamed by the slow frost of correctness."

—Christopher Morley, *Old Loopy*

"Chicago will give you a chance. The sporting spirit is the spirit of Chicago."

—Lincoln Steffens, *The Autobiography of Lincoln Steffens*

"Chicago sounds rough to the maker of verse; One comfort you have— Cincinnati sounds worse."

—Oliver Wendell Holmes

My Bloody Valentine

* * * *

During the Roaring Twenties, Al Capone ruled Chicago. Be it gambling, prostitution, or bootleg whiskey, Capone and his gangsters controlled it. Almost no one dared to stand up to him, including the police, because that meant possibly winding up on the wrong end of a gun. Still, one man was determined to dethrone Capone.

For a few years, George "Bugs" Moran and his North Side Gang had been muscling their way into Chicago in an attempt to force Capone and his men out. As 1929 began, rumors started to fly that Capone was fed up and planning his revenge. As the days turned into weeks and nothing happened, Moran and his men began to relax and let down their guard. That would prove to be a fatal mistake.

Gathering for the Slaughter

On the morning of February 14, 1929, six members of the North Side Gang—James Clark, Frank Gusenberg, Peter Gusenberg, Adam Heyer, Reinhart Schwimmer, and Al Weinshank—were gathered inside the SMC Cartage Company at 2122 North Clark Street. With them was mechanic John May, who was not a member of the gang but had been hired to work on one of their cars. May had brought along his dog, Highball, and had tied him to the bumper of the car while he worked. Supposedly, the men were gathered at the warehouse to accept a load of bootleg whiskey. Whether that is true or not remains unclear. What is known for certain is that at approximately 10:30 A.M., two cars pulled up in front of the building. Four men—two dressed as police officers and two in street clothes—got out and walked into the warehouse.

Murderers in Disguise

Once the men were inside, it is believed they announced that the warehouse was being raided and ordered everyone to line up facing the back wall. Believing the armed men were indeed police officers, all of Moran's men, along with John May, did as they were told.

Without warning, the four men began shooting, and, in a hail of shotgun fire and more than 70 submachine-gun rounds, the seven men were gunned down.

When it was over, the two men in street clothes calmly walked out of the building with their hands up, followed by the two men dressed as police officers. To everyone nearby, it appeared as though there had been a shoot-out, and the police had arrived and were now arresting two men.

"Nobody Shot Me"

Minutes later, neighbors called police after reportedly hearing strange howls coming from inside the building. When the real police arrived, they found all seven men mortally wounded. One of the men, Frank Gusenberg, lingered long enough to respond to one question. When authorities asked who shot him, Gusenberg responded, "Nobody shot me." The only survivor of the massacre was Highball the dog, whose howls first alerted people that something was wrong.

When word of the massacre hit the newswire, everyone suspected Al Capone had something to do with it. Capone stood strong, though, and swore he wasn't involved. Most people felt that Capone had orchestrated the whole thing as a way to get rid of Moran and several of his key men. There was only one problem—Bugs Moran wasn't in the warehouse at the time of the shooting. Some believe that Moran may have driven up, seen the cars out front, and, thinking it was a raid, drove away. One thing is certain: February 14, 1929, was Moran's lucky day.

Police launched a massive investigation but were unable to pin anything on Capone, although they did arrest two of his gunmen, John Scalise and "Machine Gun" Jack McGurn, and indicted them for the murders. Scalise never saw the inside of the courthouse—he was murdered before the trial began. Charges against McGurn were eventually dropped, although he was murdered seven years later, on Valentine's Day, in what appeared to be retaliation for the 1929 massacre.

A Ghost Visits Capone

Publicly, Al Capone may have denied any wrongdoing, but it appears that the truth literally haunted him until his dying day. Beginning in 1929, Capone began telling several of his closest friends that the ghost of James Clark, one of the men killed in the massacre, was haunting him. Several times, Capone's bodyguards heard him scream, "Get out! Leave me alone!" in the middle of the night. When they burst into the room believing Capone was being attacked, they would always find the room empty except for Capone, who would say that Clark's ghost was after him. Some say Clark didn't rest until Capone passed away on January 25, 1947.

Ghosts Still Linger

The warehouse at 2122 North Clark Street, where the bloody massacre took place, was demolished in 1967, and the area is now the front lawn of a nursing home. The wall against which the seven doomed men stood was dismantled brick by brick, complete with bullet holes, and sold at auction. A businessman bought the bricks and reassembled the wall in the men's room of his restaurant. However, the business failed and the owner, believing the wall was cursed, tried getting rid of it to recoup his losses. He sold the individual bricks and was successful in getting rid of many of them, but they always seemed to find their way back to him. Sometimes they would show up on his doorstep along with a note describing all the misfortune the new owner had encountered after buying the brick.

At the former site of the warehouse, some people report hearing the sounds of gunfire and screams coming from the area. People walking their dogs near the lot claim that their furry friends suddenly pull on their leashes and try to get away from the area as quickly as possible. Perhaps they sense the ghostly remnants of the bloody massacre that happened there more than 75 years ago.

* * * *

"They blamed everything but the Chicago Fire on me."

—Al Capone

The Fort Dearborn Tragedy

✳ ✳ ✳ ✳

Delays and indecision result in an 1812 massacre.

Fort Dearborn, which was situated near the current intersection of Wacker Drive and Michigan Avenue, was a major strategic site because of its access to waterways, trails, and forests. The fort had few residents until 1810, when Captain Nathan Heald was put in charge of a small garrison due to rising conflict with the British. When the War of 1812 broke out, there were approximately 100 men, women, and children living at the fort.

In July 1812 the garrison on Michigan's Mackinac Island was captured by the British army. Shortly thereafter, many Native Americans began joining with the British forces to attack U.S. forts and outposts. It quickly became clear to the U.S. forces that the Brits' next stop would be Fort Dearborn. With that in mind, U.S. General William Hull sent word to Captain Heald to evacuate the fort. He told Heald to remove the people, leave everything else behind, and head toward safer territory in Fort Wayne, Indiana.

A Fatal Delay

Unfortunately, Heald did not immediately follow Hull's command. As a result of this delay, the Potawatomi had time to gather and position themselves around the fort. On the morning of August 15, 1812, Heald realized that simply abandoning the fort was no longer an option. The only way to get out would be to reach some sort of agreement with the Potawatomi.

Heald requested a meeting with the Potawatomi council, and his request was granted. An agreement was reached in which Heald and his people would be allowed to leave the fort unharmed. In exchange, Heald promised they would leave all their extra provisions, including ammunition and weapons, inside the fort.

After Heald returned to the fort and gave the order to evacuate, some residents expressed concern that any weapons left behind might be used against them. At that point, it was decided that all the extra guns and ammunition would be disposed of in an old, abandoned well on the fort property. Unbeknownst to the people of the fort, Potawatomi scouts observed them doing this; they reported back to their leaders, who became furious.

Walking to the Slaughter

While all of this was going on, Captain William Wells arrived from Fort Wayne, Indiana, and was put in charge of helping relocate the Fort Dearborn residents. When all the arrangements were made, the soldiers, women, and children began walking south. Less than two miles from the fort (near today's intersection of 18th and Calumet), the Potawatomi turned on the group, lashing out violently. By the time the massacre ended, most of the 100 people who left the fort had been killed. A few managed to escape into the wilderness, but most of the survivors were taken prisoner and sold to the British army as slaves. However, upon hearing of the massacre, the British released all the survivors.

Grim Reminders

As news of the massacre spread across the United States, people began avoiding the Fort Dearborn area altogether. In fact, no one returned there until the War of 1812 ended. Those who went back discovered the skeletal remains of the massacre victims, who had simply been left where they had fallen. All of the victims were eventually given proper burials. Years later a small plaque and a relief panel were placed near the site of the former fort to commemorate the massacre.

When the Chicago flag was created in 1915, it featured four red stars, the first of which represents Fort Dearborn. With that, many people felt the horrible events were finally put to rest. However, in the 1980s construction workers unearthed skeletal remains that were later determined to have been from victims of the Fort Dearborn tragedy. Those remains were relocated to a nearby cemetery, but the event caused a stir. Shortly thereafter, people started reporting seeing figures dressed in period clothing wandering around in a small field near the site of the massacre. Some of the figures appeared to be screaming, although no noise was ever heard. It seemed that for a few brief moments, a portal to another era opened up, and the events of that day in August 1812 were being replayed.

The Challenge of Change

✳ ✳ ✳ ✳

By championing reform, Mayor Harold Washington left a legacy that continues to resonate.

By the early 1980s, many of America's biggest cities had undergone a political sea change. Gone were the once-powerful white "machine" mayors, who ruled over their towns like political fiefdoms, and in came a wave of reform-minded African American politicians. By 1993, nearly 70 major urban centers were headed by African American chief executives.

But for some big cities, and especially Chicago, such change came slowly. That's because, in part, the established political machine was more firmly entrenched in Chicago than almost anywhere else. But equally difficult for some in the city was accepting the notion that African Americans could be allowed access to political power. So when a relatively unknown African American state legislator named Harold Washington ran for mayor against then-incumbent Jane Byrne in 1983, few gave him a chance.

A New Face in Politics

Born in 1922 and raised in the Bronzeville neighborhood, Washington had built himself a solid career as a politician by the early 1980s—first as a lawyer, then as a member of the Illinois legislature, and later as a U.S. Representative from Illinois' First Congressional District.

Jane Byrne, Washington's predecessor, was largely ineffectual and was considered vulnerable to being voted out of office. A group of community leaders from across the city approached Washington and asked him to run against Byrne. Washington demurred, in part because the primary election was expected to include Richard M.

Daley, the previous mayor's son and a rising political force. When organizers registered 100,000 new voters in advance of the election, however, Washington changed his mind. He went on to win the Democratic primary on February 22, 1983, with 37 percent of the vote in the three-way race.

After the March general election in which he beat Republican Bernie Epton, Washington immediately ran into a firestorm of opposition. The first standoff was with the city council, Chicago's legislative branch. Known as "Council Wars," the battle pitted a group of reformist Democrats against the remnants of the white power structure that sought to block Washington's initiatives. It took a 1986 federal court order that rebalanced the city's electoral map and a second election—which Washington won by beating longtime political power-broker Edward Vrdolyak in 1987—before Washington was able to govern as smoothly as his predecessors.

Real Change in City Hall

What makes Washington's story so compelling is that for the first time in Chicago's history, whole groups of voters—African Americans, Latinos, independents, "lakefront liberals," and others long kept out of the city's power structure—found a voice and champion for reform. Washington carried out these changes by redirecting resources to long-neglected parts of the city and appointing new faces to influential city hall posts.

Washington's supporters were shocked and saddened when the mayor suffered a heart attack and died on November 25, 1987—a few months into his second term and the day before Thanksgiving. The city grieved, and soon another battle raged over how his successor would be chosen.

Washington's Legacy

In the years after Washington's death, Chicago named various institutions after the late mayor to commemorate his legacy, including the city's main library branch and the former Loop College. Perhaps Washington's greatest legacy, though, was how he changed the city's image around the world. Washington proved that city politics could be a participatory process, instead of one where who you knew and the color of your skin were all that mattered.

Delights for the Eyes

✳ ✳ ✳ ✳

Like all world-class cities, Chicago is committed to sprucing up its public spaces with artwork by both local and world-famous artists. This list provides a sampling of the classic and more obscure pieces displayed throughout the city.

- **The Fountain of Time:** Sculptor Lorado Taft created this tableau of humanity in 1922 for display in Washington Park on the South Side. The 126-foot-long work of steel-reinforced concrete depicts artists, soldiers, children, and couples streaming past the unblinking eye of Father Time.

- **Lane Tech High School Murals:** This North Side high school boasts one of the largest collections of art of any public school in the nation. The interior is adorned with 66 murals, some sponsored by the Chicago Public School Art Society in the early 20th century and others commissioned as part of the Federal Art Project during the Great Depression. Subjects range from Native American cultures to agrarian scenes to manufacturing and construction.

- **The Picasso:** In 1967, an untitled sculpture—Pablo Picasso's gift to the people of Chicago—was unveiled in the forecourt of Chicago's Civic Center building (now called the Daley Center). The controversial abstract work (which appears at the top of each page of this book) has since been hailed as a masterpiece of Cubism and is recognized around the world as a symbol of Chicago.

- **Flamingo:** This steel sculpture by Alexander Calder adorns Federal Plaza. Standing more than 50 feet tall, the bright red abstract work consists of two fluid arches that meet atop a trio of multifaceted legs. The work evokes a sense of grace and weightlessness that belies its great height and imposing mass.

- **The Four Seasons:** Working in his studio in France, Marc Chagall created this massive four-side mosaic that depicts life in Chicago. The piece was assembled for display in the First National Plaza at Monroe and Dearborn streets. The massive work contains thousands of individually painted tiles and stretches 70 feet long, 14 feet tall, and 10 feet wide.

- **Miro's *Chicago*:** Spanish artist Joan Miro created this unique sculpture in 1981 for the courtyard of the Cook County Administration building. The playful human figure incorporates both natural and synthetic shapes—a bell-like base, a moon-shape neck, and a fork-shape starry crown.

- **Monument to the Great Northern Migration:** Standing tall at the center of the intersection of 26th Street and Martin Luther King Drive, Alison Saar's statue of a solitary black traveler, suitcase in hand, represents the Great Migration of southern African Americans to Chicago and other northern cities in the early and mid-20th century. This monument was dedicated in 1996.

- ***Hopes and Dreams:*** Brightening the underground tunnel that connects three of the city's rapid transit lines at Roosevelt Road, this 1,600-square-foot mosaic was truly a collaborative creation of the entire city. Overseen by artists Juan Chavez and Corinne Peterson, this bright and hopeful work is composed of 4,000 individual tiles made by Chicago citizens at the Museum Campus throughout the summer of 1999.

- ***Cloud Gate*** **(aka "the Bean"):** This kidney-bean-shape sculpture by Anish Kapoor became a centerpiece of Michigan Avenue's Millennium Park in 2004. Made of 168 tightly fitted plates of highly polished stainless steel, each milled to a quarter-inch thickness, the  ever-changing work acts as a mirror that reflects both the city skyline and the thousands of art lovers who come to see it. At 110 tons, it is one of the largest outdoor sculptures in the world.

✳ ✳ ✳ ✳

"We dedicate this celebrated work this morning with the belief that what is strange to us today will be familiar tomorrow."

—Mayor Richard J. Daley, at the dedication of the Picasso

As Chicago as It Gets

✷ ✷ ✷ ✷

*Red, orange, yellow, green, blue, purple, brown, pink—a veritable
rainbow of colors is at the disposal of Chicagoans who want to get
somewhere in a hurry. This color-coded system of elevated trains,
known simply as the "L," is the backbone of Chicago—or, as author
Nelson Algren once described it, "the rusty iron heart" of the city.*

Headed to O'Hare? Hop on the Blue Line. Midway? That's the
Orange Line. You take the Red Line to get to Wrigley Field, home
of the Cubs. And, ironically enough, you also take the Red Line to
get to U.S. Cellular Field, home of the White Sox. (This may be the
only common ground you're likely to find between Cubs fans and
Sox fans!) There are even trains that will take you out to the 'burbs—
the Yellow Line runs to Skokie and the Purple Line runs to
Evanston. No matter your destination, the "L" can get you there—
though you may have to transfer to another line or hop a bus along
the way. There's nothing as quintessentially Chicago as standing on
an "L" train during rush hour, hanging on for dear life as the train
rattles and jerks underground (yes, despite its name, the "L" also
travels underground in places), along the Kennedy, and back up to
the elevated tracks.

Visitors to Chicago are often startled by the thunderous sound of
the elevated trains passing by overhead. Newcomers may even
unknowingly rent an apartment right next to the "L" before spending
their first night there and realizing *that's* why the rent was so cheap.

First Stop

The "L" originated in the decades following the Great Fire. As
Chicago rebuilt itself, the environs of the city crept ever farther, and
it became apparent that a modern transportation system was necessary. In 1892, the Chicago & South Side Rapid Transit Railroad Co.
opened the city's first rapid transit train system.

The line ran about four miles—between State and Wabash
streets—and towered some two stories over the muddy, congested

streets below. Though noisy and somewhat unsightly atop the imposing steel supports, the steam-powered trains proved instantly popular with commuters because they could complete their route in half the time the same journey took by streetcar.

The Loop

Over the next two decades, three other privately owned elevated lines were constructed. The start of the 20th century saw the introduction of an innovation in train technology—a control console that allowed a single operator to run an entire train from either the lead or rear car, thus eliminating the time-consuming task of turning the trains around at the end of the line. More famously, the system also added what would become its most distinctive feature—the Union Elevated Railroad, an elevated line that circled downtown and connected all four of the independently operated railways. The "Loop" soon became the nickname of both the tracks and the central downtown area. While the elevated tracks are still a major part of this sprawling mass transit system, over the years additional lines were laid both below ground and at street level.

Seeing Red . . . and Blue . . . and Green

In 1993, the Chicago Transit Authority (the government agency that now manages the trains) color-coded its elevated routes. The North Side "L" was designated the Red Line. This is perhaps quite fitting: Upscale Lakefront commuters are often literally "seeing red" when it comes to negotiating their way downtown, as the rush hour ride is often slow and inconvenient—not surprising given that much of the infrastructure dates to 1900.

And yet, despite the headaches commuters may associate with riding the "L" each day, *Chicago Tribune* readers voted it "one of the seven wonders of Chicago" in 2005. And that's no *small* wonder, considering that the "L" serves 658,524 people on an average weekday and boasted an astounding 198.1 million riders in 2008.

Ludicrous Laws

How hungry are you? . . . It is against the law to eat in a restaurant that is on fire.

Next time a tourist asks you for directions . . . Make sure you know what you are talking about! It is illegal to give "misleading information about . . . the location of restaurants or hotels."

That's what the sidewalk is for! . . . As of 1896, laws stated that visitors to Lincoln Park were to keep off the grass.

Go fly a kite! I mean, um, er, don't . . . It is technically illegal to fly a kite downtown.

It might seem totally appropriate, but . . . You cannot take your French poodle to the opera.

We speak American in these here parts . . . A 1923 declaration stated that, since we have cut all ties from England, the official language of the State of Illinois would be referred to as "American," not "English."

This place is for cleaning your clothes! . . . Customers are not allowed to sleep at any Laundromat.

Have money on you at all times . . . If you have less than a dollar, you can be arrested for vagrancy.

But be careful where you go to *get* a dollar . . . It is also illegal to be caught "prowling about banks or brokerage houses."

This kind of fun is reserved for us . . . It is against the law to give a dog whiskey.

The rest of us got dressed! . . . It is illegal to go fishing in your pajamas.

We have the utmost respect for elections around here . . . No one is allowed to gamble on presidential elections.

Fast Facts

- O'Hare's abbreviation of ORD goes back to its World War II name, Orchard Place Airport/Douglas Field. When Douglas Aircraft decided not to build planes there, it became just Orchard Field Airport, then (in 1949) O'Hare—but it kept the wartime military abbreviation.

- Butch O'Hare (for whom the airport is named) was a decorated World War II fighter pilot who disappeared over the Pacific in 1943. O'Hare's father, Eddie O'Hare, was a lawyer who helped Al Capone carry out numerous illegal activities. (In this case, the apple obviously could not have fallen further from the tree.) To save himself from jail time, Eddie O'Hare began cooperating with police in 1931. He was killed in 1939, apparently under orders from Capone.

- Early 1900s First Ward strongman "Bathhouse" John Coughlin took a personal interest in the welfare of a Lincoln Park Zoo elephant, Princess Alice, who had lost part of her trunk in an accident. Coughlin's "care" turned Princess Alice into an alcoholic; she soon learned to beg visitors for booze.

- Over the years, Chicago has not earned a reputation for deference to royalty. An example came in 1860, when Prince Albert (the future Edward VII) had a visit with the city council. Mayor Wentworth's introduction: "Prince, the boys. Boys, the Prince."

- Early Irish immigrants to Chicago faced severe discrimination. The sign "No Irish Need Apply" was commonplace, and locals bandied the slogan: "Hit him again; he's Irish." It wasn't long, of course, before that became a remarkably unwise utterance in Chicago.

- Henry Ford got the assembly line idea from Chicago's Armour meatpacking plant. Armour's method sent dead pigs down a "disassembly line," if you will, much like a dry cleaner's carousel, with each worker assigned a particular task.

This Flag Represents!

✳ ✳ ✳ ✳

The Chicago flag is pretty nice as flags go: Four red stars nestle snugly between two sky-blue stripes against a background of snowy white. And the Chicago flag isn't just good looks—it represents pieces of Chicago history and serves as a point of pride on the flagpoles (and in car windows and apartment buildings) of Chicagoans across the city.

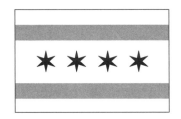

Magnificent Simplicity

In 1915, Chicago Mayor William Hale "Big Bill" Thompson decided his city needed a flag. He formed a committee and asked a popular lecturer and poet named Wallace Rice to head up a flag designing competition. Thousands of entries were received, but—in true Chicago fashion—Rice himself won the contest! What are the odds?!

Whether he won fair and square or not, Rice designed a magnificently simple flag that paid tribute to Chicago's unique geographical assets and two prominent events in Chicago's history—the Great Chicago Fire and the 1893 World's Columbian Exposition. Since then, two additional stars have been added for other influential moments.

Stripes of Blue and White

There are five stripes on the Chicago flag—three white, two blue. The white stripes signify the three geographical areas of the city. The top stripe represents the North Side, the middle stripe represents the West Side, and the bottom stripe represents the South Side.

The blue stripes pay tribute to the plentiful freshwater that surrounds the city. The top blue stripe represents Lake Michigan and the North Branch of the Chicago River, and the bottom stripe represents the South Branch of the river and the Illinois and Michigan Canal.

Four Significant Stars

The first star of the Chicago flag represents Fort Dearborn, the first United States settlement in the Chicago area. This first star was actually the fourth to be added; it was approved for addition in 1939 to commemorate the importance of this U.S. fort. The six points of this star represent some of Chicago's bragging rights: transportation, labor, commerce, finance, populousness, and salubrity, or health.

The next star commemorates the Great Chicago Fire; it represents the city's survival beyond the tragedy and honors those who lost their lives in it. This star was original to Rice's flag in 1917, and its points represent the virtues of religion, education, aesthetics, justice, beneficence, and civic pride or duty.

The third star on the flag was an original, denoting the fair that put all others to shame—the 1893 World's Columbian Exposition. The star's points symbolize the political entities that Chicago has belonged to over the years: France, Great Britain, Virginia, the Northwest Territory, the Indian Territory, and finally, Illinois.

In 1933, a fourth star was added to the flag to celebrate the Century of Progress Exposition that took place in Chicago that year. The points on this star stand for Chicago's four honorary names— Third Largest City, the Great Central Marketplace, Wonder City, Convention City—and two mottos, "City in a Garden" and "I Will."

✳ ✳ ✳ ✳

- *The Chicago flag features six-pointed stars because traditionally, five-pointed stars are reserved for flags of sovereign states.*

Tragedy at the Haymarket

* * * *

What began as a campaign for an eight-hour workday ended with a bloody event Chicago will never forget.

It was the mid-1880s, and Chicago was in a state of transition. Industry was growing more and more mechanized—good news for the corporations that were able to increase profits and lower wages, but bad news for workers who were putting in 12 to 14 grueling hours a day, 6 miserable days a week. In October 1884, the Federation of Organized Trade and Labor Unions set a goal to make the eight-hour workday standard, even if nationwide strikes were necessary to make that goal a reality. The stage was set.

The Calm Before the Storm

On May 1, 1886, hundreds of thousands of workers across the country took to the streets in support of an eight-hour workday. The first few days of the strike were relatively peaceful, but all hell broke loose on May 3, when police killed several unarmed strikers near Chicago's McCormick Reaper Works.

Workers gathered in a light rain in Haymarket Square on the West Side on May 4. Mayor Carter Harrison Sr. stopped by in a show of support for the workers, then left early when it appeared that all was peaceful. The rest, as they say, is history—and a somewhat murky history at that, as many questions remain about what unfolded in the incident now known as the Haymarket Riot.

Every Man for Himself

Once the mayor left, the police inspector sent in the riot police to disperse the crowd. At the same time, a bomb blasted the ranks of the police force. The police opened fire. Workers reportedly returned fire. A few short minutes later, eight policemen were dead, and scores of workers and bystanders had been injured. The *Chicago Tribune* later quoted an unnamed police officer, who reported, "a very large number of the police were wounded by each other's revolvers. . . . It was every man for himself, and while some got two or three squares away, the rest emptied their revolvers, mainly into each other."

The Fallout

Chicago police immediately swept across the city in search of the bomber. They arrested eight known anarchists (August Spies, Samuel Fielden, Oscar Neebe, Michael Schwab, Louis Lingg, George Engel, Adolph Fischer, and Albert Parsons) and charged them with the crime. After a well-publicized trial, the jury (which included a Marshall Field's sales rep and not a single industrial worker) returned guilty verdicts for all eight, even though only two of the men were even at the Haymarket the night of the incident. The men had clearly been tried for their incendiary speeches leading up to the Haymarket incident, not for anything they had actually done. Seven of the men were sentenced to death, and the show trial resulted in protests around the world.

Seriously, Who Threw the Bomb?

Spies, Fischer, Engel, and Parsons were hanged on November 11, 1887; Lingg had committed suicide in prison one day earlier. Governor Altgeld pardoned Schwab, Fielden, and Neebe in 1893. To the present day, no one is sure who threw the bomb, but most historians believe it was one of two anarchists who were present at the protest that day: Rudolph Schnaubelt or George Meng—neither of whom was ever arrested for the crime.

Historians consider Haymarket one of the seminal events in the history of labor, and its legacy resonates to this day. The Haymarket defendants stand as icons of the American labor movement and are remembered with rallies, parades, and speeches around the world on the anniversary of the bombing. But most important is the spirit of assembly that can be traced back to Haymarket. Today, monuments stand at the corner of Des Plaines and Randolph streets (near the spot where the bomb was thrown) and in Forest Park, Illinois, at the grave of Spies, Fischer, Engel, Parsons, and Lingg. These symbols are poignant reminders of Chicago's critical place in labor history.

Come into My Parlor

* * * *

H. H. Holmes has secured a place in history as one of the most horrifyingly prolific killers the world has ever seen.

Born in May 1860 in New Hampshire, Herman Webster Mudgett was a highly intelligent child, but he was constantly in trouble. Charming, handsome, and charismatic, he nonetheless displayed traits of detachment and dispassion from an early age. As a teen, he became abusive to animals—a classic sign of a sociopath.

Fascinated with skeletons and the human body, Mudgett decided to pursue a medical degree. After marrying Clara Lovering, he enrolled in medical school. There, he had access to skeletons and cadavers. He came up with a scheme to fleece insurance companies by taking out policies for family members or friends, using stolen cadavers to fake their deaths, and collecting the insurance money.

When authorities became suspicious, he abandoned Clara and their newborn baby, moving from city to city and taking on various jobs, most likely scheming and manipulating everyone he crossed. In 1886, the charming liar and thief with murderous intentions surfaced in Chicago with a new name: H. H. Holmes. The city would become the site of his deadliest swindle of all.

A "Castle" with a Most Intriguing Floor Plan

If you lived in Chicago in the late 1800s, you were likely consumed with thoughts of the World's Columbian Exposition. Planners hoped it would make America a superstar country and put Chicago on the map as an A-list city. The Great Fire of 1871 had demolished the town, but the fair would bring the city back—and in a big way.

With new people flooding into the city every day looking to nab one of the world's fair jobs, Chicago was experiencing a population boom that made it very easy for people to simply vanish. The handsome and charismatic Holmes recognized this as an opportunity to lure women into his clutches while most people had their focus elsewhere.

He married his second wife, Myrta, in 1887, without ever securing a divorce from Lovering. Holmes quickly shipped Myrta off to live in suburban Wilmette, while he took up residence in Chicago, free to do as he pleased. He secured a position as a pharmacist at a drugstore in Englewood. He worked for the elderly Mrs. Holden, who was happy to have a handsome young doctor to help out at her store. When Mrs. Holden suddenly disappeared, Holmes told people she had moved to California, and he purchased the store.

Next, Holmes purchased a vacant lot across the street from the drugstore and began constructing a house with a floor plan he designed himself. The three-story house at 63rd and Wallace would have more than 60 rooms and 50 doors, secret passageways, gas pipes with nozzles that piped noxious fumes into windowless rooms, chutes that led down to the basement, and an airtight vault. Holmes hired and fired construction crews on a regular basis; it was said that his swindler's streak got him out of paying for most of the materials and labor used to create this "Murder Castle."

Up & Running

Advertised as a lodging for world's fair tourists, the building opened in 1892. Holmes placed ads in the newspaper to rent rooms, but also listed classified ads calling for females interested in working for a start-up company. Of course, there was no start-up company, and Holmes hired the prettiest women or those who could offer him some sort of financial gain. One by one, they inevitably succumbed to his charm. He made false promises to woman after woman, luring them deeper into his confidence. He took advantage of their naïveté to gain their trust and steal their money.

When he was done with a woman, either because she became suspicious of him or because he had simply gotten what he needed from her, Holmes got rid of her—without remorse or emotion. Sometimes he piped gas into a victim's room to kill her in her sleep; other times he locked her in his airtight vault and listened as she slowly suffocated. Evidence shows he tortured some of them before killing them. After he had brutalized the unfortunate soul, he destroyed the evidence in a vat of acid or a kiln he had built expressly for that purpose, often selling his victims' bones and organs to contacts in the medical field.

The End of "Doctor Death"

After the world's fair ended, creditors put pressure on Holmes, and he knew it was time to flee. Strange as it seems, when Holmes was finally brought to justice, it wasn't initially for homicide; it was for one of his many financial swindles. But as clues about missing women emerged, investigators became suspicious of him for other reasons.

Detective Frank Geyer began to follow the trail of this mysterious man whose identity changed with the weather. Geyer had traced many missing world's fair women back to Holmes's lodging house. He was particularly interested in the whereabouts of three children—Howard, Nellie, and Alice Pietzel. Geyer followed their tracks across the Midwest and into Canada. In Toronto he finally found a house where Holmes had allegedly stayed with several children in tow. Buried in a shallow grave in the backyard, stuffed in a single traveling trunk, he discovered the bodies of the two Pietzel girls. Geyer found the boy's remains several months later in an oven in an Indianapolis home.

When the evidence was brought back to court, Geyer got full clearance to investigate every inch of Holmes's Chicago dwelling. The investigation turned up a lot more than detectives anticipated, and one of America's most chilling stories of murder and crime officially broke.

Inside his heavily guarded cell, Herman Webster Mudgett admitted his crimes. He officially confessed to 27 murders, six attempted murders, and a whole lot of fraud. What he didn't confess to, however, were any feelings of remorse.

Holmes was executed by hanging in 1896. He was buried in Holy Cross Cemetery near Philadelphia in a coffin lined with cement, topped with more cement, and buried in a double grave—per his own request. Was he ready to rest eternally after a life of such monstrosity? Or was he afraid that someone would conduct experiments on him as he had done to so many hapless victims?

"I was born with the devil in me. I could not help the fact that I was a murderer, no more than the poet can help the inspiration to sing."

—H. H. Holmes

🦄 Local Legends

The colorful history of the Billy Goat Tavern is a story that speaks to the gruff life of its city. And this is one story that is far from over.

The Billy Goat Tavern has likely made a difference in your life. You may be a bitter (though hopeful) Cubs fan, ruing the day your favorite baseball team was doomed to perpetual failure. You may be a follower of the *Chicago Tribune*'s political coverage, tearing through the paper each day to see what the city's famously crooked political machine has been up to. Or you may have a soft spot for John Belushi, who owed much of his success to the mania behind the counter ("cheezborgor, cheezborgor, cheezborgor") at the city's most beloved subterranean dive.

The original tavern was located on the West Side, across from Chicago Stadium (now the United Center). Built in 1934, the old Billy Goat served drinks and greasy grub for 30 years before moving to its current location, the underground intersection of Hubbard Street and Michigan Avenue. The bar was given its famous name when a wayward goat, having fallen off a truck on Madison Street, walked through the front door and struck the fancy of the bar's owner, William Sianis. Sianis, a Greek immigrant and one of the cleverest businessmen in town, renamed the bar—which was originally called the Lincoln Tavern—and grew a goatee to match that of Murphy, his new hoofed companion.

Come to Me, All You Goats

After local courts decreed that the goat be paroled into Sianis's care for life, the *Tribune* picked up the story, offering the bar a ton of publicity and, unintentionally, turning Sianis into Chicago's most famous foster parent. For decades, stray goats turned over to the Chicago police were given to Sianis, who lovingly made a home for them on a patch of grass behind his bar. Photos of the old bar show Sianis surrounded by a host of jaunty regulars and a handful of goats working the room, standing on tables, leaning against the bar, thrilled to be mingling with locals and even more thrilled not to be a plate of braised mutton.

These goats spent a great deal of time at the old tavern, looking on as their caregiver's antics brought both business and controversy to his increasingly infamous bar. During the 1944 Republican National Convention at Chicago Stadium, Sianis hung a sign outside his bar that read "No Republicans Allowed." Republican delegates, outraged by such an inhospitable gesture—just a stone's throw from their convention!—stormed the bar and demanded to be served. Sianis served drinks to the finally satisfied crowd and walked away with $2,600 in sales.

"Who Stinks Now?"

A year later, in what proved to be one of the most memorable moments in the history of baseball, Sianis again caused a scene after he and Murphy were denied entry to Game 4 of the 1945 World Series at Wrigley Field. Sianis demanded that the gatekeepers consult P. K. Wrigley, the field's owner. But P. K. Wrigley also denied them entry, noting, according to legend, goats "stink." When the Cubs lost the Series to the Detroit Tigers, Sianis fired off a telegram to Wrigley asking, "Who stinks now?"

As if humiliating the gum mogul weren't satisfying enough, Sianis used his longstanding relationships with the city's sportswriters and columnists to spread the word: As long as the Billy Goat's billy goats were locked out of Wrigley Field, the Cubs would never win another Series. Though the team had been among the best in the past—winning back-to-back Series in 1907 and 1908—it hasn't won another pennant since 1945. Goats have been ushered into Wrigley Field several times in hapless attempts to lift the curse, but Sianis's prophesy survives.

A Haven for Sportswriters

Sianis adored newspapers, for he had learned English by reading through stacks of Chicago dailies. He even ran a newsstand before buying the Lincoln Tavern, which was a popular watering hole for the city's army of reporters as soon as it opened. Sianis, who had already benefited from the hoards of fans rushing across the street for a post-game beer, installed pay phones in the back of the bar so eager sports-writers could phone reports to their newsroom—and to give them an excuse to grab a cold one on their way out.

In 1964, Sianis moved his tavern to its present location. Accessible from Michigan Avenue by descending a narrow concrete staircase, the bar is at one of downtown's many underground intersections. The tavern has managed to retain a perfect location without the pointless niceties and high prices of the aboveground cafés. Go there any night of the week and you're bound to run into dozens of reporters and editors from the *Sun-Times* and the *Tribune,* bemoaning the state of local politics and knocking back a few brews before heading home or back to work. Late-night shifts in the newsroom and early-morning deadlines keep the bar busy until the wee hours of the morning, when the youngest generations of the Sianis family stack the chairs and mop the floors.

What Part of "No Coke—Pepsi" Do You Not Understand?

The bar has opened several newer, decidedly less gritty locations throughout downtown and elsewhere in the city—on Navy Pier, in O'Hare Airport, on West Madison Avenue (home to the original tavern)—and has just opened a tavern in Washington, D.C., as well. But Billy Goat is hardly a model for the modern chain restaurant. The Hubbard Street location is lit with harsh fluorescent bulbs, and the red-and-white checkered tables are lined up like it's bingo night at the VFW. The menu remains simple—and unapologetically greasy—and the staff's reputation isn't one of extreme courtesy. It's the men behind the register, after all, who inspired one of *Saturday Night Live*'s most famous sketches, written by Chicagoan Don Novello and starring veterans from Chicago's comedy circuit. The skit plays out like this: John Belushi, Dan Akroyd, and Bill Murray stand behind a busy lunch counter and—in thick Greek accents—shout at the customers, "Cheezborger, cheezborgor, cheezborgor! No fries—chccps! No Coke—Pepsi!" The owners, delighted by the imitation and delighted, too, by the opportunity for more publicity, capitalized on the sketch.

A photo of the cast, and thousands of others—photos of regulars, of celebrities, of politicians, and of local sports heroes—adorn the walls of the Billy Goat's Hubbard Street location, where you'll find the same cheap food and drink, and the same rich company as always, with a few cloven exceptions. But watching over it all, mounted above the bar with great love and admiration, is a stuffed, bearded goat—a sign that this place has never forgotten its bizarre origins and knows what a monumental place it holds in the heart of its city.

Enter Steppenwolf, Stage Right

✴ ✴ ✴ ✴

Ensemble members who went on to work in Hollywood—such as Gary Sinise, Laurie Metcalf, John Malkovich, Gary Cole, Martha Plimpton, and Joan Allen—have all helped raise Steppenwolf's profile over the years, but for anyone living in Chicago over the past four decades, this theater company is more than a few famous faces.

Let's Put on a Show!

In 1974, suburban student Gary Sinise was approached by a pair of his Highland Park classmates. The duo wanted Sinise to help them produce a play. Sinise agreed, and several productions followed. The group, officially founded by buddies Sinise, Terry Kinney, and Jeff Perry, became a non-profit in 1975 and Steppenwolf (the name references the Hermann Hesse novel) was born. Within a year, the ensemble included the founders plus six talented friends, including John Malkovich and Laurie Metcalf. Making their home in the basement of Immaculate Conception Church and School in Highland Park, the actors produced their first season.

Act Two

By 1980, the group had gained a strong reputation for producing finely directed, passionately performed work. Steppenwolf's productions included such classics as *The Glass Menagerie* as well as works by more obscure playwrights. They moved into the city proper in 1980 and their fan base grew; audiences loved the gritty, accessible approach of the young artists. In 1982, Steppenwolf took its production of Sam Shepard's sibling rivalry tale *True West* to New York, where it garnered rave reviews. In 1985, the company was awarded a Tony for Regional Theater Excellence. More Tony Awards and nominations would follow as the group continued to work in New York, London, and various other venues.

In 1991, Steppenwolf opened the doors to its new theater complex on Halsted and North Avenue. The structure contained a main stage, offices, a studio theater, and plenty of parking for the crowds Steppenwolf shows continued to draw. Throughout the '90s, the group made tracks in the world of theater and made a name not only for them, but for Chicago as well. With Steppenwolf at the vanguard, Chicago was quickly becoming the place to be for exciting, engaging American theater.

The Future Is Bright

In 2001, Steppenwolf's production of *One Flew Over the Cuckoo's Nest* won pretty much every theater award, and the national recognition pumped up the theater's visibility. But that was only a taste of what was to come in 2008, when ensemble member Tracy Lett's *August: Osage County*—a tragically funny family comedy—rocked the theater world. Critics hailed the play, the production, the actors, the direction, and the design as creating one of the most significant moments in American theater in decades. Award after award followed, as well as an open run on Broadway. Steppenwolf reaffirmed that the edgy, in-your-face theater that got it noticed in the beginning is still the kind of work the theater produces today.

✷　✷　✷　✷

- *Steppenwolf hosts a gala each spring to celebrate its anniversary. Notable past auction prizes have included walk-on roles on* CSI: New York *and* Law and Order: Criminal Intent, *a spa weekend in New York with Joan Allen, and dinner at John Malkovich's home in France.*

- *Steppenwolf cofounder Terry Kinney became well known for his role on the HBO series* Oz *and began appearing in* The Mentalist *in fall 2009.*

You Can Thank Chicago

Ferris Wheel

In 1893, Chicago hosted the World's Columbian Exposition, which showcased the best culture, art, and science that the world had to offer. The engineering marvel of the fair turned out to be the huge rotating observatory designed and built by George W. Ferris. The world's first Ferris wheel, it soared more than 250 feet and offered a bird's-eye view of the city. The Ferris wheel remained on the Midway until 1895, when it was moved to 2643 North Clark Street. In 1903, it was moved again—this time to St. Louis, for the Louisiana Purchase Exposition. The wheel was destroyed and sold for scrap in 1906.

Cracker Jack

Cracker Jack was invented in 1896, when an enterprising Chicago-based candy maker named Louis Rueckheim figured out a way to keep molasses-covered popcorn from sticking together. Though instantly popular, the childhood treat became an icon of American culture when it was mentioned in the 1908 song "Take Me Out to the Ballgame," and its longevity was secured in 1912, when the company came up with the brilliant marketing idea of including a prize in every box. Though the brand is now owned by an international food conglomerate, the company that Rueckheim founded with his brother was a major employer on Chicago's South Side for much of the 20th century.

Dishwashing Machine

Socialite Josephine Cochrane lived in a Chicago suburb in the mid-1800s. She and her husband frequently entertained guests, and she grew frustrated over her fine china regularly being chipped as her servants cleaned it after parties. Looking for a solution to this costly problem, she began sketching out ways to automate the process of dishwashing, and by 1886 had built a functional dishwasher and earned a patent. She exhibited her invention at the World's Columbian Exposition, and before long she was selling her machines to restaurants and hotels.

Fast Facts

- From 1961 to '62, the Cubs used a harebrained managing scheme called the College of Coaches. Eight coaches rotated as managers, each doing things his own way. Records of 64–90 and 59–103 explain why no one has tried it since.

- Chris Chelios, Charles Comiskey, George Halas, Dick Butkus, Eddy Curry, and Derrick Rose share three distinctions: All are/were prominent in their sports, all were born in the Chicago area, and all played or coached there.

- The modern Arizona Cardinals called Chicago home for 40 years. Founded in 1898 as the Morgan Athletic Club, they became the Chicago Cardinals in 1922 and moved to St. Louis in 1960.

- Chicago had a third big-league baseball team in the 20th century: the Federal League's Chicago Chi-Feds (1914), renamed the Whales in 1915. The Whales won the maverick league's second and final championship. Today we know Weeghman Park, their home stadium, as Wrigley Field.

- On May 2, 1917, Cubs pitcher Hippo Vaughn dueled Reds hurler Fred Toney at Wrigley. Both threw nine innings of no-hit ball. The Cubs lost in the tenth when Olympian Jim Thorpe knocked in the winning run.

- When the Sox won the 1959 AL pennant, fire commissioner Bob Quinn decided to celebrate by blowing the air-raid sirens. Many people, conditioned to fear a nuclear attack, retreated to bomb shelters or hid under furniture.

- How cheap was White Sox owner Charlie Comiskey? He charged his players for washing their uniforms. At one point, they protested by wearing the same grimy outfits for several games. Comiskey confiscated the uniforms, had them cleaned, then fined the players for the cost of the cleaning.

Fire at the Iroquois

* * *

Newspaper ads touted the Iroquois Theatre as "absolutely fireproof." Sounds ominous, doesn't it?

The Iroquois owners had cut nearly every possible corner to open the theater in time for the 1903 holiday season. When a bit of drapery caught fire during a December 30 matinee performance of the musical comedy *Mr. Blue Beard,* all the cut corners became tragically apparent.

The scenery had been painted with highly flammable oil-based paint. The theater did not have emergency sprinklers. Installing the ventilation system had been a rush job, and it did not work correctly. As the cast opened the stage door, the lack of ventilation created a backdraft, which the audience was not protected from because the fire curtain stuck on some equipment that had been left out of place.

Most people weren't killed by the flames, however. The worst mistake the planners had made was designing the exit doors to open in toward the lobby, rather than out toward the street. Countless people were crushed to death in the rush to get through the doors. Those who got anywhere near them were rather lucky, however; few exits were clearly marked and many were obscured, so most people had a hard time figuring out where the nearest exit even was.

All told, at least 600 people died in the fire. The owners and the building inspector were eventually indicted, but they all managed to get off on one technicality or another (naturally). Today, the Oriental Theatre sits on the site of the old Iroquois.

* * *

- *Steel fire curtains, clearly marked exits, and exit doors that swing in the direction of outgoing traffic are all provisions that came out of the Iroquois tragedy.*

The Adventures of Saul Bellow

* * * *

This wanderer's observations produced numerous splendid stories.

"I am an American, Chicago born—Chicago, that somber city—and go at things as I have taught myself, free-style, and will make the record in my own way..." So says the protagonist of Saul Bellow's *The Adventures of Augie March* (1953). Bellow's free-spirited characters wandered the urban landscape looking for answers to life's questions, and Chicago was the backdrop for many of Bellow's stories.

Literature from a Scientific Mind

Bellow was born in Quebec in 1915. His Russian-Jewish family relocated to Chicago's Humboldt Park neighborhood in 1924. Bellow enrolled at the University of Chicago in 1933 but later transferred to the more economical Northwestern University to study anthropology and sociology. After beginning graduate studies in Wisconsin and then getting married, he decided to pursue writing. During the Depression, he participated in the WPA Writers' Project.

While serving in the Merchant Marines during World War II, Bellow wrote his first novel, *Dangling Man* (1944), about a young man's search for meaning as he waits to be drafted. A few years later, while living in Paris and elsewhere, he wrote *Augie March*. The book established his literary reputation, and he earned a National Book Award for the novel in 1954. Bellow's other works, many of which explore modern urban dilemmas, include *Herzog* (1964) and *Humboldt's Gift* (1975). Bellow won the National Book Award three times—the first writer to do so. He was also awarded a Pulitzer in 1975 and a Nobel in 1976.

Although he traveled extensively, Bellow identified first and foremost with Chicago—a city where, although he did not find all the answers, he certainly found inspiration.

Timeline

(Continued from p. 11)

February 1862
Camp Douglas (near present-day Martin Luther King Jr. Drive and 35th Street), a Union prison camp, accepts its first Confederate prisoners.

1865
An ailing Potter Palmer takes on two partners, Marshall Field and Levi Leiter, to form Field, Palmer, Leiter & Co. Two ownership and name changes later, the Marshall Field & Co. retail empire is launched.

October 8, 1871
A fire begins in Patrick and Catherine O'Leary's barn on DeKoven Street (where the Chicago Fire Academy now stands). By the time the last flames are extinguished, more than three square miles of the city have been reduced to ashes.

1872
Aaron Montgomery Ward launches Montgomery Ward, the first major mail order retail company. From its Michigan Avenue offices, the company will capitalize on its money-back guarantee and 1,000-page catalogs. Brick-and-mortar Montgomery Ward stores will open nationwide beginning in 1926.

1872
German immigrant brothers Harry and Max Hart establish the Harry Hart & Bro. men's clothing store downtown. The firm will eventually become Hart, Schaffner & Marx, the largest men's clothing store in the United States.

1879
Celebrated architect Louis Henri Sullivan joins forces with Dankmar Adler, fellow influential member of the Chicago School of Architecture. Together they will create the Art Nouveau Auditorium Building and other iconic structures.

1882
"Bathhouse John" Coughlin opens his first Chicago bathhouse. Along with saloon owner "Hinky Dink" Kenna, Coughlin will build a corrupt political machine in the city's First Ward, with one or the other representing the district for more than a half century.

May 4, 1886
A labor rally descends into violence when a bomb is thrown at police officers managing the crowd in Chicago's Haymarket Square. Eight officers are killed.

1892
Chicago launches its public rapid transit system. Initially dubbed the "L," for elevated railroad, the system is still known by that name despite the fact that two-thirds of it runs underground.

1892
Milton Florsheim opens Florsheim Shoe Company downtown, and will soon follow with a retail outlet. A century later, the company will be the nation's largest manufacturer of quality men's dress shoes.

(Continued on p. 110)

The Hangman's Noose

* * * *

Hanging can be one of the most painless ways to be executed.
Unless, of course, you're at the mercy of an incompetent hangman.

A skilled hangman knows exactly how far to drop a prisoner to kill him instantly. Chicago kept the identity of the local hangman a closely guarded secret—perhaps in part because whoever he was, he was really terrible at his job. Chicago hangings tended to take 15 to 20 minutes, and sometimes even longer.

Tough Breaks

Prisoner Michael McNamee held the dubious honor of being one of the first men to endure a hanging Chicago-style. On the first attempt, the rope broke, and McNamee dropped ten feet to the ground. When asked if he could stand, the prisoner seemed not to understand the question (he *had* just taken a nasty hit on the head). "I can stand that and twice that!" he barked. He was led back to the scaffold and hanged again. Which just goes to show that if at first you don't succeed, you should try again. There's no need to get hung up on perfect execution!

About 100 people were hanged in Chicago between 1840 and 1927, when Illinois switched to the electric chair. Only three men were hanged publicly (the state banned public executions in 1871). One such hanging was held in a field near what is now 26th and the lake, and the others were held in the middle of Reuben Street (now Ashland) near Taylor, a West Loop site that thousands drive over every day. Most of the other hangings took place in the prison behind the criminal court building on Hubbard; the location of the gallows was inside the jail (near the corner of Dearborn and Illinois), where the fire station is now. Few Chicagoans know the history of these places, and that's just as well. Chicagoans today are so used to efficient and skilled city officials that they'd probably have a hard time believing that incompetence was once allowed to run rampant!

The Harold Washington Library

* * * *

*In a prime bit of irony, the city that inspired countless writers was
without a central public library for more than a decade.*

The original public library, now called the Chicago Cultural Center,
was completed in 1897 and shared the same Beaux Arts aesthetic as
many other buildings of the era. It served as the city's main public
library until the 1970s, when much of the building became gallery
and event space. The "official" reason given for closing the library
was that the collection had grown too large to be housed there, but
the fact that Chicago had no plan for a new library in place before
closing the old one led many to believe that the city merely wanted
the valuable Michigan Avenue property, perhaps to build a new (and
revenue-generating) skyscraper. Whatever the reason, the library's
books were summarily moved into storage or shelved at neighborhood branches.

Thus began a decade of bickering: Where should the new library
be located? Should it be a new building or a refurbished one? How
would the city pay for it? Finally, in 1987, Mayor Harold Washington
held a design contest. Despite receiving only six entries, the contest
featured some stiff competition, notably from Helmut Jahn, whose
exciting modern glass design spanned the "L" tracks (a model can be
found in the current library). Ultimately, Jahn's design was deemed
too expensive, so architect Thomas Beeby's design won, and the
Harold Washington Library opened in 1991.

The library is clad in granite and red brick and is anchored at its
top by enormous copper owls that were added in 1993. The design
of the building is a tribute to the marble-columned museums and
theaters that shot up around the city a century before. The library
also, however, fits right in with the brick-and-mortar factories and
train stations that line the streets in Chicago's Printers Row neighborhood, which is located just south of the library and was once
home to the city's printing and publishing industry.

Fast Facts

- *While the Civil War brought many parts of the nation terrible economic hardship, it tripled Chicago's population and industry from 1861 to '70. It sure helps to be far away from the fighting!*

- *Ida Bell Wells-Barnett (1862–1931), a civil rights and suffrage activist from Tennessee, settled in Chicago just before World War I. She promptly founded African American fellowship groups and played a major role in electing Oscar Stanton DePriest, Chicago's first African American alderman.*

- *Al Capone wasn't from Chicago, though he did some of his best work there. Of Neapolitan heritage, Capone actually grew up in Brooklyn. He got his famous facial scars in his hometown, not in Chicago—a bit surprising, given his Chicago rivals' determined efforts to whack him.*

- *Just outside Soldier Field stands a 1934 present from Benito Mussolini: a column from Hadrian's era (A.D. 117–138). Mussolini sent the column to commemorate Italo Balbo's transatlantic flight from Rome to Chicago during Chicago's 1933 Century of Progress Exposition. Sending such a national treasure outside the country voluntarily was almost unprecedented, but Italians didn't argue with Mussolini.*

- *By June 6, 1944 (D-Day), the average city block in Chicago had sent seven persons into uniform. Chicago produced war goods second in value only to Detroit; half the U.S. military electronics used during the war came from the Windy City.*

- *Chicago-born William L. Shirer, author of* The Rise and Fall of the Third Reich, *helped revolutionize broadcast journalism working for CBS during World War II. He broadcast from Germany until fall 1940 and wrote several memoirs of his wartime experiences.*

The Whitechapel Club

* * *

Where the only light came from the skulls that lined the walls . . .

In the late 19th century, the area bounded by Wells on the west, La Salle on the east, Washington on the north, and Madison on the south was known as Newsboy Alley. The back room of a club on Calhoun Place housed the strangest of all Chicago's press clubs: the Whitechapel Club.

Named for the neighborhood that had been terrorized by Jack the Ripper, the club was decorated with crime-scene photos. The members surrounded themselves with such images to show that they were gritty newspapermen who had seen it all; nothing could faze them. While the club had an aura of mystery, it was regularly featured in *The New York Times.* Rumors of strange rites held in the dark headquarters circulated throughout the city.

The Truth: They Liked to Drink

In reality, the only spirits that were actually raised here were held up in a glass. Indeed, while the program at the club on any given evening might feature readings of essays and poems by the club members (some of which could probably have been categorized as "crimes" on their own), the majority of the meetings seem to have been occupied with the same thing that went on at most private clubs: drinking. But at least the Whitechapel members knew how to mix a little drama in with their cocktails: The agenda for the evening would be written out on a rolled-up curtain that would be unrolled to reveal one event at a time. The first event of the night was generally "we drink," and the second was generally "we drink again."

Just as all crime sprees must come to a close, the club ended its five-year run in 1902. The building that housed the club was demolished, and the La Salle Hotel was built in its place. The hotel included a bar known as the Whitechapel Club until the hotel itself fell victim to the wrecking ball in the mid-1970s.

This City Belongs to the Daleys—We Just Live in It

* * * *

Chicago has been governed by a Daley for the better part of 40+ years; Richard J. Daley served as mayor for 21 years and—after a few intervening years—he was superseded by his son Richard M., who has led Chicago for nearly 20 years.

Because Illinois politics have a history of frequent corruption and scandal, some view the Daley legacy with skepticism and heartily disagree with Daley politics. But, over and over again, votes are cast for the Daley ticket, proving that most Chicagoans are content with the leadership of this homegrown royal family.

Daley Senior (aka "Da Mare")

Richard J. Daley was born into an Irish American working-class family on the South Side in 1902. Chicago was a city of stock-yards and train tracks back then, chock-full of factories and ethnic neighborhoods. After spending his young adult years working in the stockyards, Daley enrolled in night courses at DePaul Law School, earned his degree, and began to make good on his dreams of being a career politician.

Daley worked his way up the ranks in precincts and ward organizations before being elected state representative in 1936. He achieved this office in a most intriguing way: He won as a *Republican* in a write-in vote 16 days after the previous office holder (David Shanahan) had died. In those days, state law held that each party had to have at least one representative per district. Since the Republican spot was open after Shanahan's death, Daley ran as a Republican. He soon fell in with the Democrats, however. Two years later, Daley was elected to the Illinois Senate. In 1953, Daley was elected chairman of the Cook County Democratic Central Committee, a position with some serious clout. Less than two years later, he narrowly defeated his opponent and became mayor of Chicago. Being both chairman of his party and mayor of the city gave Daley considerable power.

He Made Camelot Possible

Much of Daley's support came from working-class Chicagoans, who loved how "Da Mare" created jobs for the middle and working classes and greatly improved municipal services. Daley became infamous throughout the country when Republicans grumbled that Illinois had stolen the 1960 election for Kennedy. Legend has it that Daley's machine was even able to rouse voters from their *graves* to cast votes for Kennedy!

Daley had local critics as well. He was criticized for concentrating most of his efforts on the downtown area and ignoring the ethnic neighborhoods; blame for Chicago's largely segregated layout is often laid directly at Daley's feet. But as New York City faced near bankruptcy in the 1970s, Daley's shrewd business acumen secured Chicago's future, and his victory in the mayoral race of 1975 was his strongest ever. That race landed him an unprecedented sixth term, though Daley passed away in 1976 before he could complete his term.

Richard M.

In 1942, Richard J. Daley welcomed Richard M. Daley into the world. The little boy was eventually one of seven children, but it was Richard M. (the eldest child) who would follow in his father's mayoral footsteps—and surpass them in some ways.

Richard M. began his serious political career as an Illinois senator, serving from 1972 to 1980. It was no secret that his dad's powerful position helped get him elected, but it also became clear in time that the second Daley had his own supporters as well as his own way of doing things. In 1989, Richard M. ran for mayor of Chicago and won. On his 47th birthday, he took the office that he's held for more than 19 years and counting. If he is reelected in 2010, he'll beat his dad's record as the longest-serving mayor in Chicago history.

Richard M. has his fair share of fans and detractors. *TIME* magazine listed him as one of the country's five best city mayors in 2005 for his dedication to environmental improvements, urban renewal efforts, and the Millennium Park project. But critics cried foul when Meigs Field, a private airport on Lake Michigan, was suspiciously razed overnight, and plenty of critics feel Richard M.'s legislation has done more to segregate Chicago than to unify it.

Other Notable Daleys

The two Richards aren't the only Daleys who have had their day in the political realm. Eleanor Daley was wife to the first Richard and mother to the second. Most everyone knew Eleanor as "Sis," and—though she had a reputation for a strong will—she wasn't one to get involved with the politics that took up her husband's time. Sis focused on raising her children and participating in various service groups and clubs, but more than a few have said that her quiet support played a huge role in keeping the Daley legacy rolling.

Several of the other Daley kids went into politics, as well. Son William served in President Clinton's cabinet as U.S. Secretary of Commerce. Son John is a member of the Cook County Board of Commissioners. The other siblings chose a life outside politics, going into law or education, but we're pretty sure they're some of the first Chicago Democrats in line on Election Day.

✳   ✳   ✳   ✳

"What's Paris next to Chicago? Has Paris got Lake Michigan?"

—Richard J. Daley

"If a man ever reflected a city, it was Richard J. Daley . . . he was this town at its best—strong, hard-driving, working feverishly, pushing, building, driven by ambitions . . . he was this city at its worst—arrogant, crude, conniving, ruthless, suspicious, intolerant. He wasn't graceful, suave, witty, or smooth. But, then, this is not Paris or San Francisco."

—Mike Royko, "Daley Embodied Chicago,"
Daily News, December 21, 1976

One Unique Home Store

* * *

*Though in downtown Chicago you'd be hard-pressed
to find a block of buildings that look exactly alike,
there's one department store at the corner of Ohio and Wabash
that may stop you dead in your tracks.*

Today it's a Bloomingdale's home store, but for most of the last century it was Medinah Temple, home of the Ancient Arabic Order of the Nobles of the Mystic Shrine—known to most as the Shriners. A subset of the Masonic order, the Shriners are a men's club with no "ancient" or "Arabic" characteristics to speak of, but that didn't stop them from constructing a Moorish temple. Built in 1912, Chicago's Medinah Temple is just that—an eastern edifice festooned with brick and tile detailing and stained-glass windows and anchored by enormous onion domes. The temple's main space was an auditorium used for both highly secretive Shriner rites and for cultural expositions with world music and elaborate performances.

Long abandoned by the area's Shriners Club and in danger of being torn down, the building's fate was subject to intense debate. Preservationists viewed it as a significant architectural anomaly, while others viewed it as a strange, irritating eyesore.

In 2003, New York retail behemoth Bloomingdale's gutted the building and added a soaring atrium and every modern amenity. The purchase and renovation of the temple, which cost $40 million, were considered risky, but these aspects also created great publicity for the store and a new life for its famous building—or at least its shell, which continues to startle and beguile residents and visitors alike. It does look different from everything around it, and the building is now the most recognizable department store in town. Customers are always welcome, and funny hats are optional—not required.

You Can Thank Chicago

Twinkies

In 1930, Jimmy Dewar was the manager of Chicago's Continental Bakery, which was well known for its Wonder brand bread and Hostess brand cakes. Another popular item the bakery produced was a strawberry-filled shortcake, which could only be made when the berries were in season. Looking for a way to make the snack available year-round, Dewar replaced the strawberries with a banana-cream filling, and the Twinkie was born. During World War II, fruit rationing forced him to switch from the banana filling to the vanilla cream we all know today.

Tinkertoys

Stonemason Charles Pajeau loved watching children at play, and he came up with the idea for a new toy by watching neighborhood kids build models with pencils and empty spools of thread. Working out of his garage in the Chicago suburb of Evanston, he designed a set of colored wooden rods and disks with holes drilled through the center and along the sides. Partnering with business-man Robert Pettit, he introduced his Tinkertoys to local stores in 1915. Before long, the toys were a national sensation.

Cell Phones

In the mid-20th century, AT&T engineers developed a new idea for communications: a network of radio towers that would allow wireless telephone communication through telephones installed in automobiles. AT&T had some success with their car-phone service, but the true revolution in the communications industry came when Martin Cooper's research team at the Chicago-based Motorola company developed a fully portable phone in 1973. Cooper's original phone weighed two pounds and cost nearly $4,000, but consumers were nonetheless anxious to take advantage of the convenience it offered. Within a decade, the Chicago firm had reduced both the size and the cost of the cell phone, leading to a revolution in personal communications.

Wicker Park: Heart of Cool

* * * *

This storied neighborhood rose from the ashes, sunk into disrepute, and reemerged as a jewel of the North Side.

If you're going to blame Mrs. O'Leary's cow for the Great Fire, then give the star-crossed bovine some credit. After all, if it weren't for the 1871 conflagration, Wicker Park might not have emerged as a vibrant, well-heeled neighborhood.

Bordered by the Chicago River to the east and Western Avenue to the west, with Bloomingdale Avenue and Division Street forming the north-south boundaries, this neighborhood was originally designated by Charles and Joe Wicker. The brothers purchased the land and laid out the subdivision in 1870. Their timing couldn't have been better: The Great Fire ripped through the city a year later, and when it came time to rebuild, many wealthy Chicagoans settled here.

The area flourished as German and Polish merchants moved into the neighborhood. The German beer barons of the 1890s built mansions that still stand on Hoyne and Pierce streets. Toward the end of the 19th century, the area was called "the Polish Gold Coast" due to its well-heeled immigrant population and opulent churches.

A Time for Change

After World War II, the Wicker Park area, as it was now called, went through changes. The Polish and German families that had lived there over the decades gravitated to the north, and Mexican and Puerto Rican immigrants moved in. In the late 1950s, the construction of the Kennedy Expressway sliced through the city and decisively separated Wicker Park from Lincoln Park, further isolating the neighborhood and ensuring its individuality.

The Latin Kings and other gangs took over during the 1960s (perhaps in part due to the nearness of the area to the newly completed interstate), and violence gripped Wicker Park. The economic slump of the 1970s kept the area in its own kind of recession, and very little commercial or residential growth took place.

In the late 1980s, Wicker Park's fate started to turn, as artists took notice of the availability of affordable real estate in the neighborhood. Throughout the 1980s and into the early 1990s, if you were an artist in Chicago, Wicker Park was the place to be. Artists who made the area home included singer-songwriter Liz Phair, who wrote her critically acclaimed, best-selling album, *Exile-in-Guyville,* while living in a Wicker Park apartment. The fact that authors Saul Bellow and Nelson Algren had lived in the area at one time (Bellow from 1924 to 1993 and Algren from 1959 to 1975) furthered Wicker Park's artistic street cred.

Today's Wicker Park

With its proximity to downtown and its hip architectural details (the Flat Iron Arts Building at the intersection of North, Milwaukee, and Damen avenues is the area's most striking landmark), Wicker Park continues to thrive as a cutting-edge place to work and live.

Throughout the late '90s and early '00s, people with more money suddenly viewed the gritty neighborhood as a unique fixer-upper project, and soon sushi and tapas restaurants, antique shops, and entertainment venues popped up. This boom drew additional attention and created even more development: Fashion designer Marc Jacobs opened a Wicker Park store in 2007, one year after the New York shop Scoop landed in the hood, offering customers choice selections from Gucci and Prada. Houses on Pierce and Caton streets got major face-lifts, and community groups suddenly found themselves with new board members and more money.

But one of the main reasons Wicker Park continues to hold its cache as a unique spot in the city of Chicago is that there continues to be a vibrant mix of people living there. The new well-to-do residents may have cleaned up the parks and increased the area's tax revenue, but a diverse population remains. Artists, tourists, salespeople, homeless people, and street toughs all feel right at home in Wicker Park. The mix creates a city within a city, and for Wicker Park's residents, it's the only place to be.

Tired, Achy Feet?
Paging Dr. Scholl...

✳ ✳ ✳ ✳

*This "arch" Chicagoan never practiced medicine,
but he brought pain relief to millions.*

You might say that foot care was in William Mathias Scholl's blood. Born in 1882 on a farm in Indiana, Scholl had a chance encounter with his grandfather's shoemaking kit that led him to cobble together a career centered around foot care.

At age 18, Scholl set off for Chicago and soon landed on his feet, getting a job at Ruppert's, a downtown shoe store. Many of his customers complained that their dogs were barking; Scholl quickly realized that something was afoot, and bad shoe design was the culprit. Scholl enrolled in night classes at a medical school. He never wanted to practice medicine in the traditional sense, and he never did. Instead, he marched to his own drummer, inventing and patenting various foot-care devices, the first of which was an arch support called the Foot-Eazer that he developed when he was just 22 years old.

Scholl may have been a born cobbler, but he was also a born salesman. Rather than hiring salespeople, Scholl hit the ground running by personally making the rounds of Chicago shoe stores, dressed in a white doctor's coat. He would often hold a skeletal model of the foot against his products to give store owners a visual demonstration of exactly how the products would support feet.

Dr. Scholl was a pioneer who realized that an ill-fitting shoe affected the wearer's spinal alignment. This understanding led to the invention of his famous sandals, along with cushion insoles and bunion pads. By the mid-1950s, such "corny" Scholl-written slogans as "When your feet hurt, you hurt all over" were ubiquitous. When he died in 1968, the Dr. Scholl brand was worth $77 million. Today, the legacy of the doctor who never practiced medicine lives on at Chicago's Dr. William M. Scholl College of Podiatric Medicine.

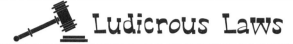

Ludicrous Laws

No one wants to see that!... Until the 1970s, it was illegal to "indecently exhibit any stud horse or stud bull" in a public place.

***Garbage* goes in a *garbage can*...** It is illegal to "dump garbage, slop, or kitchen waste down a privy."

Who's to say what's "disorderly," anyway?... In 1893, it was determined by the courts that there was no law on the books prohibiting "disorderly conduct." A judge ordered all prisoners being held on such charges freed—and there were more than 1,000 such prisoners in custody at the time!

No parking—and that applies to *everyone*... In the 1930s, laws were passed prohibiting the parking of automobiles in the Loop during business hours. More than 200 police officers were dispatched to ticket all cars parked, "regardless of political connections."

We consider stoning cruel and unusual around here... A $5 penalty may be levied against anyone who "throws a rock or casts a stone" in public.

The Willis Tower will have to come down... The Chicago building ordinance specifies that buildings may not be taller than 130 feet. By the time this law went into effect in 1893, there were already a handful of buildings much taller than that!

The phone lines are going to be jammed... It is still on the books that you must contact city officials before entering the city in an "automobile." This dates back to the days when automobiles were still quite a novelty—and terribly dangerous.

There are *some* limitations on the right to vote... A bill introduced in 1901 would have made it mandatory that assistance be given to anyone too drunk to mark a ballot at a polling place.

There's a Maze Under Your Feet

* * * *

Years ago, there were nearly as many tunnels as streets in Chicago—and many of them are still there!

Cable TV documentaries make it seem as though Al Capone personally dug out an entire network of escape tunnels. Capone wasn't anywhere near that industrious—the tunnels were already there! By the time of Prohibition, the city was full of tunnels that had been made for horse and pedestrian traffic and freight delivery years before. (During the late 19th century, intense shipping traffic on the river led to Chicago River bridges being raised much of the time; this in turn led to problems for pedestrian traffic, and the solution the city came up with was to construct pedestrian tunnels.) Many buildings were connected by tunnels, and the bootleggers of the Prohibition era found them awfully convenient. While few will ever see them, most of them are still there today!

One of the oldest tunnels went underneath the river at La Salle Street—this tunnel was dug out in 1871, just in time for it to become an escape route during the Great Fire. That tunnel was then used by cable cars, and eventually by streetcars, before being closed in the 1930s. It's still there—the entrance ramp to the parking garage in the middle of La Salle at Kinzie is the old tunnel entrance—but it was walled off and filled with damp sand in the 1950s.

Some of the old city tunnels have even been tourist attractions at times. A tunnel beneath Congress Street once connected the Congress Hotel to the Auditorium Theatre. The marble-lined tunnel was known as Peacock Alley and was one of the crown jewels of the city in the early 20th century. It's still there too—marble and all—but the entrances have been bricked off for years.

The most extensive of the Chicago tunnels were the freight tunnels 40 feet below the Loop. These narrow tunnels were originally used to deliver coal and mail. The earth dug out for them was placed along the shore and eventually became Grant Park. At one point, nearly every major building in the Loop had an entrance to these freight tunnels.

As companies switched from coal to gas heating, the tunnels became less useful. Those companies that kept using coal for heat began to have it delivered via truck. The tunnels officially stopped being used during the '50s, and the entrances were mostly bricked off. But the tunnels remain, far below the city streets. All told, there are nearly 60 miles of freight tunnels still in existence under the Loop. For many years, breaking into the tunnels to go exploring was a popular pastime, but the city always frowned on the practice—even when they were in operation, the tunnels weren't exactly safe. Security concerns about how much trouble could be caused by people breaking into the tunnels became prominent after 9/11, and today all entrances have been closed off.

At least, as far as anyone knows. Many old buildings had an entrance to the tunnels, and it's quite possible that some of them are still there in the basements of the city's oldest buildings, just waiting to be discovered.

✳ ✳ ✳ ✳

- *In 1992, the city paid dearly for neglecting the freight tunnels. A private contractor accidentally drilled into the tunnel under Kinzie Street, and Chicago River water began filling the freight tunnels. Months later, the tunnels were full, and the water had only one place to go—into the basements of the buildings that had utilized the tunnels years before. The flood was invisible to all above ground, but it paralyzed and embarrassed the city. Subway service had to be rerouted and businesses shut down. It was weeks before the Loop returned to normal. Damages resulting from the flood were estimated at around $1 billion.*

- *Another Chicago tunnel system is the Chicago Pedway, which connects the subway to many downtown buildings.*

When the Civil War Came to Chicago

* * * *

Camp Douglas, a hastily constructed prison,
spelled misery and death for Confederate POWs.

The high-rise apartment buildings along Martin Luther King Jr. Drive and 35th Street tower above a pleasant stretch of green space dotted with trees. You'd never guess that on this serene plot of land, thousands of young men met their untimely deaths.

During the Civil War, this was the site of Camp Douglas. Opened in September 1861 to serve as a training camp for Union soldiers, the facility soon housed 4,200 men. Sewers were never built, and sanitation was abysmal in the marshy lakefront terrain. By February, disease had killed 42 recruits. But the worst lay ahead.

When General Ulysses S. Grant led Union forces to victory at Fort Donelson, 4,459 captured rebels were shipped to Chicago, and the already ill-equipped Camp Douglas was pressed into service as a prison. Kind-hearted citizens donated food, blankets, and clothing, but conditions deteriorated quickly. By June about 500 prisoners had died, with dysentery the main culprit. An outbreak of smallpox in 1863 made matters worse, and the death toll soared. Escape attempts among the underfed prisoners were common.

Overall, 26,060 prisoners passed through Camp Douglas. We'll never know exactly how many died. Estimates range from 4,000 to 6,000, and the treatment of the dead was also deplorable. Medical and burial records were scandalously incomplete. Most of the bodies were buried in a sandy potter's field where Lincoln Park now stands. Later they were moved, unceremoniously, to Oak Woods Cemetery on the South Side and buried in a mass grave. A monument listing the names of the dead was not placed at the mass grave until 1912. In addition, some historians believe that the remains of some Confederate soldiers may still lie under the playing fields at North Avenue and Lake Shore Drive.

Fast Facts

- When the Treasury seized Al Capone's bulletproof Cadillac, Uncle Sam found a more legitimate use for it. The elegant armored Caddy became one of Franklin D. Roosevelt's official conveyances.

- In 1915, Mayor William Hale Thompson responded to women's concerns by appointing Louise Osborn Rowe, an inexperienced party loyalist, as the newly created commissioner of public welfare. Rowe soon resigned after getting caught taking kickbacks, just like any self-respecting male Chicago politico.

- Albert Johnson was awaiting trial in the Cook County Jail in the mid-1990s. Citing an offended sense of Christian propriety, he sued because female guards could see him nude in the shower and toilet. The U.S. Appellate Court ruled that Johnson's rights in jail didn't include modesty.

- One 1860s Chicago burglar, "Handy Andy" Lowe, always took time to do some reading in his victims' libraries. He often made intellectual notes in the margins of their books, leaving them open on a desk so the victims could appreciate his insightful wit.

- Telling it like it is: In a 1937 speech, German American George Cardinal Mundelein, archbishop of Chicago, questioned how "a nation of 60,000" could "submit in fear and servitude to . . . an Austrian paper hanger, and a poor one at that." When Mundelein died of cerebral hemorrhage in 1939, rumors (most likely false) circulated blaming Hitlerite henchmen.

- **Fact:** In the 1950s, a small-time crook named Richard Morrison got arrested. **Twist:** Morrison became the "singing burglar," not for his musical talents, but for ratting out his accomplices. **Only in Chicago:** Most of Morrison's partners in crime turned out to be CPD officers.

Little Hell

* * * *

The worst neighborhood in Chicago history?

Some of Chicago's best neighborhoods today were among the most dangerous decades ago, and vice versa. But some neighborhoods just never seem to get much better, no matter how many years pass.

One of these is the area once known as Little Hell—the patch between Halsted and Sedgwick, stretching from Chicago Avenue up to City Cemetery (which is now Lincoln Park). Originally a German enclave, after the area was leveled in the Great Chicago Fire, hastily built wooden tenements were put up. Often, two or three would be crammed into a lot that was really only large enough to hold one.

By the 20th century, the area was notorious for its gangs. The Black Hand Society, a group of extortionists, terrorized the neighborhood. Anytime a person in the neighborhood came into some property, if they didn't pay a tribute to the Black Hand, the property would be firebombed. If they still didn't pay, they might be killed.

In the middle of the neighborhood, the corner of Oak and Milton (now Oak and Cleveland) came to be known as Death Corner. For most of the 1910s, it averaged roughly a murder a week.

A combination of crime and the unsafe, unsanitary conditions of the tenements caused the buildings to be gradually torn down; the last of the tenements were gone by the end of the 1950s. In its place, Chicago put up the ambitious housing project known as Cabrini-Green, which soon became one of the most notoriously overcrowded and unsafe projects in the city. In recent years, the city has torn down most of the Cabrini high-rises in an attempt to once again reinvent the neighborhood. Only the passing of the years will tell if the city gets it right this time around.

Chicago Chatter

"I give you Chicago. It is not London-and-Harvard. It is not Paris-and-buttermilk. It is American in every chitling and sparerib, and it is alive from snout to tail."

—H. L. Mencken

"Chicago never seems to go to bed, and the streets at night are a blaze of electric light and thronged with people. I asked a man at a saloon once what time they shut up, and his answer was, 'Well, I've been here over ten years, and it's never been closed since I've been here.'"

—Martindale C. Ward, *A Trip to Chicago: What I Saw, What I Heard, What I Thought* (1895)

"There are bonds that can't be broken. I spent so much of my life there [Chicago] that I carry it with me when I'm gone."

—Saul Bellow

"Chicago is a more interesting place to write about than many places could be. It's a shot and a beer kind of town, not a quiche and chardonnay kind of town, which is part of the excitement. It still has enormous energy that sets it apart."

—Sara Paretsky, author

"Chicago is the Napoleon of cities. A city of colossal vices and colossal virtues."

—Hamlin Garland, *Rose of Dutcher's Coolly*

"It isn't hard to love a town for its greater and lesser towers, its pleasant parks or its flashing ballet. Or for its broad and bending boulevards . . . But you never truly love it till you can love its alleys too."

—Nelson Algren, *Chicago: City on the Make*

Marilyn and the Babe Stayed Here

✳ ✳ ✳ ✳

*Near the top of Lake Shore Drive sit the remnants of
the Edgewater Beach Hotel, a pink, stucco birthday cake of
a building that for more than 90 years has represented a history of
luxurious decadence on Chicago's Far North Side.*

The original 400-room building, which was demolished shortly after
the hotel closed in 1967, was constructed in 1916 and was designed
in the shape of a cross to offer the majority of the guests unobstructed views of the lake. The hotel became so successful that
several other structures were added, including a 600-room addition
in 1922, a matching—and still-standing—apartment building in
1927, and an elaborate network of restaurants, bars, swimming
pools, tennis courts, and gardens.

Throngs of Chicagoans were drawn to the hotel's most market-
able features—its lakeside promenade and wide stretches of sandy
beaches—while plush amenities and stunning vistas attracted
wealthy and powerful guests from all over the country. For decades,
such stars and athletes as Marilyn Monroe, Bette Davis, Babe Ruth,
and Lou Gehrig could be spotted lounging in the sun while
Chicago's elite hosted weddings and cocktail parties in the hotel's
marble-clad dining rooms. Even presidents Franklin D. Roosevelt
and Dwight D. Eisenhower are said to have stayed at the hotel, a
retreat from campaign stops and the rat race in Washington.

But with the rise of air conditioning in the 1950s and '60s and

the Lake Shore Drive extension
(which cut off the hotel's immediate beach access), the hotel lost its
luster and began to lose business.
The old-fashioned, 18-floor high-
rise didn't stand a chance against
the climate-controlled skyscrapers

going up downtown; all it had to offer was an outdated Baroque facade and the sound of traffic coursing by. The hotel was forced to close in 1967.

After the '60s ended, the hotel's buildings traded hands many times; one was even used for a Loyola University Chicago dormitory before it was demolished. The 1927 Edgewater Beach Apartment building is still in operation, its street-side storefronts and restaurants leased to new generations of Chicagoans. Located at the corner of Bryn Mawr and Sheridan roads in the Bryn Mawr Historic District, the apartment building is not without its own illustrious past: It was home to legendary Chicago Bears coach and owner George Halas, who lived in the 18th-floor penthouse. There's no word on what he thought of the hotel's choice of paint color.

- *In 1941, Ed McCaskey visited Halas at the Edgewater Beach Apartments to request permission to marry Halas's daughter, Virginia. Halas never gave his consent, and the couple eloped in 1943.*

- *Benjamin Marshall, the architect of the Edgewater Beach Hotel, also designed the Drake Hotel and the Iroquois Theatre, which was consumed by flames a month after it opened.*

- *A 1949 incident at the Edgewater Beach Hotel provided the inspiration for Bernard Malamud's book* The Natural *(which was later made into a movie starring Robert Redford). Ruth Ann Steinhagen was a 19-year-old Chicagoan who became obsessed with Cubs player Eddie Waitkus. When Waitkus was traded to Philadelphia, Steinhagen was devastated. When the Phillies came to Chicago to play the Cubs, Steinhagen checked into the Edgewater Beach Hotel because she knew that was where the Phillies would likely be staying. Steinhagen lured Waitkus to her room and shot him; later she stated she knew she could not have him and didn't want anyone else to have him either. Waitkus recovered and helped the Phillies win the pennant the following year.*

Chicago Cuisine

Food historians generally cite Raffaele Esposito, a citizen of Naples, Italy, with inventing pizza in 1889. His original creation had a delicate crust topped with thin layers of tomato sauce, mozzarella cheese, and basil. The toppings were meant to reflect the colors of the Italian flag—in honor of King Umberto I and Queen Margherita of Italy. (Many contemporary Italian restaurants offer "Margherita Pizza" as a tribute to this first pizza.) The tasty dish soon became popular around the world, including in the United States, as a light snack or premeal indulgence.

In 1943, two Chicago businessmen decided to open a new eatery in lumber baron Nathan Mears's refurbished mansion at Ohio and Wabash streets. Richard Novaretti and his partner, Texan Ike Sewell, first considered a Mexican restaurant, but—after failing to come up with a viable menu—they decided to switch to Italian fare under the banner of The Pizzeria. Seeking to offer something distinctive, they experimented in the kitchen until they hit on a hearty variation of Esposito's original recipe—the Chicago-style pizza.

This Pizza Means Business

Their recipe called for a thin crust lightly dusted with cornmeal and spread across the bottom and up the sides of a deep, heavy pan. The crust was then topped with a generous helping of crumbled Italian sausage, a preposterous amount of cheese, and finally a layer of rich tomato sauce. The novel dish not only greatly increased the amount of toppings normally found on pizzas of the day but also inverted the order in which they were layered. The gooey, indulgent creation, which required a knife and fork for diners with any interest in maintaining tableside decorum, proved more than a match for even the heartiest of appetites. Few diners could eat more than one slice.

The restaurant and the new dish became an instant success, and before long the pair opened a second site a few blocks away. Both restaurants, now called Pizzeria Uno and Pizzeria Due, are still in operation, pulling in an astonishing $6.5 million in sales annually between them. The business has also expanded to offer franchises in 31 states and several foreign countries, including South Korea, Honduras, and the United Arab Emirates.

The Plot Thickens (and Bubbles, and Spills over the Side of the Pan...)

But the story of the recipe's creation is not as clear cut as it might seem. No one seems to know for sure whether it was Sewell, Novaretti, or the pair working together that hit upon the formula for the famous Chicago "uber pizza." Further complicating the origin story is Adolpho "Rudy" Malnati, a bartender who was brought into the mix as the restaurant's business manager. Malnati would later leave to open his own Chicago-style pizzeria, and his family members still operate two popular local pizza chains (Lou Malnati's and Pizano's). His son Rudy Jr. would later contend that his father was a key contributor to the original recipe but has no clear evidence to back up the claim.

There's no doubt, however, that the Chicago-style pizza did originate at the Ohio Street restaurant that opened in 1943 and that imitators sprang up quickly, first across the city and then across the country. Many of Uno's contemporary competitors were started by former employees of Pizzeria Uno. Former Uno waitress Helen Delisi set up Delisi's in West Rogers Park on the North Side, and Chicago cabbies Sam Levine and Fred Bartoli and their friend George Laverde opened Gino's East on Superior Street after hiring former Uno cook Alice Mae Redmond. Chicagoans frequently debate which culinary institution offers up the best version of the distinctive dish, but there's no question that it is truly a Chicago original.

* * * *

- *Ike Sewell did finally get his Mexican restaurant. Su Casa opened down the street from Pizzeria Uno in 1963.*

- *Stuffed pizza is sometimes mistaken for Chicago-style pizza, but the two are not the same. Stuffed pizza has a layer of dough on top, and Chicago-style pizza does not.*

Chicago Rocks!

✳ ✳ ✳ ✳

The Windy City is no slouch when it comes to rockin' out.
Here are six great examples of world-famous Chicago bands.

- Might as well start with the obvious! Still going strong after four decades, the beloved, horn-fueled **Chicago** is the biggest rock band to ever come out of the city after which it is named. No other band charted more U.S. singles in the 1970s, and Chicago has sold a mind-boggling 120 million albums worldwide since its founding in 1967 as "Chicago Transit Authority" (the group tweaked their moniker in 1969 after the real transit organization threatened legal action). Fans still flock to their concerts to revel in such nostalgic hits as "Beginnings," "Make Me Smile," and "Saturday in the Park."

- Formed in 1988 by guitarist/vocalist Billy Corgan, guitarist James Iha, and bassist D'arcy Wretzky, no other "alternative" Chicago band has had as much success as **Smashing Pumpkins.** Encompassing everything from metal to goth to psychedelia, the band was an instant favorite of music critics, who praised their 1993 sophomore album *Siamese Dream* to the skies. It was not until their smash-hit 1995 double album *Mellon Collie and the Infinite Sadness,* however, that Smashing Pumpkins broke through to the mainstream.

- Though technically from Rockford, Illinois, **Cheap Trick** is thought of by many as a "Chicago band," as they cut their performing teeth there in the mid-1970s. Cheap Trick produced radio-friendly, irresistible pop songs such as, "I Want You to Want Me," "Surrender," and "So Good to See You," but they struggled for success in the United States. In Japan it was a different story—indeed, the Japanese greeted them as "the New Beatles" when they embarked on their first Japanese tour. The frenzy proved contagious, and the live album they made there, *Cheap Trick at Budokan,* was what finally put them over the top in the United States. In recent years, Cheap Trick recorded the theme song for *That '70s Show.*

- Hugely popular but critically reviled, **Styx** was formed in Chicago in 1970 and went on to great success in the next decade, becoming the first band to score four multiplatinum albums in a row. Early hits included both arena rockers ("Come Sail Away") and sickly sweet power ballads ("Lady"). When founding

member Dennis DeYoung began pushing a more theatrical "concept" agenda in the early '80s, however, the rest of the band rebelled. The result was unbearable tension, barf-inducing synth dreck ("Mr. Roboto"), and the band's first breakup in 1984. The band still tours and even made a stop at the White House in 2009.

- When alternative country group Uncle Tupelo broke up in 1994, vocalist/guitarist Jeff Tweedy and bassist John Stirratt decided to form a new band, **Wilco.** Though not widely known to main-stream audiences, Wilco has been hugely influential among other alternative rockers and a critics' darling since day one. Their most famous album, 2002's *Yankee Hotel Foxtrot,* sold a respectable 590,000 copies, and the band has been a pioneer in using the Internet to get its music out to its fans. Wilco won a Grammy Award for Best Alternative Music Album in 2004 for the album *A Ghost is Born.*

- Born in the Chicago suburb of Wilmette in 2001, **Fall Out Boy** sold 2.5 million U.S. copies of its 2005 major-label debut, *From Under the Cork Tree.* Though ostensibly fronted by vocalist/ composer Patrick Stump, bassist/lyricist Pete Wentz has received the lion's share of attention. Whether overdosing on the sedative Ativan, marrying poptart Ashlee Simpson, founding his own fashion line, or guest-starring on *CSI: NY,* the past several years, nary a week has gone by in which Wentz has not made the news. Indeed, his overexposure has cost Fall Out Boy dearly in the alternative cred department, though the band continues to sell albums and tour successfully. Their fifth album, *Folie a Deux,* a largely collaborative effort that includes such artists as Elvis Costello and Lil Wayne, was released in December 2008.

The Green, Green Grass of Home

✳ ✳ ✳

It's definitely not easy being green, but from its first public parks to today's wetlands conservation, Chicago has worked hard to maintain its unique environment.

Think of Chicago, and the first image that comes to mind may not be "green"—a quality that signifies a clean environment filled with trees and fresh air. But these days, Chicago is living on the edge—that is, the cutting edge of environmentalism. The city has embraced all manner of environmentally friendly initiatives, from encouraging people to be pedal pushers during their daily commutes to fostering rooftop gardening.

An Early Commitment

Chicago's very history is littered, if you will, with a sense of commitment to nature and its healing powers for an urban citizenry. Starting with the city's motto, *Urbs in Horto* (City in a Garden) from its earliest days, Chicago modeled itself on the majestic capitals of 16th- and 17th-century Europe, which placed a high value on public parks and other green spaces.

However, much of the inspiration for these grand spaces came from a less-than-majestic source: workers who were often cooped up in factories and tenements all week long. City officials believed that exposure to clean air and green grass would improve the health and lives of these workers, so they made a commitment to create the spaces that would provide these benefits.

The project started right in Chicago's own "front yard," its 29-mile lakefront. In 1909, renowned architect Daniel Burnham convinced city officials to create Grant Park, 319 acres of open space on Lake Michigan. Throughout the late 19th and early 20th centuries, a wealth of world-renowned park designers—including Burnham, the Olmsted brothers, William Le Baron Jenney, and Jens Jensen—contributed to the development of Chicago's parks.

Leading the Charge

Today, Mayor Daley and others are heeding the call to help make Chicago the greenest big city in the country. From building the first municipal rooftop garden on city hall to establishing a Department of the Environment in 1992, green initiatives are among the cornerstones of Daley's administration. Using his clout as one of the most powerful mayors in the country,  he has helped lure green technology businesses, such as solar-panel manufacturers, to the city, and he has worked to improve wastewater management, overhaul the city's recycling program, and restore the Lake Calumet region, which is one of the largest wetland areas in North America.

But not everything is coming up roses. Chicago still struggles with brownfields, abandoned or underused industrial and commercial facilities that contain high levels of hazardous waste and other pollutants. The city also has one of the highest commuting times in the country, as public transportation fails to entice drivers out of their cars. And the Chicago River, long the lifeblood of the city, still suffers from a host of problems, including pollution, erosion, and loss of wildlife.

A Model City

Still, Chicago is taking responsibility for its problems, and it has made great strides. The city is retrofitting its alleyways using recycled materials that allow stormwater to drain into the ground instead of collecting on hard surfaces or draining into the sewer system. The city also coordinated the planting of the nation's first public orchard at Kilbourn Park in 2008.

As people around the globe become increasingly aware of the need to protect the environment, big cities like Chicago can help provide models for how urban dwellers can do their part. With its wealth of programs and activities to help make Chicago green, the city already has a head start.

The Poetry Slam: A Perfect 10

* * * *

We know you've scribbled a poem down on a napkin or in your journal with dreams of sharing your brilliant verse with a world that could never understand. The good news, fair poet, is that a Chicago construction worker has invented something called the poetry slam!

In 1984, a Chicagoan named Marc Smith decided that poetry needed a little livening up. He enjoyed poetry but not poetry readings—they were too stiff and hoity-toity, making them inaccessible to the general public. Smith organized the first poetry slam (named after the grand slam in baseball) at the Green Mill. The rules are simple: The work had to be original, and no props or costumes were allowed.

Smith picked judges from the audience and gave them markers and napkins on which to write their scores from 0 to 10. Smith instructed the rest of the audience to get involved too. If they hated a poet, they were encouraged to boo. If they liked him/her, they should cheer. The winner of the slam received a Twinkie.

Slam On, Crazy Poet!

Smith's idea caught on. By 1993, the first National Poetry Slam was held in San Francisco; the event continues to be held in a different U.S. city every year and brings more than 80 teams from across the country together for five full days of fierce poetic competition.

Slams have popped up in small towns and big cities across America, as well as in France, Nepal, and the Czech Republic. Marc Smith still hosts the Original Uptown Poetry Slam at the Green Mill every Sunday night. The show's been running for more than 20 years and shows no signs of slowing.

* * * *

- *President Barack Obama and First Lady Michelle Obama hosted a poetry slam at the White House in May 2009. James Earl Jones was among the performers.*

Fast Facts

- Why does a grave in Woodlawn Cemetery say only "Baldy; June 22, 1918"? That was the day a circus train got rear-ended in Hammond, killing 86. The wreck mangled most of the remains beyond identification. "Baldy," known only by his carny alias, was one officials were able to identify.

- Italian tradition considers death in childbed to be martyrdom. One such martyr, Julia Petta, died in 1921 and was interred in Mount Carmel Cemetery. Her mother began having dreams about Julia, and in 1927, she convinced a judge to order exhumation. Julia's body had not decayed.

- October 4, 2004, was one of the strangest days in Chicago history. Not a single homicide was reported that day. No one could remember a day like it in Chicago, which typically had 600–900 homicides per year in the preceding decade.

- In the 1920s, Johnny Torrio bossed his minions from the Four Deuces (2222 S. Wabash). If you suspect that it was a hive for all forms of criminal activity, you have a pulse. Despite a near-successful assassination attempt on him in 1925, Torrio died of natural causes in 1957.

- With the rise of the interstate freeway in the late 1950s, Chicago knocked down thousands of homes to make way. This unleashed ten million Norway rats on the rest of the city as the dispossessed rodents sought new lodging.

- Cub Stan Hack (played 1932–47) was famous for his friendly disposition. Bill Veeck sold "Smile With Stan Hack" mirrors in the bleachers. After fans began using them to blind opposing batters, umpires called the mirrors "Out!"

- **Fact:** Taylor Street scoffed at Prohibition. **Twist:** Police officers tried to break up the hooch operation of one Taylor Street family, the Montanas. **Only in Chicago:** The police retreated under fire from matriarch Grandma Montana

The Era of the Dance Halls

* * * *

*Chicago's grand ballrooms offered residents an escape into
a world of beauty and fantasy.*

After the horrors of World War I, people all across America were
ready to let loose and celebrate. Some of the biggest, most elegant
ballrooms in the land were built in Chicago to showcase the hot new
sounds of jazz and big band swing.

The Roaring Twenties

One early Chicago dance hall was the Trianon, built by entrepreneur
Andrew Karzas in 1922. Karzas put a lot of thought into this project.
He strategically located his ballroom at Cottage Grove and East
62nd Street so that it was easily accessible by Chicago's elevated
train system. Realizing that his middle-class patrons were caught up
in the frenzy of luxury and high living that defined the 1920s, he
designed the interior in an over-the-top Louis XVI style.

The Trianon became an emormous success,
but Andrew Karzas was not about to rest on his
laurels. He and his brother William decided to
open another ballroom, one that would be even
grander than the Trianon. In 1926, they unveiled
the Aragon Ballroom on Lawrence Avenue, which
could welcome up to 8,000 dancers a night. Since
the Trianon's French interior design had been
such a hit, the brothers Karzas decided to try
something even more exotic with the Aragon—a
Spanish/Moorish decor. The venue featured
mosaic tiles, a terra-cotta ceiling, and majestic
arches. The second level of the Aragon was
accessed by way of an ornate double staircase.
This upper ballroom was built to resemble a huge
Spanish courtyard, and "stars" twinkled in the
blue-black "sky" above. The Karzas brothers had

done it again; even Chicago's mayor, "Big Bill" Thompson, came to the grand opening of the Aragon.

In 1929, America experienced the most devastating stock market crash of its history, and the American people were facing a depression that would hold them in its exhausting grip for the next decade. One might think this would have spelled the end for Chicago's great ballrooms, but they continued to flourish. Like motion pictures, dance halls allowed weary citizens an escape for relatively little money. Those who could not afford a new car or a vacation could still afford a night of dancing.

In addition to the Trianon and the Aragon, there were ballrooms all over the city, such as Green Mill Gardens (4802 N. Broadway) and the Moulin Rouge (416 S. Wabash). Most were constructed near "L" lines, so as to be easily accessible to patrons from every corner of the city. Jazz bands and big bands from all over America and Europe came to Chicago, bringing new tunes in exchange for taking away some of that distinctive "Chicago Sound." Rules varied from club to club; some were racially integrated and some were not. Bored with "square" music, whites began to demand African American bands— even in dance halls that were off-limits to African American patrons. Seeing the popularity of the grand ballrooms, many of Chicago's finest hotels, such as the Drake and the Palmer House, initiated renovations in their ballrooms in order to offer their guests the most elegant surroundings as they danced.

The dance halls continued to draw large crowds throughout the Depression and World War II, but with the dawn of the '50s came the dawn of rock 'n' roll, which dealt a deathblow to Chicago's grand ballrooms. Most of the ballrooms have been demolished, but a couple (the Aragon and the Green Mill) survive as reminders of days when elegance reigned.

✳ ✳ ✳ ✳

- *Beginning in 1940 and lasting through most of the decade, Lawrence Welk performed regularly at the Trianon.*

Chaplin in Chicago

* * * *

It wasn't the first film studio in Chicago, but the success of the films it produced—and the star power it commanded—made Essanay Studios one of the most competitive and powerful motion-picture companies of the silent era.

Essanay was founded by George Spoor and Gilbert Anderson, who combined the sounds of the first initials of their last names to produce the studio's moniker. Spoor, who owned a film distribution company, and Anderson, a veteran of vaudeville and a rising motion-picture star, proved to be particularly acute businessmen who knew their market and—for a decade—knew how to deliver. They cultivated a stock of profitable onscreen talent and paid exorbitant salaries to keep their stars churning out hit after hit.

The studio early productions were so successful—especially 1907's *An Awful Skate* (or *The Hobo on Rollers*)—that in 1908, just a year after it was established, Essanay moved to a sprawling location along West Argyle Street on Chicago's affluent North Side. The studio's directors filmed both on set and on location, choosing between Chicago's breathtaking lakefront, nearby farms, and, of course, its industrial cityscape.

Soon, banking on its successes in Chicago, Essanay built a second studio, this time closer to the bourgeoning film industry in another American boomtown, a stretch of arid, waterless turf known as Hollywood. (Hollywood's first movie studio, the Selig Polyscope Company, originated in Chicago as well.) Essanay was able to produce pictures that could appear to have been shot in any number of exotic locales. And, at a time when producing moving pictures was still a wonder and the industry lacked a home, that kind of flexibility was a valuable asset.

Essanay's four biggest names were Gilbert Anderson himself, who originated the much-loved western hero Broncho Billy; Ben Turpin, a mawkish, cross-eyed clown; decadent starlet Gloria Swanson, whose career was launched at Essanay; and Charlie

Chaplin, the much-beloved English actor whose graceful slapstick never ceases to entertain. These stars helped Essanay refine genres, and the studio produced many of the era's most successful westerns (starring Anderson) and comedies (starring Chaplin).

On to Drier Pastures—But the City of the Big Shoulders Had Left Its Mark

Chaplin's legacy at Essanay was both short and unpleasant, but proved highly profitable for both the star and the studio: Chaplin received $1,250 a week, one of the highest salaries in the industry, but left Chicago after less than a month on the job, frustrated by the company's management and annoyed by Chicago's unruly weather. Chaplin, used to milder climates, headed first to the Essanay's newer, sunnier studio space in California, but, after disputes over his salary, Chaplin left for good. His exit proved to be the studio's death knell: It closed both its California stage and its Chicago headquarters in 1918, just three years after Chaplin signed with a new company.

Still, a few weeks of Chicago's industrial hoopla could well have contributed to Chaplin's anguishing urban comedy, and, surely, to his famous "Tramp" character, donning a bowler and wielding a bamboo cane. He debuted the Tramp while he was working for Essanay— though it was for a film made elsewhere—and performed it in his one finished project for Essanay, *His New Job,* a movie about a film extra who stumbles into an acting job before clumsily destroying a soundstage and ripping the dress of his modest ingenue.

Essanay's glory was brief yet wondrous. Chaplin may have only spent 23 days with the company, but his rise to fame—and that of his Essanay costars—was meteoric and much deserved. And, perhaps, after their flight to the foothills of California, they brought some of the city with them. Today many studios still film in Chicago, which has had a leading role in such famous Hollywood-produced movies as *The Untouchables, Ferris Beuller's Day Off,* and *The Dark Knight.* But the decadent lives of glamour queens and matinee idols only collided at full speed with that of the "hogbutcher of the world" once—for a few fleeting, silent years.

Radical Chicago

✳ ✳ ✳

Chicago has a long history of social and political activism. As a major industrial urban center, it became a hotbed of labor activity in the 19th century and has produced more than its share of crusaders in support of women's rights, civil rights, and various other causes. Below are a few of the more notable—and controversial—activists that Chicago has sent to the national stage.

- Mary Harris was a tiny, grandmotherly figure who adopted the name **Mother Jones** and was one of the most effective organizers of mine workers during the 19th and early 20th centuries. While she is best known for traveling from one hot spot to another, she spent many years in Chicago, where it is generally believed she developed her passion for workers' rights by observing the dire conditions of the city's working poor.

- **Lucy Parsons** was an outspoken advocate for workers' rights whose husband, Albert, was executed in connection with the infamous Haymarket bombing of 1886. She continued her radical agitation for labor reform and became one of the founding members of the Industrial Workers of the World.

- **Jane Addams** was an Illinois socialite who completely redefined the approach to social services and community activism in 1889 by founding Hull House on South Halsted Street. While living among Chicago's urban poor, Addams helped bring improvements to virtually every aspect of their lives, from public education to improved city services to judicial and political reform.

- A fearless supporter of African American civil rights in the 19th century, **Ida B. Wells** began her career by working for a crusading newspaper in Memphis, Tennessee. She continued her work after moving to Chicago in 1895 and went on to become one of the founders of the National Association for the Advancement of Colored People.

- In 1939, when he was just 30 years old, **Saul Alinsky** created the Back of the Yards Neighborhood Council, bringing economic and social development to the neighborhood by channeling the residents' collective antipathy toward the area's meatpacking industry. For this effort, the Chicago native is generally credited with creating the modern notion of community organizing. Many of his principles and tactics are still widely employed today, and Alinsky's philosophies have influenced such leaders as Hillary Clinton and Barack Obama.

- **Fred Hampton** was a leader of the Chicago chapter of the Black Panther Party in the 1960s. The group, which advocated both community service and militant action, drew the ire of conservative groups and local government figures. Hampton was killed in a controversial police raid in 1969.

- A native of Greenville, South Carolina, **Jesse Jackson** moved to Chicago in the mid-1960s as a civil rights organizer for the Southern Christian Leadership Conference. He eventually broke from the group to form Operation PUSH (People United to Serve Humanity) and went on to become one of the most influential African American activists on both the national and international scenes.

- A son of Commonwealth Edison chairman Thomas G. Ayers, **Bill Ayers** was raised in Glen Ellyn, a Chicago suburb. He attended Lake Forest Academy and the University of Michigan, then became a founding member of the Weather Underground, a radical group that bombed numerous government buildings to protest the Vietnam War. All charges against him were dropped when he surrendered to authorities in 1980, and he went on to become a respected professor of education at UIC. He found himself at the center of the 2008 presidential election when Barack Obama was criticized for having a professional relationship with the activist.

Hull House

✳ ✳ ✳ ✳

In the late 1880s, Hull House represented a bastion in social equality.
Unfortunately, Hull House also became known for its ghost stories.

In 1856, businessman Charles J. Hull constructed a mansion at
Halsted and Polk streets on Chicago's Near West Side, a fashionable
section of the city. But the Great Fire of 1871 sent wealthy
Chicagoans elsewhere, and the Near West Side began to attract a
large population of immigrants. It became one of the most dangerous slums in the city, and by the 1880s, Hull House was surrounded
by factories, bordellos, taverns, and rundown tenement houses.

Jane Addams Moves In

Born into an affluent Illinois family in 1860, Jane Addams knew
nothing of poverty as a child. When her father died, she sank into
a depression, and she traveled to Europe to distract herself from
her grief.

Jane and Ellen Gates Starr, her friend and traveling companion,
volunteered with the poor at Toynbee Hall, a settlement house in
London's Whitechapel neighborhood. There, Jane and Ellen offered
food, education, and medical care while lobbying for social reform
and improved standards of living. Jane was invigorated by her work
and soon made plans to start a similar project in Chicago.

By the time Addams came to the Near West Side with the
intention of starting a settlement house, the crowded neighborhood
was teeming with poverty and crime. Brothels and dope houses
victimized the immigrants who came to the United States with little
money and were often unable to speak English.

Impressed by Jane's plans for a settlement house, Helen Culver,
Charles Hull's niece, offered the mansion to Addams with a rent-free
lease. Addams and Starr converted the mansion into a place that
offered food, shelter, and education. As the operation increased in
popularity, 12 more buildings were added, until eventually Hull
House spread out over an entire city block.

When Jane Addams died in 1935, the Hull House Association took over the property and continued her efforts until the 1960s, when the University of Illinois at Chicago bought the property.

Lingering Spirits

Charles Hull's wife had died of natural causes in a second-floor bedroom of the mansion several years before Jane Addams took up residence in the home. After her death, some of the staff of the house claimed to hear footsteps pacing back and forth in the room from time to time. Visitors and overnight guests experienced Mrs. Hull's presence too.

Author Helen Campbell claimed to see a ghostly woman standing next to her bed when she spent the night in the haunted room. When she turned on a light, the apparition disappeared. In Jane Addams's autobiography, *Twenty Years at Hull House*, she stated that earlier tenants of the mansion believed that the attic was haunted, so they always left a bucket of water on the steps because they thought a ghost would not be able to pass it and descend to the lower floors. The ghostly tale of Mrs. Hull is still recounted today, but this would not be the only supernatural tale surrounding Hull House.

By 1913, rumors were circulating that Hull House was the refuge of a "Devil Baby," and the organization's reputation as a great example of social reform was superseded. According to the story, this deformed child was the son of a Catholic woman whose husband was an atheist. When the young woman hung a picture of the Virgin Mary in her home, her husband angrily tore it down, screaming that he would rather have the devil himself in his home than a picture of the Virgin Mary. He soon got his wish!

When his wife became pregnant, it was said that she was carrying the "Devil Baby" in her womb. Allegedly, the baby was born with pointed ears, horns, a tail, and the ability to speak both English and Latin. Unable to endure the insults and tormenting by his neighbors, the husband abandoned the child at Hull House, where he continued to be a nuisance. Unable to make him behave, Jane Addams had him locked away in the attic.

People flocked to Hull House, hoping to get a peek at the freakish child. The pandemonium eventually died down, but decades later, many people still believe that the story of the "Devil Baby" had some elements of truth to it. People have speculated that the child was actually a badly deformed infant brought to Hull House by a poor, young mother who could not care for it.

Those who believe the "Devil Baby" tale insist the disfigured boy was hidden away in the attic of Hull House for many years. They claim this explains why a deformed face was often seen looking out the windows. Believers state that the boy grew up at Hull House, and when Jane Addams died, he was moved to another settlement house on the North Side, where he later died.

Jane Addams considered the story more a sociological study than anything else. She believed that women of the time clung to the story as a way of keeping their husbands and children in line. The story aroused Addams's sympathy for the plight of the people who believed the strange tale.

Hauntings Today

Today, Hull House is a National Historic Landmark. The University of Illinois at Chicago built its campus around the mansion in the 1960s, leaving no trace of the old neighborhood that once existed. The crumbling tenements and brothels have been replaced by lofts and ethnic restaurants.

Hull House remains an attraction for tourists, history buffs, and ghost enthusiasts. It is not uncommon for motion sensors to be triggered, even when no one is at the house. Officers report that no other building on campus gets as many false-alarm calls as Hull House.

Visitors who have come to Hull House during the evening hours often report strange occurrences. There are many claims of lights turning on and off, shadowy figures seen moving inside, babies crying, and shutters that open and close by themselves.

There are many possible suspects in the haunting of this house, including the ghost of Mrs. Hull, the lingering spirit of one of the poor people that Jane Addams tried to save, and, of course, the "Devil Baby." Some believe a portal to another realm surrounds Hull House. You can visit Hull House today and find out for yourself— but we would venture to guess that the only spirit that will follow you as you leave is the spirit of community service.

Quiz

Chicago's Daleys are among the best-known big-city mayors of the 20th century, but other memorable politicians have served in the city's top elected office. See if you can match the selection of Chicago mayors below to the clues about their careers.

Answer Choices:
Michael Bilandic
Jane Byrne
Anton Cermak
Carter Harrison Jr.
Carter Harrison Sr.
William B. Ogden
"Big Bill" Thompson

1. Gangster Al Capone was a regular contributor to this mayor's campaign fund.

2. An experienced businessperson, this mayor kept the city financially sound during the depression of 1837.

3. This mayor was voted out after the Haymarket tragedy and was assassinated during the last days of the World's Columbian Exposition.

4. This mayor caused a sensation by moving into Cabrini-Green in 1981.

5. This mayor cleaned up the red-light districts, battled with streetcar developer Charles Yerkes, and left works by Gauguin and Toulouse-Lautrec to the Art Institute upon his death.

6. This mayor was a founder of Chicago's machine politics and was murdered during a public appearance with President Franklin Roosevelt in Miami.

7. This mayor brought free public festivals and the Chicago Marathon to the city, but lost a bid for a second term as a result of a poor snow-removal job after a heavy blizzard.

Answers: 1. Big Bill Thompson, 2. William B. Ogden, 3. Carter Harrison Sr., 4. Jane Byrne, 5. Carter Harrison Jr., 6 Anton Cermak, 7. Michael Bilandic

Kingmaker City

✳ ✳ ✳ ✳

Presidents past and present have tipped their hats to Chicago.

Long before Hyde Park resident Barack Obama became the nation's 44th president, Chicago was an important stop on the road for any candidate. Other political hotspots (Alaska, anyone?) may take the limelight, but few places have played a bigger role in electing the nation's chief executives in the past 150 years than Chicago.

A Gracious Host City (for the Most Part)

Chicago has hosted more presidential nominating conventions (14 for Republican, 11 Democrat) than any other American city, and many of these conventions went well beyond the scope of merely nominating a candidate. In 1896, Democratic candidate William Jennings Bryan gave his famously fiery "Cross of Gold" speech in Chicago, whipping the crowd into a frenzy, and in 1968, the nation watched anxiously as protestors and police clashed outside of that year's Democratic convention.

Much of the city's historical attractiveness for political conventions comes from its central location, but right from the start, the city also simply had more space than other locations. The 1860 Republican convention was held in a temporary structure called the Wigwam, a great place for a powwow of 12,000 participants. In 1880, Republicans met in the Interstate Industrial Exposition Building, a huge, barnlike structure on Michigan Avenue at Monroe Street. The Chicago Coliseum at 63rd Street and Stony Island Avenue, was home to the 1896 Democatic convention, and between 1952 and 1968, the 9,000-seat International Amphitheater at 43rd Street and Halsted held no fewer than five conventions.

A Cherished Right

Beyond these gatherings, Chicago is best known for its ability to get out the vote. The expression "Vote early and vote often" is variously attributed to Al Capone, Richard J. Daley, and William Hale "Big Bill" Thompson. Historically, Chicago's citizenry prepared to vote (whether only once or several times a day) by marching in a torchlight parade each Election Eve. No parade was more significant than that of 1960, when Mayor Richard J. Daley accompanied John F. Kennedy and hundreds of thousands of marchers to the Chicago Stadium, where Kennedy spoke to a massive rally. Kennedy's narrow victory over Richard Nixon is often credited to the ability of Mayor Daley to turn out the vote: Kennedy won Cook County by a staggering and somewhat suspicious 450,000 votes.

The Lowest Lows and the Highest Highs

No Chicago political event is as notorious as the 1968 Democratic convention. Fueled by opposition to the Vietnam War, protesters clashed with police in battles beamed around the world by television. So divisive were the events of 1968 that Chicago didn't host another convention until Bill Clinton accepted his reelection bid in the newly constructed United Center in 1996. In between, however, Chicago continued to be a fertile hunting ground for votes, and with the rise of Barack Obama in 2008, Chicago once again became the epicenter of presidential politics.

✳ ✳ ✳ ✳

- *One of the most memorable moments from the 1968 convention was when Abraham Ribicoff of Connecticut took to the podium to endorse George McGovern of South Dakota. In his speech, Ribicoff was critical of the tactics the Chicago police were using to handle the protestors outside the convention. Ribicoff's words enraged Mayor Daley, who was sitting in the front row. Daley's response was not caught by microphones, but television viewers had no problem reading his lips.*

First City of Comedy

* * * *

A group of U of C students staged a theatrical revolution.

Who comes to mind when you try to think of the funniest people you've ever seen? Stephen Colbert of *The Colbert Report*? Tina Fey of *30 Rock*? Steve Carell of *The Office*? Bill Murray or John Belushi of *Saturday Night Live*?

All these comedic actors have something in common: They honed their skills in Chicago. Forget hog butchering, deep-dish pizza, and architecture. The City of the Big Shoulders' real gift to the world is comedy. From Mike Nichols directing *The Graduate* to Tina Fey taking time out from *30 Rock* to transform herself into Sarah Palin, a long parade of Chicago-trained actors, writers, and directors have kept America in stitches.

Games Lead to Brilliance

How did a working-class midwestern city become a major source of showbiz talent? It started in the 1950s at the University of Chicago, where the lack of a drama department did not stop students from forming their own theater group. One of those students was Chicagoan Paul Sills, who had learned improvisational theater games from his mother, Viola Spolin, and taught them to his fellow actors as a way to develop their skills. In improv, actors build a sense of trust and timing among themselves by performing scenes created on the spot—out of their own imaginations—rather than from scripts.

Inspired by their improv work, Sills and a group of actors established their own cabaret-style comedy theater group, the Compass Players, and made improv a part of the show. Audiences were encouraged to suggest types of characters and settings, and the actors would use that information to create comedy sketches that focused on political and social humor. Buoyed by their success, Sills and other Compass members opened their own club on North Wells

Street in 1959 and called it the Second City. The troupe gained notoriety as a proving ground, propelling Alan Arkin, Joan Rivers, David Steinberg, Robert Klein, and others to national fame.

By the 1970s, Second City's workshops were as renowned as its shows, and young actors from around the country made the pilgrimage to Chicago to learn comic improv, hoping for a shot at the big time. The shows themselves had evolved into polished, rehearsed revues, though the material continued to be developed through improv. Second City went from notable to legendary in the late 1970s after alums Belushi, Murray, Gilda Radner, and Dan Aykroyd helped establish *Saturday Night Live* as one of the funniest shows on TV.

A Comic Boom

In the 1980s, with its hot reputation and an influx of eager young performers, Chicago saw an explosion of improv-based comedy shows and workshops, each offering its own spin on the form. At ImprovOlympic (later called iO), Second City veteran Del Close taught a technique he called "the Harold," a long-form style of improv that created complex performances that were more like short plays than comedy skits. Annoyance Theatre, established by Mick Napier, a respected director at Second City, succeeded in pushing improv into darker, more experimental areas. Annoyance's *The Real Live Brady Bunch* was a breakout hit that was remounted successfully in New York and triggered a nationwide revival of interest in the popular 1970s sitcom, while *Co-ed Prison Sluts* ran for an amazing 11 years—a record in Chicago musical-theater history.

As the growth of cable TV offered more room for comedy programming in the 1990s and 2000s, Chicago continued to funnel talent to the coasts. Andy Dick, Rachel Dratch, Jeff Garlin, Sean Hayes, Mike Myers, Bob Odenkirk, Amy Poehler, Andy Richter, Amy Sedaris, and others maintained the city's 50-year tradition of breeding comic innovation.

✳ ✳ ✳ ✳

"I went to Second City, where you learned to make the other actor look good so you looked good."

—Bill Murray

Crawford? Pulaski? Same Difference.

* * * *

Most of us probably don't give too much thought to the street names in our community, other than learning them in order to get around. But sometimes the naming of a street can become quite contentious.

In the early 1930s, Mayor Ed Kelly championed an effort to rename Crawford Avenue, an 18-mile-long thoroughfare on the West Side, to honor Revolutionary War hero Casimir Pulaski, who created and led the Continental Army's cavalry unit. Though Kelly's idea sounds honorable enough on the surface, most observers saw it as a blatant attempt to court the city's ever-growing numbers of Polish voters.

One stretch of the street in the central part of the city was a highly successful retail district, and local merchants there objected to the change. They cited the cost of having to alter their signs and reprint business cards, forms, and so on (though many accused them of simply having an anti-Polish bias). When the change was put through by the city council in 1933, the merchants started legal proceedings. Kelly won out after a two-year legal battle. Some Crawford backers actually tore down the Pulaski street signs, and one streetcar conductor got into a scuffle with a Polish passenger when he called out the stop as Crawford. Residents submitted several petitions over the next 15 years to have the name changed back, but the city council dutifully ignored all of them. A second legal case went to the Supreme Court of Illinois in 1952, when the matter was settled once and for all in favor of the Polish horse master.

* * * *

- *Drivers who head north on Pulaski will find themselves on Crawford Avenue once they pass out of the city limits. Although Chicago changed the name of the street in the '30s, the suburbs retained the original name.*

Fast Facts

- Chick Gandil, the 1919 Black Sox ringleader, had a memorable fight with the Indians' Tris Speaker at Comiskey Park earlier that year. Speaker slid into first base with spikes high, slashing Gandil. After the inning ended, the fisticuffs began. It took seven policemen to break them apart.

- Banished "Black Sox" post-baseball occupations: Eddie Cicotte, game warden; "Shoeless Joe" Jackson, liquor storekeeper; Buck Weaver, drugstore operator; Lefty Williams, pool hall owner; Chick Gandil, plumber; "Happy" Felsch, tavern keeper; "Swede" Risberg, dairy farmer.

- ChiSox shortstop and Hall of Famer Luke Appling (played from 1930 to 1950) was one of the most annoying batters of his day from a pitching standpoint. Always deadly with two strikes and expert at fouling off disliked pitches, he typically struck out just 30 times per season.

- While the Cubs' double-play combination of Tinker (Joe, SS) to Evers (Johnny, 2B) to Chance (Frank, 1B) went down in history, less often recorded is that Tinker and Evers weren't on speaking terms. As for Chance, a tall, strong, opinionated former catcher, neither cared to trifle with him.

- What exactly was wrong with Cubs great (played from 1904 to 1912) Mordecai "Three-Finger" Brown's pitching hand? Two separate injuries, both in his farming youth. A feed chopper accident severed his index finger and broke the rest; while healing, Mordecai fell and broke them again. His middle finger healed crookedly.

- The Harlem Globetrotters are not from Harlem. They started out in Chicago as the Savoy Big Five (after Bronzeville's Savoy Ballroom) in the 1920s. They didn't play in Harlem until 1968.

Folk Music in the Big City

✳ ✳ ✳ ✳

The Old Town School of Folk Music has nurtured generations of folkies, guaranteeing that traditional American music will be heard well into the future.

American folk music is the traditional sound of the common people, passed down through the generations with little thought of profit or fame. Folk music has been an important part of American culture since colonial days, but it was considered a "lower" form of music for most of its history. Things began to change with the advent of radio in the 20th century; suddenly folk music could be heard far and wide.

In the 1930s and '40s, folk singers Woody Guthrie and Pete Seeger began to record commercially and tour nationally, but it was in the 1950s and '60s that folk music experienced its greatest boom in the United States. As more traditional groups such as The Weavers and The Kingston Trio gave way to "progressive" folkies Bob Dylan, Joan Baez, and Phil Ochs, an argument began as to what "folk music" really meant and how far an artist should be allowed to push its boundaries. That argument has never been settled and probably never will be, but both traditionalists and rebels have found plenty to love at the Old Town School of Folk Music.

Art Through Expression

The Old Town School opened its doors at 333 North Avenue (in Chicago's Old Town neighborhood, of course) on December 1, 1957, the brainchild of musicians Frank Hamilton and Win Stracke. Hamilton and Stracke believed it was important for the school's teaching methods to reflect the type of music it was promoting: organic, communal, and participatory. While other music schools concentrated on note reading and performance perfection, the Old Town teachers encouraged students to play by ear and play joyfully, rather than nervously stressing out about the "proper" way to play.

Just because they had a more laid-back approach to teaching, however, didn't mean those at Old Town weren't eager to use traditional methods to collect and preserve folk songs for future generations. In the early years, Old Town musicians put together a songbook of almost 100 folk songs—mostly from North America, but also from England, Ireland, Israel, and other countries. This songbook contained not only the actual music and lyrics of each song, but also what was known of the song's history and geographic origin. It will no doubt prove to be a priceless document to musical historians for years to come.

At Home in the Square

The Old Town School moved to 909 West Armitage Avenue in Lincon Park in 1968. In the 1970s, interest in folk music waned and for a while, the school teetered on the edge of bankruptcy. Luckily, a new board of directors realized that with increased awareness, more effective fundraising, and change of venue, the Old Town School could be bigger and better than ever. In 1998, the school moved into a much larger building that once served as a library: 4454 North Lincoln Avenue in Lincoln Square.

Enrollment at the Old Town School is now a healthy 6,000 students per week, and the school is in the process of expanding into an annex across the street from its current location. There is a class for everyone, from the wiggleworms classes for babies to group guitar and dance classes for adults to world music workshops. All music-lovers enjoy the venue's 400-seat concert hall, where greats such as Pete Seeger, Mahalia Jackson, and Roger McGuinn of The Byrds have performed.

✳ ✳ ✳ ✳

- *My wild Irish Rose*
  The sweetest flow'r that grows,
  You may search ev'rywhere,
  But none can compare
  With my wild Irish Rose.

  —Lyrics from the traditional folk song "My Wild Irish Rose"

One Side or the Other: Chicago's Baseball Rivalry

* * * *

If there's only one thing you learn about Chicago, it should be this: You can't be a fan of both the city's baseball teams at the same time.

When it comes to sports, can a city be in a rivalry with itself? If the subject is baseball, and the town in question is Chicago, the answer is a resounding "Yes!"

In fact, few rivalries in all of sports are as intense or have as long a history as the one between the fans (and sometimes even the players) of the Chicago Cubs and the Chicago White Sox. While the two teams haven't met in the World Series or even a playoff game in more than a century—and only began playing official games against each other in 1997—pledging allegiance to either the Cubs or the Sox can be as important to a Chicagoan as where they live, what they do for a living, or whom they're married to.

So Near, Yet So Alien

Storied sports rivalries are usually built around a few key ingredients: geographic proximity, a history of intra-league competition, or legend-ary games that are still debated by fans. From the Chicago Bears and the Green Bay Packers in professional football to North Carolina versus Duke in college basketball to the New York Yankees and the Boston Red Sox in baseball, what matters is the competition—who won and who lost, and what will happen the next time the teams meet. Few cities have more than one professional home sports team, how-ever, and while New York has two baseball teams to argue over, in Chicago, it is so much more than just which team is better.

With the Cubs and the Sox, the rivalry is as much a mind-set or a lifestyle choice as it is a question of batting averages and pitching stats. Take the two teams' home stadiums, for example. For the Cubs, home is the storied, ivy-covered Wrigley Field on the city's gentrifying and middle-class North Side. Wrigley is known as the

"Friendly Confines" and is hallowed ground for legions of tourists and college kids who some say outnumber the true baseball fans. The Sox, on the other hand, play in the relatively new U.S. Cellular Field, called "The Cell" by fans and foes alike and the shrine for a critical and passionate fan base on the city's grittier South Side. Fans see themselves as "North-Siders" or "South-Siders," and this alone provides more than enough fodder for a slew of insults and scorn, baseball-related and otherwise.

On—and Off—the Field

Of course, the rivalry does have its sports competition angle. Dating back to the creation of the American League in 1900, the Cubs and Sox have competed for fans' loyalty as well as bragging rights as the best team in town. The early rivalry reached a peak with the two teams' only World Series appearance to date in 1906, which the Sox won in six games.

For decades the only meetings between the two teams was the occasional exhibition game that mattered for little more than bragging rights. With the introduction of interleague play in 1997, however, the games started to matter in the standings, and the regular season games between the two teams became one of the hottest sports tickets in town. Through 2009, the Sox have a slight edge in the series (37–35).

White Sox fans got a major boost over their rivals in 2005, when their beloved team won the World Series for the first time in 88 years. The following season, the rivalry boiled over onto the field when Cubs catcher Michael Barrett punched his White Sox counterpart, fan favorite A. J. Pierzynski, after a close play at the plate at U.S. Cellular Field. After a bench-clearing brawl, the White Sox went on to win the game, 7–0.

Today, the rivalry continues. And while differences may not be settled anytime soon by punch-ups like the one on the field in 2006, if you're a Chicago baseball fan, it may be best to remember one hard and fast rule: Never flash your South Side pride anywhere on the North Side. Never. At any time. And vice versa.

All the Right Moves

* * * *

*A dance show for Chicago kids
gave new meaning to the phrase "generation gap."*

By 1965, Jack and Elaine Mulqueen had been on the Chicago airwaves for two years with their WBKB children's show *The Mulqueens.* The couple's ratings weren't bad—about 180,000 viewers—but still, Jack felt a change was needed. *The Mulqueens'* mix of comedy, puppetry, and short films just wasn't that different from its competitors. What could they do to stand out, to ensure they could hang in there for the long haul?

An Untapped Market

Dance shows such as *American Bandstand, Shindig,* and *Hullabaloo* had been popular with teens and young adults for quite some time, but Jack realized that there were no such shows for children. Kids were tired of "corny" children's music and wanted to listen to rock 'n' roll like the big kids.

These young Chicagoans also often had young, stay-at-home moms who would rather turn on a dance show than sit through yet another sickeningly sweet kiddie show. And it was usually these mothers who made the record-buying decisions in their families. Jack Mulqueen knew if he could satisfy both segments of his audience, he would have a hit on his hands.

A Mod Makeover

Elaine Mulqueen underwent a makeover—complete with miniskirt and go-go boots—to become Pandora, the perky hostess of the show they decided to call *Kiddie-A-Go-Go.* But there was one big problem: Elaine had never done any of the popular dances of the day (the Swim, the Monkey, and the Jerk), and these dances weren't taught at traditional dancing schools. Finally Jack called a nightclub and had them send over a go-go dancer to teach Elaine all the right moves.

Even Dick Clark Busts a Move

Kiddie-A-Go-Go debuted on WBKB on January 1, 1966. Jack Mulqueen cultivated relationships with record company executives, who were always looking for new ways to sell vinyl. The first band to appear on the show was The New Colony Six, a Chicago pop band with the upbeat sound the Mulqueens were looking for. Acts that followed included The Flamingos and The Four Seasons, along with such singers as Leslie Gore and Roger Miller. Even Dick Clark, the host of *American Bandstand,* appeared on *Kiddie-A-Go-Go,* and Pandora was able to persuade him to dance with the kids. Clark later told the Mulqueens that it was the only time he'd ever danced on television.

Kiddie-A-Go-Go was an instant hit. Before the end of the school year, its ratings had shot up to 247,600 viewers. Jack Mulqueen's hunch that young viewers and their mothers were looking for something different had been correct. That April, the department store Carson Pirie Scott began marketing *Kiddie-A-Go-Go* sweat-shirts, and it seemed that the show had found a home in its timeslot.

Contributing to the Delinquency of Minors?

That very same month, however, WBKB's station manager, Tom Miller, was fired. The new station manager, Dick O'Leary, was not a fan of *Kiddie-A-Go-Go.* Though he refused to even watch the show, he told Jack Mulqueen that it was contributing to the delinquency of minors and teaching children to dance like strippers. O'Leary canceled the show despite its high ratings, and the Mulqueens were forced to carry on at a UHF station, WCIU, which reached less than half of WBKB's viewing audience. Still, the show survived until 1969, when the Mulqueens themselves pulled the plug after Elaine suffered a health scare.

The spirit of *Kiddie-A-Go-Go* lives on in Chicago in the form of Channel 19's *Chic-A-Go-Go,* which has been on the air since 1996 and features dancers of all ages. Jack and Elaine Mulqueen are retired and live in a suburb of Chicago.

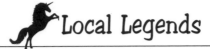Local Legends

Mary Alice Quinn was just 14 years old when she died in 1935, but she left a lasting impression on many of the more mystically inclined believers in Chicago's Catholic community.Some were of the opinion that she healed the sick only while alive; others believe her spirit hovers over a South Side cemetery, and that she continues to use her healing powers to this day.

Mary Alice Quinn was born on December 28, 1920. Like many children in Chicago, she was born into a poor immigrant family; her parents often felt overwhelmed by their adjustment to urban American life. To make matters worse, Mary Alice had been born with a serious heart condition and was never really healthy during the few years she had to live. Her life consisted of little more than lying in bed and praying continually. One day she saw an image on the wall of her bedroom and was convinced it was a message from God. She could not have known how radically her life was about to change.

Mary Alice's neighbors in the Grand Crossing area soon began to request specific prayers from her, and Mary Alice never refused any appeal if she felt it was honest and well-intentioned. Her reputation for healing grew by word of mouth, and eventually she was praying for hundreds of people. Mary Alice's family was shocked at her growing fame and worried about the toll her "work" might have on her health, but Mary Alice felt sure of her destiny.

Devoted to St. Thérèse

In order to understand Mary Alice Quinn, one must understand St. Thérèse of Lisieux, to whom Mary Alice was devoted. St. Thérèse was born in Alençon, France, as Francoise-Marie Thérèse Martin on January 2, 1873. She became a Carmelite nun while still a teenager and entered the convent at Lisieux. At first Thérèse seemed quite unremarkable; before long, however, her devout faith and simple kindness impressed all who knew her. (This should be starting to sound familiar at this point...)

St. Thérèse is known for her "Little Way," her acknowledgement that as a mere mortal, there was not much she could do to alleviate the pain and suffering in our world. "Great deeds are forbidden me," she once said. "The only way I can prove my love is by scattering flowers and these flowers are every little sacrifice, every glance and word, and the doing of the least actions for love." These sentiments appealed to Mary Alice, and she strove to pattern her life after St. Thérèse's as closely as possible.

All who knew her were deeply saddened when the ailing Mary Alice Quinn took a turn for the worse at age 14. Strengthened by her intense faith, on her deathbed Mary Alice told her family that, like St. Thérèse, she wanted to be a "little flower of Jesus" and continue to intercede for the sick even after her passing.

Word Gets Around
About a Misleading Headstone

Because of the almost fanatical devotion of her followers, Mary Alice was buried at Holy Sepulchre Cemetery under a headstone bearing the name "Reilly"; word got around, however, and her devoted followers began visiting her grave. Her apparition was supposedly seen by many on Chicago's South Side in the 1930s and '40s. To this day, many still visit Mary Alice's grave (which now includes her name on the headstone). Some claim a strong scent of roses can always be detected there, even on the coldest winter day.

✳ ✳ ✳ ✳

• *Holy Sepulchre Catholic Cemetery is also the final resting place of Richard J. Daley, former mayor of Chicago.*

Timeline

(Continued from p. 56)

1893
Richard Sears and Alvah Roebuck found Sears, Roebuck & Co. in Chicago.

May 1, 1893
The gates to the Columbian Exposition, the grand world's fair held to celebrate the 400th anniversary of Christopher Columbus's expedition, open to the public.

October 28, 1893
The night before the closing of the Columbian Exposition, Mayor Carter Harrison Sr. is gunned down by Patrick Eugene Prendergast. An unemployed Irish immigrant, Prendergast was upset by his failure to earn a city government post. He will be hanged for Harrison's murder.

June 2, 1894
The Field Museum of Natural History opens. Funded by Marshall Field and filled with artifacts from the Columbian Exposition, the museum is housed in the building that served as the Palace of Fine Arts during the exposition.

July 4, 1894
America's first modern amusement park featuring mechanical attractions, Paul Boyton's Water Chute, is opened at 63rd and Drexel. The centerpiece of the park is the country's first Shoot-the-Chutes ride. Boyton ("the father of America's amusement parks") will go on to found New York's Coney Island.

May 1, 1897
Chicago "Sausage King" Adolph Luetgert murders his wife.

1900
Dr. Wallace Abbott founds Abbott Alkaloidal. Renamed Abbott Laboratories, the company has enjoyed success and growth through the 20th century and into the 21st.

January 17, 1900
The Sanitary and Ship Canal opens, reversing the flow of the Chicago River. This "solves" the sewage problem—once the sludge leaves the city limits, it just falls off the face of the earth, correct?

February 1900
Sisters Ada and Minna Everleigh open the Everleigh Club, an opulent house of prostitution on South Dearborn Street.

1901
The White Sox franchise arrives in Chicago following stints in Sioux City, Iowa, and St. Paul, Minnesota. They will win the pennant race for the upstart American League that same year.

1903
Canadian immigrant James Kraft launches a Chicago-based cheese delivery business. Within 30 years Kraft will become a global food-processing giant.

(Continued on p. 147)

A Fair to Remember

* * * *

*When the gates of the World's Columbian Exposition opened in
1893, the fate of Chicago was forever changed.*

Long before television and the Internet, expositions provided a way
to galvanize resources and people—and make money, of course.
When it was announced that the House of Representatives was
accepting petitions from cities that wanted to hold America's world's
fair to commemorate the 400th anniversary of Columbus's voyage to
the New World, competition was fierce.

Chicago, New York, St. Louis, and Washington, D.C., all clam-
ored for the honor of hosting the fair, but none fought harder than
Chicago. The city's "who's who" were all in on the campaign:
Marshall Field, Potter Palmer, Philip Armour, Cyrus J. McCormick
Jr., and Joseph Medill all gave time and big money to secure the
right to the fair. Chicago at that time was a city of immigrants and
class struggle, known for manufacturing and not much else. City
leaders believed that if they could nab the fair, they could change
the way America and the world saw the city they loved.

On February 24, 1890, after months of deliberation, the House
of Representatives gave Chicago its wish—as long as it raised
another $5 million. The city's elite forked over the cash, and the fair
was Chicago's.

Boss Burnham & Crew

Once Chicago was given the green light, there was a lot to do. A
governing body was put in place to oversee what would be officially
called the World's Columbian Exposition. Congress created a
national oversight board comprised of two representatives from each
state and territory. A local group of representatives was formed as
well, and planning began.

The fair would be held on 600 acres of land, and heading up the
architectural plans was Burnham & Root, a firm that had helped
rebuild Chicago after the devastating fire not 20 years prior. Daniel

Burnham was not only an architect, he was a cracker-jack businessman whose input in the planning stages of the fair shaped the entire event. Burnham wisely chose Frederick Law Olmsted to help create the fairground environment; Olmsted was far and away the best landscape architect money could buy. Artist Francis Millet supervised all painting, and all things related to sculpture were handled by Augustus Saint-Gaudens.

Daniel Burnham

Burnham was a fan of the Beaux Arts style of architecture and so the fair, he decided, would have a decidedly classical look and feel. The buildings were to be built near Michigan Avenue, smack-dab on the most primo lakefront area of the city. The millionaires who lived there vetoed this choice and lobbied successfully for the fair to be moved south to Jackson Park.

Within a year, 40,000 skilled laborers were hard at work. The layout was simple: A Court of Honor would make up the center of the fairgrounds and would include such structures as the Electricity Building and the Palace of Fine Arts. Olmsted used the natural geography of the area to influence his plans; waterways threaded themselves through the park and emptied into Lake Michigan. Sculpture abounded, including a gilded statue of the Republic, located in the Grand Basin at the center of the Court of Honor.

At a time when the world was dingy with factory soot, the grandeur of these buildings and waterways defied comprehension. Burnham's enormous structures were covered with gleaming white stucco, which gave them a regal, heavenly quality. Early photos showing the construction of such buildings made their way to the newspapers of the world, and anticipation of what was to become the world's most extraordinary exposition intensified.

If You Build It... Everyone Will Come

The gates to the world's fair opened in 1893, and in walked more than one hundred thousand people on the first day alone. When fairgoers got to Chicago, they were presented with 65,000 exhibits, amusement rides, and parks and boulevards. The Midway Plaisance charmed young and old alike; a person could spend an entire day exploring the Midway alone. An elevated railway system shuttled people around, and electric boats ferried folks across the many waterways. Hundreds of "Columbian Guards" and undercover detectives patrolled the grounds while the cleanup crew kept the fair neat and tidy. Merchants numbered in the hundreds, selling such newfangled treats as the hamburger, bubbly drinks (commonly known as "soda" these days), and Cracker Jack. Scott Joplin performed a new kind of music called "ragtime," and a group of hula dancers introduced their style of dancing. Visitors who rode the first Ferris wheel marveled at the size and scope of the fair.

Those who attended the world's fair took home stories of invention and innovation. Word spread that Chicago was "the White City," named for the gleaming buildings and the illumination of gas and electric lights. Industry in Chicago soared, and many saw the city as a thriving center of commerce—a reputation it still holds today.

Closing Time

The fair closed its gates in October 1893. What was to become of the buildings and exhibits? Many of the artifacts filtered out of the city. The hugely popular Ferris wheel spent some time in a North Side neighborhood but was eventually moved to St. Louis for the 1904 world's fair.

As for the buildings, most of them were razed. The majority of the structures weren't built to last, after all; only the Palace of Fine Arts remains. After the fair ended, the Palace of Fine Arts housed the Field Columbian Museum (known today as the Field Museum of Natural History) until 1920, and then in 1933, the building reopened as the Museum of Science and Industry.

Even though the majority of the buildings were destroyed, the layout of the fair influenced public works projects in America throughout the decades to come. The National Mall and countless college campuses took their cue from the architecture and landscaping exhibited at the Columbian Exposition.

Indeed, Chicago's daily hustle and bustle proves that the legacy of the world's fair lives on. The fair put the city on the map and brought a world in transition into the 20th century with style, innovation, and hard work. Now *that's* the Chicago way.

All the Drama Started Here

✴ ✴ ✴ ✴

When two Chicago radio stations first put soap operas on the air in the '30s, they revolutionized the broadcasting industry.

Steamy romantic trysts, strained family relationships, mysterious medical conditions—these plot twists set soap operas apart from all other programming. While daytime serials have both their dedicated fans and their contemptuous detractors, there's no question that they make up one of the most enduring genres of mass media.

Enter Irna

In the 1920s, the young radio industry was growing in popularity, but the majority of its regular programming went out over the airwaves at night. In both national and local markets, no one believed daytime shows could draw enough listeners to make a profit. That all changed when Irna Phillips, who was earning a living as a radio actress at Chicago's WGN, proposed a daytime program called *Painted Dreams*. Developed with a female audience in mind, the saga followed Mother Moynihan and her troubled family. The station managers took a gamble on the 15-minute serial, which debuted in October 1930, and found an eager audience of housewives who embraced the melodrama as a welcome distraction from their daily routines. From that day to this, the soap opera has been a staple of daytime programming.

Phillips both wrote and acted in the show for the next two years, until an ownership dispute drove her to WMAQ, where she put on a similar show called *Today's Children*. She soon struck deals with the national networks and created several more daytime dramas, including *The Guiding Light*. Thanks almost entirely to the genre Phillips invented in

Chicago, the national networks saw their revenue from daytime programming triple during the 1930s.

Temptresses, Cliff-Hangers, and Intense Organ Music

As her shows evolved, Phillips created many of the familiar conventions we all expect from a soap opera. She structured each episode as a series of brief vignettes that moved back and forth between storylines. Her shows relied on organ music to stress important actions or facial expressions, and cliff-hangers kept audiences coming back day after day. She was also the first to introduce a temptress character—a conniving woman who thrives on using deception or trickery to steal men away from her competition.

By the early 1940s, Phillips had five of her soap operas in national syndication, and she soon moved them to television. She gave up acting but continued to write all the shows; at one point she estimated that she was churning out two million words of script per year. She developed a peculiar working style in which she would create the scenes by acting them out herself, switching back and forth between characters; her assistants would write up the scripts as they watched her.

Over the years Phillips created some of the best-known soap operas in American history, including *Days of Our Lives* and *As the World Turns*. Two of her employees eventually went on to create enduring soaps of their own; William Bell and Agnes Nixon, both also Chicagoans, were responsible for *The Young and the Restless, One Life to Live,* and *All My Children.* Phillips continued working on her shows from Chicago until shortly before her death in 1973, but her influence has endured to this day. During the 1990s, eight of the eleven nationally broadcast television soaps could be traced directly to her or to one of her protégés, earning the Chicago native the undisputed title of "Queen of the Soaps."

✳ ✳ ✳ ✳

- *Phillips was never one to shy away from controversial topics. Her soap* Another World *was the first to deal with the subject of abortion.*

More Than Just a Pretty Facade: Chicago's Architectural Masterpieces

* * * *

If you build it, they will come: Chicago's skyline draws crowds with its unique combination of lofty formal aesthetics, heavy structural elements, and playful innovation.

- **Reliance Building** (32 N. State; Atwood, Burnham, and Root; 1895): A major problem of urban skyscrapers was the canyon effect: Each building was in the shadow of the next, so owners faced the choice of paying to light the buildings 24/7 or letting workers drone on in the dark. The construction of this skinny skyscraper shed some light on the problem—literally—by employing a new construction method that allowed nearly the whole facade to be covered by "Chicago windows." Large central panes let the light stream in (even today when the building is dwarfed by its neighbors), and the smaller flanking windows could be opened to get in a cross-breeze, a factor that couldn't be underestimated in the fragrant days before central air.

- **UIC Campus** (Harrison & Halsted; Walter Netsch; 1968): Even before it was constructed, the Brutalist campus of UIC was a polarizing project—105 acres of the Near West Side were paved over to allow the school to move in, and in turn, the residents were forced to move out. Things didn't get better once Walter Netsch's creations were in place. The walled-in campus kept the city out and earned the bitter nickname "Fortress Illini." The confusing geometrical silhouettes of the buildings—University Hall actually gets wider as it gets taller—drew harsh criticism, and the warren of elevated walkways cast deep shadows, causing students to fear that muggers lurked everywhere. Eventually, the walls came down, and part of the concrete jungle made way for a traditional quad, but many of the buildings remain, relics of an experimental era.

- **Illinois Institute of Technology (IIT) Campus** (State and 31st–35th; Ludwig Mies van der Rohe; 1968): At a dinner reception in honor of Mies van der Rohe shortly after he started work on the IIT campus, he was introduced by architectural frenemy Frank Lloyd Wright: "I give you Mies, my Mies. Love him as much as I do and he will reward you." And reward he did: Over the next 40 years, the blighted Bronzeville neighborhood gained an oasis of simple elegance in the High Modern heaven of squat, simple buildings of steel, glass, and gray brick. And the "crowning" achievement of all was Crown Hall, an expansive glass structure that houses—of course!—IIT's School of Architecture.

- **Carson Pirie Scott & Co.** (1 S. State; Louis Sullivan; 1904): Influential architect Louis Sullivan came to Chicago to help the city rebuild after its Great Fire, and in doing so, fanned the flames of architectural influence for the next century. And none of his properties was hotter than the Carson Pirie Scott building, a marvel of gleaming windows (the better to display merchandise!) and exterior ironwork over the entry (the better to attract customers from both State and Madison streets!), which gives the building a fluidity that almost makes it seem to be in perpetual motion.

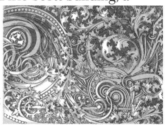

Carson Pirie Scott ironwork

- **Seventeenth Church of Christ, Scientist** (55 E. Wacker; Harry Weese; 1969): Though his most famous work may be the metro in Washington, D.C., Harry Weese was no stranger to Chicago, where his buildings run the gamut from a jailhouse, Metropolitan Correctional Center, to a house of worship, the Seventeenth Church of Christ, Scientist. Architectural pilgrims flock to the conspicuous corner of Wacker Drive and Wabash Avenue to pay homage to the Brutalist, windowless cylinder. Its modern form, recessed fountains, and massive skylight draw gazes from both baffled tourists and reverent Christian Scientists. The identifying text engraved along the top of the structure adds a trademark graphic element to the cityscape.

One Determined Detective

✳ ✳ ✳ ✳

Graphic novels have come into their own over the years, receiving accolades for great storylines and artistic merit. They all owe a debt of gratitude to one of the biggest names in the business—Chester Gould, creator of the Dick Tracy universe.

From a young age, Chester Gould dreamed of creating a comic strip for the *Chicago Tribune*. Gould finished his studies at Northwestern and the Art Institute, got a little room on North La Salle Street, and set about getting his foot in the door at the paper.

It took Gould almost 10 years, but the *Tribune* finally liked one of his ideas. The strip that got him the job was a detective story, filled with fast-paced action and colorful characters. Gould named the first-of-its-kind strip after its protagonist: Dick Tracy.

The strip first appeared on October 4, 1931, in the *Detroit Mirror*, a paper owned by the *Tribune*. The *New York Daily News* soon began running it as well, and finally the *Tribune* ran it too. Before long, the strip, which readers had begun to follow religiously and loved for its gritty subject matter, had become so popular that it appeared on the front page of many papers.

For 46 straight years, Gould created the *Dick Tracy* world. His characters were borderline outrageous (i.e., "The Mole," "Flattop," and "Breathless Mahoney") and his use of fantastic gadgets kept readers' imaginations firing (i.e., the classic "2-Way Wrist Radio"). The character of Tracy went through changes over the years; Gould experienced periods of great success, but times of backlash too (for instance, readership dropped during the "space period," when Gould catapulted Tracy and company into space adventures).

Gould stopped drawing the strip in 1977, but the cult of *Dick Tracy* lives on. A successful 1990 live-action movie featured Warren Beatty, Al Pacino, and Madonna. There have been various television adaptations of the comic strip, countless comic books, cartoon versions, and several films, as well, so it's still easy to get your fill of the crime fighter with the banana yellow hat and trench coat.

chicago chatter

"Here on the shore of Lake Michigan has risen a great and growing city, worthy to bear the title of the Empire City of the West."

—Noah Brooks, "Empire City"

"I wish I could go to America if only to see that Chicago."

—German Chancellor Otto von Bismarck,
to General Philip Sheridan

"I can't see why anyone would want to live anywhere else in the world."

—Jack Woltjen

"Chicago is a stew of contradictions. Coarse yet gentle. Idealistic yet restrained. Grappling with its promise, alternately cocky and unsure."

—Alex Kotlowitz

"Being a Cubs fan prepares you for life—and Washington."

—Hillary Rodham Clinton

"An October sort of city even in spring."

—Nelson Algren, *Chicago: City on the Make*

"It is hopeless for the occasional visitor to try to keep up with Chicago—she outgrows his prophecies faster than he can make them. She is always a novelty; for she is never the Chicago you saw when you passed through the last time."

—Mark Twain, "Speculations and Conclusions,"
Life on the Mississippi

"It is given to some cities, as to some lands, to suggest romance, and to me Chicago did that hourly. It sang, I thought, and in spite of what I deemed my various troubles, I was singing with it."

—Theodore Dreiser, *A Book About Myself*

"Chicago is a great American city. Perhaps it is the last of the great American cities."

—Norman Mailer, *Miami and the Siege of Chicago*

Putting Out the Welcome Mat: The Everleigh Club

* * * *

The Everleigh sisters cashed in on the sins of the Second City.

At the turn of the 20th century, life was changing for American women, who enjoyed the freedom of working outside the home. Never before had more young women been out on the street—and some were *really* out on the street. Prostitution was a legal option in some areas, and many street-smart women realized that they could make enough money to live on by selling their most precious asset: themselves. In 1910, there were more than 600 brothels in Chicago.

Meanwhile, in Omaha, sisters Ada and Minna Lester—who later changed their name to "Everleigh" after their grandmother's "Everly Yours" letter sign-off—ran a successful brothel. When their Omaha establishment looked as if it had come to a climax, the sisters looked to Chicago—a juicier, more lucrative market.

In a business often linked with desperation and debauchery, the Everleigh sisters had a unique and oddly effective hook: class. The sisters claimed they had gone to finishing school; their supposed well-groomed background gave them an air of dignity.

Perfumed Fountains and Mirrored Ceilings

Ada and Minna found a place they liked at 2131–2133 South Dearborn in the Levee district. The finest linens, furnishings, and lighting were installed to make the new club stand out. Perfumed fountains were installed in every room, and a $15,000 gold-leafed piano was wheeled into the music room for some auditory stimulation. The dining room was modeled after a Pullman train car. A few mirrored ceilings and lush oriental rugs later, the Everleigh Club was ready to open. For a house of ill repute, the sisters certainly garnered a reputation for offering the most luxurious "amenities."

The doors of that house wouldn't open for just anyone, however. As the sisters would say, the club was "not for the rough element, the clerk on a holiday, or a man without a check book." No kidding—simply to enter the club cost $10, and any kind of hunger—carnal or otherwise—came at a stiff price. Dinner included caviar and was $50. A bottle of champagne would run you $12. If you wanted to spend private time with one of Ada and Minna's girls, that would take another $50. Considering the average wage for a typical worker of the time was about $6 a week, not just anyone was walking through the doors of the Everleigh.

Girls, Girls, Girls

There were also standards for the girls who worked inside the club. The sisters would say that to be given a job at the club, "a girl must have a pretty face and figure, must be in perfect health, and must look well in evening clothes." Though prostitution was rampant at the time, it wasn't glamorous; the Everleigh Club was an exception. The Everleigh girls were also exceptional for the era: They were well fed, their health was monitored, and they were paid well for less work.

And as for the kind of work they were doing, well, let's just say that Minna and Ada had a clear business plan: sell, sell, sell—and not just sex. The booze and food tabs were just as important as the tabs for "other" services. Said the sisters, "Contemplation of devilment was more satisfactory than the act itself."

The End of an Era

In 1911, Mayor Carter Harrison Jr. ordered the club to close. The Everleigh sisters went to Europe, then settled in New York. They changed their names back to Lester and spent the rest of their lives socializing and going to the theater. As for the club itself, it was razed in 1933. Today, a housing development (the Hilliard Homes) stands on the ever-so-sinful Everleigh grounds.

✳　✳　✳　✳

- *Marshall Field Jr. died of a gunshot wound in 1905. It was rumored that he was shot at the Everleigh Club, but his family maintained that he accidentally shot himself at home, while cleaning his rifle in preparation for a hunting trip.*

Shoot for the Sky

* * * *

*How naked Chicago would feel
without its elegant Buckingham Fountain.*

In 1927, Chicagoan Kate Buckingham (daughter of a grain elevator mogul) commissioned a fountain to honor her late brother Clarence, a former director of the Art Institute. Positioned at Columbus Drive and Congress Parkway, the Georgian pink marble fountain was designed by Edward H. Bennett, coauthor of the Plan of Chicago. The fountain gives a nod to Lake Michigan with four Art Deco seahorses representing the four states that touch the Great Lake: Wisconsin, Illinois, Indiana, and Michigan. The design was influenced by the Latona Basin in Louis XIV's gardens at Versailles (though in typical Chicago fashion, the Buckingham is twice as large as the French fountain).

The fountain's central water shoot reaches heights of 150 feet, and the water displays are powered by pumps that churn up to 7,000 gallons of water per minute (though thankfully, the water is recirculated). The water show can be viewed every hour on the hour from April to October, 8:00 A.M. to 11:00 P.M. daily, weather permitting. The fountain lights, which come on at dusk, give what Kate Buckingham described as a "soft moonlight" look.

Though the fountain closes down during the winter, it sports twinkling lights during the holiday season. Any repairs are taken care of before spring comes, and thanks to Kate Buckingham, there's always money for fixes: At the time of the presentation of the fountain, a trust fund of $300,000 was established to fund repairs and upkeep, so the fountain would never be a burden on taxpayers.

You Can Thank Chicago

Mail Order

Aaron Montgomery Ward got his start as a Marshall Field clerk. He then worked for a St. Louis dry goods wholesaler as a sales rep assigned to the rural market. In 1872, Ward started his own company using a new distribution method—mail order. His first catalog was just a page long, but by 1876 he was offering 3,000 products. His innovative sales approach opened up a whole new market by making big-city goods available to frontier families. Just before the turn of the century, another Chicago firm, Sears, Roebuck & Co., entered the mail-order business and soon surpassed Ward's annual sales by allowing patrons to buy on credit. Together, these Chicago-based retail giants pioneered the national distribution model that we know today.

The Skyscraper

As a result of its ambitious plan to rebuild the city in the wake of the Great Fire, Chicago became a leader in urban planning and architecture. In what was likely the most significant architectural feat of the 19th century, William Le Baron Jenney devised an entirely new way to construct large office buildings. His Home Insurance Building, put up in 1885 on the corner of La Salle and Adams, relied on an interior steel frame to bear the load of the building, which allowed the exterior walls to be lighter and the building to be taller. This innovation is still used in the designs of modern skyscrapers. Three of Jenney's skyscrapers still stand: Robert Morris Center (403 S. State St.), the Manhattan (431 S. Dearborn), and the Ludington (1104 S. Wabash), which is now part of Columbia College.

Boy Scouts of America

The Scouting movement was founded in Britain by military figure Lord Robert Baden-Powell. According to Scouting legend, William D. Boyce, a publishing magnate from Chicago, became lost in a dense fog while visiting London. One of Baden-Powell's Scouts helped him find his way and told the American about the British organization. Impressed with the selfless mission of the group, Boyce set up a similar organization after returning to Chicago, and the group grew into the Boy Scouts of America.

Literature of the Lost

* * *

Chicago's down-and-out inspired one up-and-coming writer.

Nelson Algren was fixated on Chicago's seamy side—the areas where drug addicts, crooked politicians, and criminals felt right at home. Algren published his harsh opinions of the city, and it came as a surprise to exactly no one that they weren't warmly received—especially at city hall. Algren said that Chicago is "the only major city in the country where you can easily buy your way out of a murder rap." Yet beneath such criticisms lay a sense of understanding. "You may find lovelier lovelies," he said of the city, "but never a lovely so real."

Algren grew up in a South Side neighborhood full of material to fuel his fascination with the grittier aspects of life. He studied journalism at the University of Illinois, graduated in 1931, then drifted through New Orleans and Texas. At one point, Algren stole a typewriter from an abandoned classroom. Whether the typewriter itself—or the four months of jail time he got as a result of the escapade—was the catalyst, Algren made up his mind around this time to be a writer, chronicling the ills of society. Believing his hometown to be even sicker than most, Algren headed for Chicago.

Algren's first novel, *Somebody in Boots* (1935) did something worse than garner attention—it bombed. His second, *Never Come Morning* (1942), achieved a much higher profile: Nothing says "read me" quite like getting banned from the Chicago Public Library for violent themes. *The Neon Wilderness* (1947) received much praise, and *The Man With the Golden Arm* (1949) garnered Algren the first National Book Award for fiction. His masterpiece, *City on the Make* (1951)—with its gritty portrayal of Chicago's working people—remains one of the most famous literary portraits of the city.

Literati Not Invited:
The Underground Library

✳ ✳ ✳ ✳

Forget posterity—this collection is one for obscurity!

The Chicago Underground Library (CUL) has specialized in compiling Chicago's hidden history through its fringe literature. It's a whole new genre of library, one that boasts an inspired collection of early '80s punk rock zines cheek by jowl with handwritten works from the turn of the century. One thing you won't find in its card catalog, however, is a work from a traditional large press.

Founders Nell Taylor and Emerson Dameron began with their "tome sweet tome," a small collection of local indie works that they kept in their Ukrainian Village apartment. Since then, the CUL has been "underground" in both a literal and a figurative sense: For a while, it was housed in the basement of MoJoe's Hot House, a coffeehouse that itself went under, ousting the CUL in the process. The collection then moved to an unlicensed art space on the Near West Side, where it couldn't be publicized at all for fear of bringing down the wrath of the authorities. But networking within Chicago's art and literature scenes eventually paid off, and the CUL is now housed in the Congress Theater building in Logan Square.

The CUL is all about shelving predetermined notions of what a library is and what types of reading material it should house. In the beginning, Taylor and Dameron didn't even want to separate the material into categories because they felt that smudging the lines between genres would help visitors notice new connections among the documents. In the end, however, the collection was split into five sections: Books, Journals, Newspapers, Magazines, and Zines. (The word *zine* is an abbreviation of *fanzine* or *magazine* and is used to describe noncommercial publications with limited circulations.) There are no qualifications as far as subject. In fact, even printing isn't a requirement! Handwritten, typed, photocopied . . . any written material that was produced in any way in or about Chicago is welcome.

A Chicago Connection to the Boston Tea Party?

* * * *

Is the last surviving participant of the Boston Tea Party buried in Lincoln Park?

The place now occupied by Lincoln Park used to be City Cemetery. While the gravestones were moved in the 1870s, many of the bodies remained. In the 1890s, a memorial boulder was set up to mark the burial spot of one of Chicago's earliest heroes: David Kennison, the last surviving participant of the Boston Tea Party. The boulder is still in place, despite the fact that we now know that Kennison is probably buried about a block from the spot . . . and that Kennison was full of it.

Before his death in 1852, Kennison claimed that he had reached 115 years of age. He would regularly regale Chicagoans with stories of the Revolution and the War of 1812, both of which he claimed to have fought in. He even donated a vial of tea leaves that he claimed were from the Boston Tea Party to the Chicago Historical Society. The institution (which now calls itself the Chicago History Museum) still has them, even though historians no longer believe Kennison's story. Genealogists today have determined that Kennison was at least 30 years younger than he claimed to be, making him only about six years old at the time of the Boston Tea Party. Historians do believe he served in the War of 1812, however.

While his stories were outrageous, if people in Chicago doubted him in his day, they never said so. He became one of the first heroes of the fledgling city, and, when he died, he was granted a full military funeral. A marching band—his favorite kind of band—followed the casket from a Clark Street church up to City Cemetery. He may have been a liar, but he inspired a generation of Chicagoans.

Fast Facts

- A veteran of Waterloo, Andreas von Zirngibl emigrated to Chicago as a farmer. He died in Chicago in 1855. He wanted his grave to remain inviolate on his own farmland. It still does—amid the junk at the American Fastener Salvage Yard (E. 93rd and S. Ewing).

- One of the few remaining tombs in Lincoln Park to hint at its former cemetery days is the Couch Mausoleum. No one buried their favorite sofa there; Ira Couch was a local businessman who died in 1858. In 1859, physicians and scientists began voicing concerns about having a cemetery so close to the source of the area's drinking water. Most of the bodies were moved by 1887; the Couch Mausoleum likely remains because it was deemed too costly to move.

- One of the world's odder amusement parks, Old Chicago, opened in Bolingbrook in 1975. Enclosed against the elements, people could enjoy it all year round. Cost overruns, structural problems caused by hasty building, un-savvy retail planning, and competition from Six Flags killed Old Chicago in 1981.

- Is Straight Dope and Chicago Reader "Smartest Human Being" Cecil Adams really Ed Zotti? The reclusive Adams insists they're different persons and that he has never been photographed (a dubious claim, given school picture-taking). The controversy generates interest in Adams's work, so he has little motivation to quell it.

- **Fact:** Daley Center puts up a nice nativity scene each Christmas. **Twist:** On two occasions, someone has stolen the baby Jesus from the manger. **Only in Chicago:** The setup crew now wires the infant Savior into his manger to make Jesus-jacking more difficult.

"Hyde" and Seek History

* * * *

Hyde Park claims more Nobel Prize winners per capita than any other neighborhood in the country, and locals (President Obama among them) claim that its Italian Fiesta Pizzeria cooks up the best pizza in this pizza-laden city. Brilliance and pepperoni? We're there.

In the 1850s, businessman Paul Cornell decided to purchase a piece of land near Lake Michigan, about seven miles south of the hustle and bustle of downtown Chicago. Cornell opened up a hotel called Hyde Park House, which quickly became the center of Hyde Park Township—what we know as the neighborhood today was actually separate from Chicago until it was annexed in 1889.

Soon after the annexation, oil tycoon John D. Rockefeller and a group of Baptists founded the University of Chicago, and within a few years, the World's Columbian Exposition set much of its scene in and around Hyde Park. These and other events in the late 19th and early 20th century contributed to the boom time for the area.

Nobels upon Nobels (Yawn...)

This Hyde Park university continues to thrive as one of the country's most revered schools of higher learning. The curriculum is intense, and the campus is gorgeous—maybe designed that way to take the students' minds off their mountains of homework? If you stroll through the grounds of the U of C, you might feel like you've been transported to some other world—and you're not imagining things. The quads on the main campus feature neo-Gothic limestone buildings patterned after the layouts of Oxford and Cambridge.

More than 82 Nobel Prize laureates have been affiliated with the university, including T. S. Eliot, Enrico Fermi, and Bertrand Russell. The list of distinguished U of C alumni is just as long and varied. It includes director Mike Nichols, writer Susan Sontag, philosopher John Dewey, composer Philip Glass, and Supreme Court Justices Antonin Scalia and John Paul Stevens, among many others. (We told you it was a classy place.)

The World's Fair Was Here

Chicago was host to the 1893 world's fair, the Columbian Exposition. Much of the event was held in and around Hyde Park, and the fair put the neighborhood on the map forever. The Midway Plaisance, a parklike boulevard that extends west from the nearby Jackson Park neighborhood and forms part of the University of Chicago campus, was built for the fair and can still be strolled today. Millions of people from across the country and around the world came to Chicago for the fair and left with the sense that Chicago was a center for progress; this impression still fuels the area today.

A Mies over There,
A Frank Lloyd Wright over Here

With all its Gothic edifices and sleek modern buildings, Hyde Park features some magnificent pieces of architecture. Notable structures include the Promontory Apartments, the first high-rise designed by Mies van der Rohe, and Frank Lloyd Wright's Robie House, which, with its low roof and horizontal lines, looks as though it has arisen of its own accord out of the flat prairie that surrounds it.

Hyde Park also boasts the Museum of Science and Industry. The venerable institution is housed in the only remaining building from the Columbian Exposition. During the 1893 world's fair, it served as the Palace of Fine Arts. All the other exposition buildings were created using inexpensive materials because the buildings had to be constructed quickly and were not intended to last. It was necessary to create the Palace of Fine Arts using fireproof materials, however, because it was to house numerous pieces of valuable art.

Hyde Park residents delight in whizzing by all these structures along their recently refurbished lakefront bike path; on any given day (yes, even in the dead of winter) those traveling via bicycle to and from Hyde Park can be seen, taking in all the sights and sounds of their historic neighborhood.

Chicago Killers

* * * *

You've no doubt heard of H. H. Holmes,
but the infamous killer was far from Chicago's only one.
Here are some of the most notorious names in American crime,
born and bred in the "hog butcher for the world."

- **I love you—really, I do:** Chicagoan **Tillie Klimek** poisoned her husband, remarried, and then did the same thing three more times, collecting life insurance and claiming that she'd foreseen her husbands' deaths in her dreams. Earning her the monikers "Black Widow" and "Mrs. Bluebeard," Klimek is also suspected of having murdered a handful of her children, cousins, and a boyfriend who didn't take the bait. She was sentenced to life in prison in 1922 and died in 1936.

- **"Supermen" they weren't: Richard Loeb** and **Nathan Leopold** grew up in the Kenwood neighborhood. Loeb's father was a Sears, Roebuck & Co. vice president, Leopold's was a wealthy box manufacturer. Loeb was obsessed with crime novels, and Leopold was obsessed with Loeb—and with the idea of Nietzsche's superman, a superior individual who was above the law and could do as he pleased. Leopold believed that a superman could even commit murder. When Loeb conceived of the idea to attempt a perfect crime—one for which they would never be caught—Leopold was his willing accomplice.

  In 1924—when Loeb was 18 and Leopold was 19—the two lured Loeb's 14-year-old cousin Bobby Franks into a car and beat the unsuspecting child to death. They attempted to hide the body near Wolf Lake; they did a poor job, however, and a passerby found the body the next day. Investigators then discovered Leopold's glasses in the area where the body was found, and the boys were quickly apprehended.

  The trial was a sensation; because the boys had pleaded guilty, the main point of the trial was to determine if the boys would go to prison or be hanged. Defense attorney Clarence Darrow claimed that both boys were mentally unstable because they had been abused by their governesses; using this defense among others, Darrow persuaded the judge to spare the boys' lives, much to prosecutor Robert Crowe's chagrin.

Loeb was killed in prison in 1936. Leopold was a model prisoner and was released in 1958. Even prosecutor Robert Crowe had become convinced of Leopold's reform and considered writing a letter to the parole board on his behalf. Leopold lived most of the rest of his life in Puerto Rico. He died in 1971.

Bobby Franks is buried in Rosehill Cemetery. Some cemetery workers claimed to see a young boy wandering the cemetery at times; when they approached him, he would disappear, however. The workers claimed the ghost did not rest until Leopold's death in 1971.

- **Keep your ground-floor windows locked:** A raging alcoholic and a sociopath, **Richard Speck** sneaked into a dorm through an unlocked window and brutally murdered eight nurses in 1966. The systematic killings of the students shocked the nation. The Chicago Police Department sent 60 officers on a hunt for Speck. After listening to the testimony of Corazon Amurao (the sole surviving nurse), the jury at his trial deliberated for only 49 minutes and sentenced him to death. The death penalty was declared unconstitutional in 1972 (while Speck was on death row), and Speck was sentenced to eight consecutive terms of 50 to 150 years each.

  Speck's bizarre, cold-blooded persona became the subject of much clinical and popular debate throughout his years in prison. As a child, Speck was abused by his stepfather and suffered several serious falls; he had the IQ of a ten-year-old, and many specialists believe he had undiagnosed brain damage. Speck died of a heart attack in 1991. After no one claimed the body, Speck was cremated, and his ashes were scattered in an undisclosed location.

- **The number one reason so few people like clowns anymore:** A beloved neighborhood fixture in the suburb of Norridge, **John Wayne Gacy** wore clown makeup to block parties and contributed to numerous local charities. Adoring friends were shocked when it was revealed that he tortured and strangled more than 30 young men and buried them in the crawl space under his house. Police believe he was able to abduct many of his victims by using a handcuffs trick. Gacy would show the victim handcuffs, handcuff himself, then release the cuffs. He would then handcuff his victim and abduct him. Gacy was convicted of 33 murders and was executed in 1994. Prosecutors were able to go forward with the execution by choosing the lethal injection option, which was not considered cruel or unusual.

- **Beyond our reach:** A brilliant but tormented mathematician, **Ted Kaczynski** (aka "the Unabomber") traded his position at Berkeley for a life in Montana, where he read philosophy and became one of the country's most infamous domestic terrorists. Kaczynski, who was raised on Chicago's Southwest Side, was the subject of a massive FBI manhunt after nearly 20 years of mailing bombs to academics and businessmen—and attempting to blow up a plane in 1979. The fact that Kaczynski's preferred targets were universities and airlines led FBI agents to dub him the "Unabomber."

    Kaczynski has intense suspicions about technological progress and the effect it has on human beings and nature. One prison psychiatrist diagnosed Kaczynski with paranoid schizophrenia in 1998, but others are not convinced. Specialists will likely be studying his case for years to come to determine the root of his psychological distress; conjecture lays blame across the spectrum, from an illness he contracted as an infant to psychological experiments he underwent while he was a Harvard undergrad. Investigators still are not sure how he chose his specific targets. Kaczynski was sentenced to life in prison and is currently in a maximum-security lockup in Colorado.

* * * *

"I wonder now, Nathan, whether you think there is a God or not. I wonder whether you think it is pure accident that this disciple of Nietzsche's philosophy dropped his glasses or whether it was an act of Divine Providence to visit upon your miserable carcasses the wrath of God."

—State's Attorney Robert Crowe,
in his summation during the Leopold & Loeb case

A Wife Disappears

* * * *

The story of Louisa Luetgert, the murdered wife of "Sausage King" Adolph Luetgert, is a gruesome tale of betrayal and death.

Adolph Luetgert was born in Germany and came to America after the Civil War. He opened his first business—a liquor store—in 1872. Luetgert married his first wife, Caroline Roepke, that same year. She gave birth to two boys, only one of whom survived childhood. Just two months after Caroline died in November 1877, Luetgert quickly remarried a much younger woman, Louisa Bicknese. He gave her an unusual gold ring that had her initials inscribed inside the band. Little did Luetgert know that this ring would prove to be his downfall.

In 1892, Luetgert built a sausage factory at the corner of Hermitage and Diversey. But just a year later, sausage sales declined due to an economic depression. Luetgert had put his life's savings into the factory, along with plenty of borrowed money, so when his business suffered, creditors started coming after him. Instead of trying to reorganize his finances, Luetgert answered an ad posted by an English millionaire and made a deal to sell him the majority of the sausage business. The Englishman proved to be a con man, and Luetgert ended up losing even more money. Luetgert eventually laid off many of his workers, but a few remained as he attempted to keep the factory out of the hands of creditors.

Luetgert's marriage seemed to be failing, as well. Neighbors frequently heard the Luetgerts arguing, and he began carrying on with several mistresses. When Louisa discovered that he was fooling around with a relative of hers, she became enraged. One night, during a shouting match with Louisa, Luetgert allegedly took his wife by the throat and began choking her. After noticing alarmed neighbors watching him through the parlor window, Luetgert reportedly calmed down and released his wife.

Louisa disappeared on May 1, 1897. When questioned about it days later, Luetgert stated that Louisa had left him and was possibly staying with another man. When Louisa's brother, Dietrich Bicknese, asked Luetgert why he had not informed the police of Louisa's disappearance, the sausage maker told him that he'd hired a private investigator to find her because he didn't trust the police.

When Bicknese informed the police of his sister's disappearance, Captain Herman Schuettler and his men began to search for Louisa. They questioned the couple's neighbors, who detailed the violent arguments they had overheard. Schuettler summoned Luetgert to the precinct house on a couple of occasions and each time pressed him about his wife's disappearance. Luetgert stated that he did not report Louisa's disappearance because he could not afford the disgrace.

During the investigation, a young German girl named Emma Schimke told police that she had passed by the factory with her sister at about 10:30 P.M. on May 1 and remembered seeing Luetgert leading his wife down the alleyway behind the factory.

Police also questioned employees of the sausage factory. Frank Bialk, a night watchman at the plant, told police that when he arrived for work on May 1, he found a fire going in one of the boilers. He said Luetgert asked him to keep the fire going and then sent him on a couple of trivial errands while Luetgert stayed in the basement. When Bialk returned to the factory, he went back to the boiler fire and heard Luetgert finishing his work at around 3:00 A.M.

Later that morning, Bialk saw a sticky, gluelike substance on the floor near the vat. He noticed that it seemed to contain bits of bone, but he thought nothing of it because Luetgert used all sorts of waste meats to make his sausage.

On May 3, Luetgert asked another employee, Frank Odorofsky, to clean the basement and to keep quiet about it. Odorofsky put the slimy substance into a barrel and scattered it near the railroad tracks as Luetgert had requested.

Sausage Sales Decline Again

On May 15, the police search was narrowed to the factory basement and a vat that was two-thirds full of a brownish, brackish liquid. Officers drained the greasy paste from the vat and began poking through the residue. Officer Walter Dean found bone fragments and two gold rings—one a band engraved with the initials "L. L." Believing they had a solid case against Luetgert, prosecutors indicted him. The details of the crime shocked the city. Even though he had been charged with boiling Louisa's body, rumors circulated that she had actually been ground up into sausage that was sold to local butcher shops and restaurants. Sausage sales dropped dramatically in Chicago in 1897.

Luetgert's trial ended in a hung jury on October 21. A second trial was held in 1898, and Luetgert was convicted and sentenced to life.

Louisa's Revenge

By 1899, Luetgert was a shadow of his former self, often babbling in his cell at night. Legend has it that Luetgert claimed Louisa haunted him. Based on the fact that neighbors reported seeing Louisa's ghost inside her former home, one has to wonder if she did indeed drive Luetgert insane. Luetgert died in 1900, likely from heart trouble.

The sausage factory stood empty for years, looming over the neighborhood as a grim reminder of the horrors that had taken place there. Eventually, the Library Bureau Company purchased the factory to store furniture and supplies.

On June 26, 1904, the old factory caught on fire. Despite the damage done to the building's interior, the Library Bureau was able to reopen its facilities. In 1907, a contracting mason purchased the old Luetgert house and moved it from behind the factory to another lot in the neighborhood, hoping to dispel the grim memories—and the ghost—attached to it.

Hermitage Avenue no longer intersects with Diversey, and by the 1990s, the factory stood empty. But in the late '90s, around the 100th anniversary of Louisa's death, the former sausage factory was converted into condominiums; a brand-new neighborhood sprang up to replace the aging homes from the days of the Luetgerts. Fashionable brick homes and apartments appeared around the old factory, and rundown taverns were replaced with coffee shops.

One thing has not changed. Legend has it that each year on May 1, the anniversary of her death, the ghost of Louisa can still be spotted roaming Hermitage Avenue near the old sausage factory.

An Ominous Chain Reaction

* * * *

*Few events have changed the course of history as greatly as the
movement of a few simple particles at the University of Chicago one
sobering December afternoon in 1942.*

As the United States braced itself for a second year of war both
in Europe and in the Pacific, the world's top scientists set off a
mesmerizing chain reaction that proved possible the development of
nuclear technology. Its consequences were also, however, devastating
and final, capable of obliterating civilization with the press of a
button. The atomic bomb was born at 3:25 P.M. on December 2, 1942.

The Split Heard 'Round the World

By the close of the 1930s, the Axis powers were said to have begun
developing a weapon that would harness atomic energy in order to
cause vast, devastating damage. Urged by a letter from physicists
Albert Einstein and Leó Szilárd, U.S. President Franklin Roosevelt
created a committee of scientists to research the feasibility of such a
project, the first in a series of official measures taken by the
American government to develop the bomb. After Allied scientists
working in England discovered Uranium's fissile properties (or, more
specifically, the fact that the isotope Uranium-235 had the ability to
split), the project was given the full resources of the military.
Physicists and engineers were recruited from throughout the world
to work on what became known as the Manhattan Project.

Numerous labs and thousands of personnel throughout the
country worked overtime to understand, first, how to enact nuclear
fission and, second, how to safely harness its energy. Under the
auspices of the now-defunct Office of Scientific Research and
Development, the Manhattan Project constituted the most complex
integration of science and military technology in modern history.

The Chicago Metallurgical Laboratory, the ultra-secret midwestern arm of the project, was overseen largely by Leslie Groves, a
meat-and-potatoes brigadier general, while Enrico Fermi, an Italian

academic and Nobel Laureate—and namesake of
Fermilab, which still conducts nuclear research
outside Chicago—worked with a team of physicists to create the conditions necessary for nuclear
fission and the subsequent chain reaction.

A Most Imposing Pile

Using the work of such theorists as Szilárd, who had discovered the
process of nuclear chain reaction, and the expertise of his engineering team, Fermi constructed a block—a "pile"—of Uranium and
other materials called Chicago Pile 1. This was the famous reactor,
and it stood almost 26 feet high. From the pile, a rod coated in the
element Cadmium would be withdrawn, causing neutrons to collide
with and split the Uranium isotopes, and by doing so, cause more
collisions. Slowed by the non-Uranium materials and quickly shut off
by reinserting the Cadmium rod, the reactor showed the potential
for larger reactions in an uncontrolled setting.

Though his famous reactor was meant to be constructed outside
of the city, at the Argonne National Laboratory in nearby DuPage
County, a labor strike forced Fermi to find another space.

Since named a historic landmark by the federal government, the
room Fermi chose was a squash court beneath some rusty bleachers
at the University of Chicago's long-abandoned Stagg Field. While
scores of fellow scientists, officials, and dignitaries looked on, Fermi's
team completed a successful self-sustaining nuclear reaction—the
world's first. Just three years later, detonated in a split second, the
same type of reaction would annihilate a city.

Sources say that the mood that day was both exhilarating and
terrifying; after the war, Fermi and Szilárd expressed ambivalence
about the consequences of their work, which held immense promise
for energy production but could also result in such destruction and
utter despair. Today these themes resonate on the spot of that first
detonation. Just above that old squash court stands a sculpture that
is, in its raw power and simplicity, as beguiling as the sight of that
reactor must have been. A vague, amorphous shape, the bronze
statue *Nuclear Energy* by British sculptor Henry Moore is a
reminder of the totality of that day. And, of course, it serves as a
reminder that it all happened here, in Chicago.

Bubbly Creek

* * * *

Where no current flows, but the surface bubbles...

Bubbly Creek is the nickname given to an area along the South Fork of the Chicago River's South Branch that was once at the very center of Chicago's notorious Union Stockyards, for decades the nation's largest cattle processing and meatpacking operation. At the height of the stockyards' activity, the area around Bubbly Creek became an open sewer for meatpackers, who dumped animal waste and carcasses into the river in hopes they would just disappear.

Unfortunately, the creek received so much blood and offal that it began to bubble methane and hydrogen sulfide as the various waste pieces were decomposing. Years ago, the creek would churn violently at times, and the bubbles were as large as basketballs. The creek water never froze because of the surface scum and the thickness of the "water."

From Marsh to Open Sewer

The area surrounding Bubbly Creek was originally a shallow marsh, but during the 1800s the area was dredged to speed up the rate of water flow into the river and increase the amount of buildable land in the fast-growing city. Soon, the neighborhood, long known as "Back of the Yards" due to its proximity to its biggest employer, saw the Union Stock Yard & Transit Co., or simply the Yards, become the center of the American meatpacking industry. From the Civil War

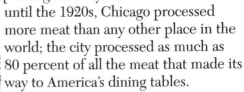

until the 1920s, Chicago processed more meat than any other place in the world; the city processed as much as 80 percent of all the meat that made its way to America's dining tables.

At a time when there was little or no effort to protect the environment or regulate the dumping of waste into the river, residents watched as the area around 35th and Racine became more and more polluted. So prominent was Bubbly Creek fixed in the public imagination that it even earned a mention in *The Jungle,* Upton Sinclair's classic 1906 novel about the city's meatpacking industry. Sinclair wrote, "[Bubbly Creek] is really a great open sewer a hundred or two feet wide.... Here and there the grease and filth have caked solid, and the creek looks like a bed of lava; chickens walk about on it, feeding, and many times an unwary stranger has started to stroll across, and vanished temporarily."

Hope for Restoration

The Yards closed in 1971, and experts say that the stockyards waste is now stable sediment. The creek is still contaminated, mostly due to untreated sewage that is released into Chicago waters during heavy rains. In recent years, a number of projects have been undertaken to help clean up the site, each of which has met with limited success. For example, Mayor Daley created the Bubbly Creek Task Force, while the Wetlands Initiative (an environmental group working to preserve Midwest wetlands) and the Chicago District of the U.S. Army Corps of Engineers have worked on plans to restore the creek. Until this stretch of the Chicago River is restored to what it was like before the stockyards arrived, it will continue to stand as a living reminder of the days when Chicago was "Hog Butcher for the World."

✳ ✳ ✳ ✳

- *Bubbly Creek's unsavory reputation did not stop an Arlington Heights developer from building Bridgeport Village, an upscale housing development along Bubbly Creek, in 2003. Buyers paid $655,000 for the smallest homes, and the largest were priced as high as $1.2 million. Residents of the development have expressed surprisingly few complaints about the waterway, merely remarking about a "strange smell" on warmer days.*

- *Brave souls now boat, canoe, kayak, and fish in the waters of Bubbly Creek, but swimming is still prohibited.*

From Chicago to Hollywood

* * * *

Some of Hollywood's brightest stars, past and present, have roots in Chicago and its environs. Here are 20+ Chicagoans who have dazzled Tinseltown with their talent.

- **Jim Belushi** (Wheaton)
- **John Belushi** (Wheaton)
- **Jack Benny** (Waukegan)
- **Joan Cusack** (Evanston)
- **John Cusack** (Evanston)
- **Dennis Farina** (Chicago)
- **Harrison Ford** (Park Ridge)
- **Charlton Heston** (Evanston)
- **Bonnie Hunt** (Chicago)
- **Jennifer Hudson** (Chicago)
- **Bernie Mac** (Chicago)
- **Michael Madsen** (Chicago)

John Cusack

- **Virginia Madsen** (Chicago)
- **Jenny McCarthy** (Chicago)
- **Mr. T** (Chicago)
- **Bill Murray** (Wilmette)
- **Bob Newhart** (Oak Park)
- **William Petersen** (Evanston)
- **Jeremy Piven** (Evanston)
- **Gary Sinise** (Highland Park)
- **Vince Vaughn** (Lake Forest)
- **George Wendt** (Chicago)

Gary Sinise

Fast Facts

- During the Silurian period—long before the glaciers carved out Chicago—the area that would become Illinois was located south of the equator and was covered by a vast sea. The sea's coral reefs formed what is now Thornton Quarry, a large limestone quarry just south of Chicago.

- In the early 1900s, locals called the neighborhood around Chicago and Michigan avenues "Towertown," after the old Water Tower. From 1917 to 1933, the Dill Pickle Club in Towertown served as the indoor hangout for local eccentrics— much as Bughouse Square was the outdoor venue for such characters.

- Another Towertown cultural center throughout the 1950s was the College of Complexes, which harbored intellectuals, writers, and anyone else with something on his or her mind. The College has moved around a lot but functions to this day. The group meets weekly and tags itself as "a debate group that attracts outsiders and political obsessives."

- The June 26, 1954, monster Lake Michigan wave was caused by storms that created extremely heavy air pressure over the lake. The right set of circumstances occurs on Lake Michigan every few centuries. The 1954 wave was ten feet high and swept numerous fishermen into the lake. Many were rescued, but eight drowned.

- **Fact:** People bought Extra-Strength Tylenol in and around Chicago in September 1982, as always. **Twist:** Some sicko had inserted potassium cyanide into some capsules and reshelved the bottles, killing seven headache sufferers. **Only in Chicago:** For years, people called the painkiller "Extra-Strength Tylenide." The tamperings led to the tamper-proof bottles we all struggle with today. The case was never solved, though in February 2009 the FBI conducted a search of prime suspect James Lewis's home, citing forensic advances and new tips following the 25th anniversary of the killings.

Frank Lloyd Wright's Chicago

* * *

Long considered one of America's greatest architects,
Frank Lloyd Wright's life and work
took early and important shape in Chicago and its suburbs.

Stand on the corner of Woodlawn Avenue and East 58th Street on any given day, and you'll likely see a gathering of architecture fans from around the world. That's because 5757 South Woodlawn is the site of the Robie House, a crowning achievement in the catalog of Frank Lloyd Wright.

More than 40 years after his death, Wright remains one of the world's best known and loved architects. He is most closely associated with Chicago, and for good reason: He got his start here, lived in the nearby suburb of Oak Park, and designed and built some of his greatest works in and around the city.

Trying to get a grasp on the life and work of Wright is challenging. Few public figures lived a life as full of artistry and achievement as Wright, and simply cataloging his buildings can be dizzying. In his lifetime, he designed more than 1,000 structures (of which 400 were built), making him one of history's most prolific architects. While his personal life was often in turmoil—and he ran his business in a haphazard fashion—as an architect, he is considered unmatched.

His Structures
Take a Cue from Their Surroundings

The list of Wright works in and around Chicago is long, but any appreciation of Wright in Chicago has an easy starting point: Robie House. Long and low, the Robie House hugs the ground and employs a projecting cantilevered roof, continuous bands of stained-glass windows, and thin bricks that emphasize the building's horizontal design. Seen by many as the best example of Prairie-style architecture, the Robie House brings to life Wright's belief in the need for a design philosophy that emphasizes the relationship between architecture and nature.

For other examples of Wright's Prairie style, there's the Emil Bach House, a private residence built in 1915 at 7415 North Sheridan Road; the J. J. Walser House, an earlier, 1903 version of the Prairie style at 42 North Central Avenue; the Raymond W. Evans House at 9914 South Longwood Drive; and the James Charnley House, an early example of Wright's emerging style located at 1365 North Astor Street. All in all, there are nearly 20 surviving examples of Wright's work within the city's boundaries.

Oak Park Treasures

A treasure trove of Wright's work lies beyond Chicago's western border, in Oak Park. The village has the largest collection of Wright-designed residential properties in the world. The best place to start is the Frank Lloyd Wright Home and Studio, which served as Wright's home and workplace for the first 20 years of his career. In addition, there are more than 25 residences within the town, as well as Unity Temple, a revolutionary Cubist structure. Wright took special interest in this project because he was a member of the congregation. This unique place of worship was made from poured concrete. Its high windows allow for plentiful natural light but also ensure privacy and encourage contemplation.

A World of Wright

In the Chicago metropolitan area as a whole, more than 100 Wright buildings and historical sites can be found, not to mention countless examples of his influence and legacy when it comes to architectural design. Since his death in 1959, Wright has taken on a kind of larger-than-life image that places him as an iconic figure of the art form, one who left behind a truly American style of architecture.

✳ ✳ ✳ ✳

- *Unity Temple is currently endangered. It was constructed without expansion joints, and the walls are beginning to crack. The congregation is working to raise funds to renovate the worship space, but it will not be cheap or easy.*

Hep Cats and Scat Singers: Chicago Gets All Jazzed Up

* * * *

Ask a tourist what music they associate with Chicago, and the answer is likely to be blues. And that's a shame, in some ways, for as important as Chicago was to the creation of blues, it has an equally large and historical legacy as one of the most important cities for jazz. When it comes to jazz, the Windy City sure can blow!

Soon after the first jazz notes played in New Orleans in the 1890s, southern musicians began moving north to start playing Dixieland, or hot jazz, in Chicago. Noted jazz trumpeter Louis Armstrong blew into the city in 1922 to join Joe "King" Oliver, then the best and most influential hot jazz band in Chicago. Armstrong, who almost single-handedly changed jazz from music played collectively to one that featured improvised solos, including vocal scats, later recorded with his famous Hot Five and Hot Seven bands for Chicago's OKeh Records.

Jazz Thrives in Chicago's Nightclubs

By the time swing and big bands were bopping nationwide, Chicago was one of the most important cities for live concerts and radio broadcasts because of its large number of supper clubs and hotel ballrooms. All the heppest cats, from Duke Ellington to Tommy Dorsey to Glenn Miller, settled in for extended concert seasons in front of adoring Chicago fans. Chicago developed a host of important figures in the first half-century of jazz, including cornetists Muggsy Spanier, Jimmy McPartland, and Bix Beiderbecke; saxophonist Bud Freeman; clarinetist Benny Goodman; and drummer Gene Krupa.

When bebop began to hit its crescendo in the 1950s, Chicago had already established itself as a hotbed of talent and opportunity for jazz musicians. While few major record labels were based in Chicago (other than OKeh and Chess), the city boasted plenty of recording studios and nightclubs. Stars such as Charlie Parker, Dizzy Gillespie, and Miles Davis made Chicago—particularly the city's South and West sides—a kind of second home. But just as Chicago and Louis Armstrong helped push jazz in new directions in the 1920s, by the 1970s, Chicago also became the musical and intellectual home to much of the "free" or avant-garde jazz scene. Centered around the Association for the Advancement of Creative Musicians (AACM), composers Henry Threadgill and Anthony Braxton, drummer Jack DeJohnette, trumpet player Leo Smith, violinist Leroy Jenkins, and the band Art Ensemble of Chicago spearheaded a movement of risk-taking and experimentation, even if they were relatively unknown outside of the global jazz community.

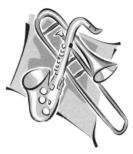

Today, Tomorrow, and Beyond

Jazz continues to thrive in Chicago today. Most visible is the long-running Chicago Jazz Festival, a free, three-day celebration in Grant Park that features local musicians, as well as musicians from around the world. There are even workshops and an area that showcases high school and college acts. Even though the last performance of the night is at 9:30, attendees who haven't had their fill can move on to clubs such as Andy's, the Jazz Showcase, the Velvet Lounge, the Hungry Brain, the Green Mill, Katerina's, or the House of Trend, where some fest performers are sure to pop up.

Chicago area universities continue to produce outstanding musicians at a seemingly inexhaustible pace. Now and into the future, Chicago looks poised to remain true to its legacy as one of the most important and exciting cities for jazz.

✳   ✳   ✳   ✳

- *Headliners at the 2009 Chicago Jazz Fest included Gonzalo Rubalcaba, Esperanza Spalding, Madeleine Peyroux, and Amina Figarova.*

A Battery on the Lakefront

✷ ✷ ✷ ✷

Chicago's lakefront was once braced for an invasion.

In the cold war years following World War II, bomb shelters were commonplace; it seemed it would only be a matter of time before the United States fell victim to an air strike perpetrated by Soviet bombers. The solution the U.S. military came up with was to build Nike missile bases at strategic points across the country as a last line of defense. Three of the points selected were in Chicago, along the Lake Michigan shore: Montrose Point on the north (designated C-03, C-standing for Chicago Defense Area), Burnham Park (C-40), and Promontory Point in Jackson Park (C-41).

On the Alert

There were two components to each missile base—a control center and the actual missile bunker. The two components were two and a half miles apart. The missile was 40 feet long and located in an underground magazine; it could be launched in 15 minutes and had a range of 25 miles. Some installations were armed with nuclear missiles that were twice as powerful as the weapon that was dropped on Nagasaki. Though it seems that planning to use a weapon like that above your own airspace would be self-defeating, there were systems in place (radar and interceptor aircraft) that made the missiles the absolute last means of defense. Although there were frequent alerts from the 1950s through the 1970s, most were drills. There were, however, occasional unknown aircraft sightings.

Local leaders were not happy to have missiles on park land, but they did not resist the federal effort because Chicago was considered a top potential target. When the Soviets launched *Sputnik* in 1957, however, it became clear that the Nike missiles were obsolete; they would be useless against intercontinental ballistic missiles. All of the Nike bases were dismantled by the late 1970s. A memorial to the Nike site missile mission can be seen in Chicago's Hegewisch neighborhood at Wolf Lake Park.

(Continued from p. 110)

December 30, 1903
Chicago's "absolutely fireproof" Iroquois Theatre burns 37 days after its grand opening.

1909
Chicago union organizer Agnes Nestor successfully lobbies for a state law that limits women to a ten-hour workday.

September 1, 1909
Edward P. Brennan's revised house and street numbering system is implemented. It is the basic system in use today, with State and Madison at the city center, eight blocks to every mile, even address numbers on the north and west sides of each street, and odd address numbers on the south and east sides of each street.

1910
Comiskey Park is built at 35th Street and Shields Avenue. Named for Charles Comiskey, the first owner of the White Sox, the team will play at the park until 1990.

1910
Some 40,000 Chicago garment workers walk off the job in response to a wage cut. The strike will lead to the organization of the Amalgamated Clothing Workers of America labor union.

1911
The U.S. Navy opens the Great Lakes Naval Training Station in North Chicago. Some one million sailors will pass through its gates en route to naval battles in the Atlantic and South Pacific during the Second World War.

1914
Weeghman Park is built to house the Chicago Whales baseball club. When their league folds, Charlie Weeghman buys the Cubs franchise and moves it to his new ballpark. He will sell the team to Charles Wrigley in 1920, and the park will take Wrigley's name in 1926.

1915
John Hertz, a Chicago car salesman, establishes the Yellow Cab Co. with a fleet of 40 yellow trade-in vehicles. He will eventually sell the taxi company to focus on growing the car rental interest that bears his name.

July 24, 1915
Nearly 850 people die when the disastrously top-heavy steamship *Eastland* capsizes while still at port and holding its capacity of approximately 2,500 passengers. It remains the worst maritime disaster in the history of the continental United States.

1919
Brooklyn-born Alphonse Capone, a dropout and a street thug, arrives in Chicago to help John Torrio with his bootlegging business. Capone and his family move into a house at 7244 South Prairie Avenue.

(Continued on p. 171)

Bragging Rights

- In its heyday as a boomtown, the city's growth rate was swifter than that of any other city in U.S. history. Its population skyrocketed from around 29,000 in 1850 to more than 1.5 million in 1900.

- The enormous Tiffany dome that caps Chicago's Cultural Center is the largest in the world, at 38 feet across. Valued at $35 million, the dome is made up of 30,000 pieces of Tiffany glass.

- Built in 1930, the Adler Planetarium was the first in the Western Hemisphere. With astronomers' ever-expanding knowledge of space, the planetarium has expanded too: Today it has 3D shows, several theaters, and a "staircase to the stars."

- Chicago is home to Skidmore, Owings & Merrill, LLP, one of the world's most famous architectural firms. The company has produced some of the tallest buildings on earth, including Chicago's Willis Tower (formerly known as the Sears Tower) and the Hancock Building.

- Chicago is the home of Barack Obama, the 44th president of the United States of America. Obama came to Chicago to work as a community organizer, then taught constitutional law at the University of Chicago. Obama got his start in politics by representing his South Side neighborhood in the Illinois Senate. He went on to represent Illinois in the U.S. Senate and then—of course—assumed the presidency in 2009.

- A number of literary luminati have honed their skills in Chicago, including Henry Blake Fuller, Finley Dunne, Sherwood Anderson, Carl Sandburg, James T. Farrell, Richard Wright, Nelson Algren, Studs Terkel, Saul Bellow, Gwendolyn Brooks, Mike Royko, Stuart Dybek, Sandra Cisneros, Richard Powers, and Aleksandar Hemon.

- With several of the world's most famous candy companies, Chicago produces more confections than any other city. Among other purveyors of the sweet stuff, Chicago houses the Wrigley Company, Ferrara Pan Candy Company, and the Blommer Chocolate Company.

A Liner Capsizes on the River

* * * *

*One of the most tragic events in Chicago history
took place on July 24, 1915. On that overcast summer afternoon,
hundreds of people died in the Chicago River
when the* Eastland *capsized just a few feet from the dock.*

July 24 was going to be a special day for thousands of Chicagoans. It was reserved for the Western Electric Company annual summer picnic, which was to be held across Lake Michigan in Michigan City, Indiana. And although officials at the utility company had encouraged workers to bring along friends and relatives, they were surprised when more than 7,000 people arrived to be ferried across the lake on the five excursion boats chartered for the day. Three of the steamers—the *Theodore Roosevelt,* the *Petoskey,* and the *Eastland*—were docked on the Chicago River near Clark Street.

On this fateful morning, the *Eastland,* a steamer owned by the St. Joseph-Chicago Steamship Company, was filled to its limit. The boat had a reputation for top-heaviness and instability, and the new federal Seaman's Act, which was passed in 1915 as a result of the RMS *Titanic* disaster, required more lifeboats than previous regulations did. All of this resulted in the ship being even more unstable than it already was. In essence, it was a recipe for disaster.

The Ship Overturns

As passengers boarded the *Eastland,* it began listing back and forth. This had happened on the ship before, so the crew emptied the ballast compartments to provide more stability. As the boat was preparing to depart, some passengers went below deck, hoping to warm up on the cool, cloudy morning, but many on the overcrowded steamer jammed their way onto one side of the deck to wave to onlookers on shore. The *Eastland* tilted once again, but this time more severely; passengers began to panic. Moments later, the *Eastland* rolled to her side, coming to rest at the bottom of the river, which was just 18 feet below the surface. One side of the boat's hull was actually above the water's surface in some spots.

Passengers on deck were tossed into the river. The overturned ship created a current that pulled some of the floundering swimmers to their doom, while many of the women's dresses snagged on the ship, tugging them down to the bottom.

Those inside were thrown to one side of the ship when it capsized. The heavy furniture onboard crushed some passengers, and those who were not killed instantly drowned when water rushed inside moments later. A few managed to escape, but most didn't. Their bodies were later found trapped in a tangled heap on the lowest side of the *Eastland*.

Firefighters, rescue workers, and volunteers soon arrived and tried to help people escape through portholes. They also cut holes in the portion of the ship's hull that was above the water line. Approximately 1,660 passengers survived the disaster.

In the end, 844 people died, many of them young women and children. Officially, no clear explanation was given for why the vessel capsized, and the St. Joseph-Chicago Steamship Company was not held accountable for the disaster.

The bodies of those who perished in the tragedy were wrapped in sheets and placed on the *Theodore Roosevelt* or lined up along the docks. Marshall Field's and other large stores sent wagons to carry the dead to hospitals, funeral homes, and a makeshift morgue, the Second Regiment Armory, where more than 200 bodies were sent.

After the ship was removed from the river, it was sold and later became a U.S. warship as the gunboat U.S.S. *Wilmette*. The ship never saw any action but was used as a training ship during World War II. After the war, it was decommissioned and eventually scrapped in 1947.

Lingering Spirits

At the time of the *Eastland* disaster, the Second Regiment Armory (located on the Near West Side) was the only public building large enough to be used as a temporary morgue. Chicagoans with missing loved ones filed through, searching for familiar faces. In 22 cases, there was no one left to identify them—those families were completely wiped out. The names of these victims were learned from neighbors who came searching for their friends. The weeping, crying, and moaning of the bereaved echoed off the walls of the armory for days.

As years passed, the armory building went through several incarnations, including a stable and a bowling alley, before Harpo Studios, the production company owned by talk-show maven Oprah Winfrey, purchased it. A number of *The Oprah Winfrey Show* staff members, security guards, and maintenance workers claim that the studio is haunted by the spirits of those who tragically lost their lives on the *Eastland.* Many employees have experienced unexplained phenomena, including the sighting of a woman in a long gray dress who walks the corridors and then mysteriously vanishes into the wall. Some believe she is the spirit of a mourner who came to the armory looking for her family and left a bit of herself behind at a place where she felt her greatest sense of loss. Staff members have also witnessed doors opening and closing on their own and heard sobbing sounds and phantom foot-steps on the lobby staircase.

Chicago River Ghosts

In the same way that the former armory seems to have been impressed with a ghostly recording of past events, the Chicago River seems haunted too. For years, people walking on the Clark Street Bridge have heard crying and moaning sounds coming from the river. Some have witnessed the apparitions of victims splashing in the water. On several occasions, some witnesses have called the police for help. One man even jumped into the river to save what he thought was a person drowning. When he returned to the surface, he discovered that he was in the water alone. He had no explanation for what he'd seen, other than to admit that it might have been a ghost.

So it seems that the horror of the *Eastland* disaster has left an imprint on these spots and continues to replay itself, ensuring that the *Eastland* victims will never be forgotten.

Chicago Titans

✳ ✳ ✳

Chicago was and is a town that's all about business. The following six titans helped mold the Windy City into what it is today.

- **Potter Palmer** (1826–1902) started out as a clerk in a dry goods store in New York and soon opened his own New York store. Palmer visited Chicago in 1851; he envisioned great opportunity and quickly moved here. He opened a store, and it grew to be the largest in the Midwest. By 1865 Palmer was in ill health; his doctor advised him to retire, and Marshall Field and Levi Leiter took over his store.

  In 1868, Palmer's health was restored, and he was not content to be idle. At the time, Chicago's retail district was centered around Lake Street, but the street's location along the polluted river was a detriment to business. Palmer believed a new location was needed. He quietly began buying up land along State Street and lobbied for businesses to move there. His plan was eventually realized.

  The Palmer House Hotel was Palmer's luxurious wedding present for his bride, Bertha, whom he married in 1870. Palmer was also instrumental in the creation of Chicago's "Gold Coast" along Lake Shore Drive. Chicago's wealthiest citizens had lived along Prairie Avenue, but once industry began encroaching on that area, Palmer moved to Lake Shore Drive. Other wealthy citizens quickly followed, as the Palmers controlled the social lives of the elite. They often entertained at their Lake Shore Drive mansion. Their dining room could sit 50 people, and many came just to view Bertha Palmer's vast art collection.

- No businessman on this list was as controversial as **George Pullman** (1831–97), founder of the Pullman company town south of Chicago. Here Pullman built comfortable homes for his workers, but he also ruled them with an iron fist, trying to regulate their activities even during their off hours. His patronizing ways eventually led to the infamous and violent Pullman Strike of 1894, which had to be put down by federal troops.

- **Philip Danforth Armour** (1832–1901) revolutionized meat production. Armour & Co., headquartered in Chicago, was one of the first factories to use an assembly-line system and was the very first to offer canned meat. The importance of this canning process cannot be overstated; in the late 19th century, meat spoilage was a major problem for families all across America, and canning and refrigeration were the only answers. Armour was also the first to realize that the so-called "waste" of hog slaughtering could be used to make glue, fertilizer, and other products. He infamously stated that his goal was to sell "everything but the squeal."

- A Massachusetts blue blood who descended from some of the earliest Puritan settlers, **Marshall Field** (1834–1906) ventured west in search of fortune. He found it in Chicago, where he took over Potter Palmer's dry goods establishment, renamed it Marshall Field & Company in 1881, and turned it into one of the most luxurious department stores in the country. Field also helped found the Field Museum of Natural History and donated land to the University of Chicago. Marshall Field & Company was acquired by Macy's Inc. on August 30, 2005, after 154 years in business.

- **Aaron Montgomery Ward** (1844–1913) began his career as Marshall Field's protégé. He worked in Field's Chicago dry goods business, then became a traveling salesman for Wills, Greg, & Co. As he drove all over southern Illinois, he heard complaints from rural merchants and farmers about the difficulty of buying well-made products at decent prices. Ward invented the mail order industry in 1872, cutting out the middle man and shipping goods directly to customers. The Montgomery Ward catalog became known as the "Wish Book," and Sears and other competitors soon began their own direct-mail divisions.

- Losing a finger in a shoe factory accident was perhaps the luckiest thing that ever happened to **Charles Walgreen** (1873–1939), the son of Swedish immigrants. The doctor who treated him in his hometown of Galesburg, Illinois, encouraged him to go to Chicago and become a pharmacist. By the late 1920s, Walgreen presided over a chain of 110 drugstores.

Showing the Klan the Door

* * *

Riding a wave of resentment against African Americans, Jews, Catholics, and immigrants, the Ku Klux Klan enjoyed a startling surge of popularity in the early 1920s. Championing "100 percent Americanism," the Klan reached out to white Protestant men who felt threatened by the hedonism of the Jazz Age and the encroachment of diversity in big cities.

Nowhere was the clash of cultures more pronounced than in Chicago, home to 110,000 African Americans, 125,000 Jews, 1,000,000 Catholics, and 800,000 immigrants. By late 1922 the Klan claimed 100,000 members in the city and another 100,000 in the suburbs. A unifying force was a weekly local newspaper called *Dawn* that featured Klan-related news and advertising, such as a coffee company that promoted its "Kuality Koffee and Kourtesy."

As the Klan began to influence local politics, the African American community and its newspaper, the *Chicago Defender,* decried the organization. The city council reacted, officially condemning the Klan and passing a worthless ordinance outlawing masks. But as a legal entity that remained largely nonviolent in Chicago, the KKK thrived.

A Force from the South

The city's most organized anti-Klan forces rallied behind an unlikely figure—Grady K. Rutledge. Born in Alabama, Rutledge was a reporter who claimed to be a direct descendant of Edward Rutledge, the youngest signer of the Declaration of Independence. Grady Rutledge had recently moved to Chicago to start a publicity firm that raised money for several large charities. He hired Ben Hecht, a popular Chicago journalist, and together they raised millions of dollars.

In 1922 Rutledge joined with various community leaders to form an anti-Klan association called the American Unity League (AUL). The league launched a newspaper called *Tolerance* and also published booklets with such catchy titles as "Is Your Neighbor a Kluxer?" Using a network of spies, *Tolerance* obtained and printed lists of Klansmen's names; they figured that, since the Klan reveled in secrecy, the best way to attack them would be through exposure. The approach was novel and effective; circulation reached 150,000 by year's end.

A Wrigley-Size Whoops

One AUL operative claimed that chewing gum magnate William Wrigley Jr. was a Klansman. Rutledge was skeptical and resisted printing the story, but other AUL leaders overruled him. Wrigley was implicated in the December 31, 1922, issue of *Tolerance,* based on what was later proved to be fraudulent evidence. *Tolerance* was soon crushed under the weight of lawsuits filed by Wrigley and others. In a bizarre twist, Rutledge joined the Klan and wrote a series of articles for *Dawn* exposing the AUL's shady tactics.

Dawn lasted about a year longer than *Tolerance.* Its last issue appeared in February 1924. By 1925 interest in the Klan had dissipated as quickly as it had erupted. Exposure had ruined many Klan-friendly businessmen, and internal squabbling weakened the organization.

Hecht became a renowned literary figure and prolific Hollywood screenwriter, winning an Oscar for *Underworld* and working on many films, including *Wuthering Heights* and *Gone with the Wind.* In his autobiography, Hecht portrayed Rutledge as witty but temperamental, a heavy drinker, and a fraud who skimmed the funds he raised for charity. Perhaps Rutledge's conscience caught up with him. In September 1926 he was found dead in his Park Ridge home, an apparent suicide at age 35.

＊　＊　＊　＊

- *The American Unity League's stated goal was "the creation of better feeling between the several racial and religious groups making up America."*

Bluebeard in the Flesh

* * * *

"All of the women for Johann go crazy!"

In 1905, when the police finally caught up with Johann Hoch, he had already proposed to what would have been his 45th wife. His habit was to meet a lonely middle-aged woman, propose, marry her, and take her money in the space of about a week. Depending on Johann's mood, about a third of the women were murdered; the others were simply abandoned.

Hoch's method of murder was slipping his new bride some arsenic, which was a perfect crime in those days. Arsenic was used in embalming fluid, so the minute an undertaker came into the house, convicting someone of arsenic poisoning was impossible.

The press was fascinated—how could an ugly man who spoke like a comedian with a German accent convince so many women to marry him? Why, his last Chicago wife (his 44th overall) had agreed to marry him while her sister (wife #43) was lying dead on her bed! *The Herald American,* which could be counted on to print the wildest rumors in town, claimed that Hoch used hypnosis on the women and that he had learned all he knew about murdering from the infamous H. H. Holmes.

Hoch's power over women made it seem as though he *must* have had access to some sort of magic spell. As his trial continued, wife #44, the woman who had first reported him to authorities, came to his cell daily to bring him money and beg him to forgive her. He received numerous letters containing marriage proposals while in prison. Any marriage would have been a short one—Johann was hanged in 1906.

* * * *

- *Legend has it that as Hoch was about to be hanged, he said to the guards, "I don't look like a monster now, do I?" After the deed was done, one of the guards quietly replied, "Well, not anymore."*

Fast Facts

- When the Great Fire broke out in 1871, Father Arnold Damen of Holy Family Church was out of town. Hearing of the fire by telegraph, he held an all-night vigil, praying that the church be spared. The fire did indeed shift northward— away from Holy Family. Now that's some praying.

- Daniel Hale Williams, M.D., performed one of the first successful open-heart surgeries in Chicago in 1893. When the American College of Surgeons formed in 1913, Dr. Williams was its lone African American charter member.

- Being in a labor union is usually safe today. In 1937, it wasn't. The Steel Workers Organizing Committee was working to unionize steel plants, and several smaller steel-makers (Republic Steel among them) were refusing to recognize the union. During a protest in front of Republic Steel (114th and Avenue O), strikers clashed with police, and ten strikers were killed. A congressional investigation determined that the police used excessive force, and the event went down in history as the Memorial Day Massacre.

- A sea lion named Big Ben escaped from Lincoln Park Zoo in November 1903. The hapless wanderer was found washed up on shore near Bridgman, Michigan, the following spring.

- Chicago will never forget December 1, 1958—the day of the Our Lady of the Angels School fire. Death toll: 92 children and three nuns. The cause of the fire was never pinpointed, but the building's fire preparations were certainly inadequate. Many of the children are buried at Queen of Heaven Cemetery in suburban Hillside, which now features a memorial to the victims of the fire.

- **Fact:** Colorful Chicago Mayor "Big Bill" Thompson first took office in 1915. **Twist:** He sympathized with the Central Powers during World War I. **Only in Chicago:** This earned him the popular nickname "Kaiser Bill" Thompson.

Pullman:
A Lesson for Control Freaks

✳ ✳ ✳ ✳

*Railroad magnate George Pullman thought he was doing his workers
a favor by building them a brand-new town with all the amenities.
Instead, he helped bring about the country's first nationwide strike
and nearly brought the country to its knees.*

George Pullman

In the years following the Civil War,
American companies were focused on one
key facet of business: increased worker
productivity. Through the use of such new
methods as the assembly line and such
new technologies as the Bessemer con-
verter to make steel or the mechanical
thresher to increase agricultural production, American workers and businesses
enjoyed a period of industrial production
like the world had never seen. At the same
time, progressives and liberals of the day
sought better conditions for workers. These conflicting goals led to
a violent 1893 uprising in Pullman, a company town 13 miles south
of Chicago.

If Something Seems Too Good to Be True . . .

George Pullman built the town to house the thousands of workers
who helped manufacture his company's luxurious sleeper cars. It was
the fruition of Pullman's idea of a model community, built to replace
the rundown tenements that often housed workers. The town
consisted of strips of neat, tidy rowhouses. By providing such living
quarters, Pullman hoped to better the health, environment, and
spirit of his employees and thereby attract skilled workers, increase
productivity, and avoid strikes. The town was, for the most part, built
by Pullman factory workers and was completed in 1884.

The houses had all the most modern amenities, and Pullman made sure the town had everything the workers could ever want or need (a school, a bank, a post office, a library, a theater, shops, and restaurants); this way, workers would never feel the need to leave, and the days and weeks would progress exactly as Pullman planned.

For a while, everything went smoothly. Workers bristled at certain policies in the company town (alcohol was forbidden, there were inspectors on the payroll to make sure workers were "behaving," and homes were only leased, never sold), but for the most part, the workers were happy.

Frugality's a Cinch When You Have No Money

Tempers flaired during a financial panic in 1893, however. As demands for the company's train cars plummeted, Pullman laid off workers. He cut the wages of the workers who remained by 30 percent, even though more work would likely be required of them. To make matters even worse, Pullman continued to deduct the same rent from workers' paychecks to ensure investors would continue to get the 6 percent return he had promised them. Pullman preached frugality from his Prairie Avenue mansion as his workers' families went hungry.

The Strike

Soon, matters came to a head. The American Railway Union (ARU), led by Eugene Debs, a fiery speaker who later ran for president on the Socialist ticket, called for a strike. Railroad workers across the nation refused to handle Pullman cars, and within four days, 125,000 workers on 29 railroads had quit work rather than handle the company's products.

The strike became a national issue. Many workers were left without jobs as the company hired scabs. The strikers appealed to Illinois Governor John P. Altgeld, who wrote George Pullman three times, asking him to do something about the "great distress" among his former workers. Pullman blamed the workers for their problems, arguing that if they had not gone on strike, they would not be suffering.

The Larger Battle

Beyond the plight of the workers, a debate rose up across the country over the role of workers, their rights, and the rights of businesses and managers to set wages and working conditions. Since the strike had halted the transportation of goods across the country, business owners and some newspaper editors began painting the union as a lawless, violent gang and called for the strike to be broken up—and by force, if necessary.

President Grover Cleveland, faced with nervous railroad executives and interrupted mail trains, declared the strike a federal crime. He deployed 12,000 troops, many of whom set up camp in Grant Park. By the end, 13 strikers were killed and 57 were wounded, with railroad workers also causing millions of dollars in property damage.

On August 3, 1894, the strike ended. Many workers and their supporters around the country were devastated as the Pullman employees were forced back to work. Debs went to prison, the ARU was disbanded, and the power of industrial workers' unions was effectively diminished until the Great Depression. Many did lay the blame at Pullman's feet, however; a presidential commission chastised him for ignoring his workers' plight.

An Ongoing Legacy

From a worker's perspective, not all was lost. For one, while serving his time in jail, Debs decided that labor needed to win political power to balance that of their employers. He became the Socialist Party's presidential candidate and received nearly a million votes in 1912. For another, the strike helped set in motion the Progressive Era in U.S. history, a period when President Theodore Roosevelt and others began to question the unchecked power of major industries.

In the years following the strike, railcars began losing ground to automobiles, and the company and the town gradually shut down. The state filed suit against the company's ownership of a town, and today, Pullman is an historic district of narrow streets and tidy row houses on Chicago's Southwest Side. Visitors come from around the world to recall a critical period in American history and an industrial tycoon who thought he had it all figured out.

You Can Thank Chicago

Car Radios

In the 1920s, Paul and Joseph Galvin started a business in Chicago selling devices that allowed home radios to be run on regular electric current rather than on batteries. In 1930, the innovative brothers rolled out a remarkable new invention—a radio that could be mounted in a car, so that motorists could be entertained and informed as they toured the dusty roads of America. Taking advantage of the popularity of their new device, the brothers renamed their company Motorola (a combination of "motor" and "Victrola"), and went on to become one of the largest electronic communications manufacturers in the world.

Italian Beef Sandwich

A Chicago Italian Beef sandwich consists of thinly sliced seasoned beef on a hearty Italian roll, adorned with sautéed peppers—either sweet or hot according to the customer's preference. Now a staple of caterers and fast-food stands around the country, the sandwich was introduced in Chicago during the 1930s. According to Al's Beef and the Scala Packing Company (leading Chicago Italian beef purveyors), the sandwiches became a staple of Depression-era Italian family gatherings because the thinly sliced meat and hearty rolls offered a cheaper way to feed large crowds.

Lemonheads

The Ferrara Pan Candy Company was founded in Chicago in the early 1900s by Italian immigrant Salvatore Ferrara and was originally known for the popular sugar-coated almonds it sold. In 1962, the company introduced Lemonheads, a small, round, sour candy that remains a popular treat today. The candies are made by the "pan" process referred to in the company's name, in which layers of flavoring and coloring are added to a hard candy center as it spins around in a rotating pan. Still owned by the same family today, Ferrara Pan produces more than 500 million Lemonheads a year.

Poet of the Big Shoulders

* * * *

*Who knew a scrappy high school dropout from Galesburg, Illinois,
would one day give the City of the Big Shoulders
its most fitting nickname?*

Carl Sandburg's ability to capture the feel of Chicago in the industrial age through his lyrical-yet-gritty poetry secured him a place in the hearts of the working people and in the annals of literary history. Sandburg's vision of the city shaped it for generations to come.

Portrait of Sandburg as a Young Man

The house where Carl Sandburg's remains now rest is the same house in which he was born. The son of Swedish immigrants, Sandburg was the second of seven kids. After finishing eighth grade, Carl went on to various odd jobs, from shining shoes to delivering milk.

Ten years later, Sandburg decided to see the world. He got around as best he could, hitchhiking and riding the rails. Later, when he began to write, these hobo days would provide plenty of inspiration.

Influences and Experiences

When the Spanish-American War broke out in 1898, Sandburg—who was still working odd jobs—joined the Sixth Illinois Volunteers. During his service, Sandburg wrote dispatches for the *Galesburg Evening Mail*. When the fighting was over, Sandburg returned to Illinois and entered college (he never received his high school diploma, but his status as a war veteran earned him admission and free tuition at Lombard College in Galesburg). Once in school, he found that he enjoyed writing and reading—poetry, especially—and soon joined a group that called themselves the Poor Writer's Club. The club was made up of socialist thinkers, and Sandburg was heavily influenced by conversations with these peers.

Never one for the conventional path, Sandburg took only the courses that interested him and quit college before he graduated.

He began working on his first poetry collection and took odd jobs to support himself. Over the next few years, several volumes of Sandburg's poetry would be published by a small press owned by one of his professors.

Poetry for the People

The poetry that Carl Sandburg wrote was different from much American poetry that had come before it. While Sandburg's poems were rich with imagery and offered exquisitely crafted words and phrases, there was a realism to his work that readers found refreshing and inspiring. This was because much of the writer's poetry turned a reporter's eye on what was happening in America at the turn of the 20th century. Sandburg was used to approaching writing from a journalist's perspective: He had written dispatches during the Spanish-American War and World War I, and he wrote for the *Chicago Daily News* for a number of years.

The country was booming during the early part of the 20th century; Rockefeller, Carnegie, and other tycoons were funneling massive wealth into various industries that created jobs in steel mills, slaughterhouses, and agriculture. But the boom caused problems too. Great numbers of people swarmed into the rapidly growing cities, and soon there were far more people than jobs. Poverty and illness raged through these communities, and Sandburg, along with other socialist thinkers, grew disgusted with a country that would allow a few to get rich while the masses suffered.

In *Chicago,* his most famous poem, he personifies the city, elevating the plight of workers into an almost heroic quest:

> Hog Butcher for the World,
> Tool Maker, Stacker of Wheat,
> Player with Railroads and the Nation's Freight Handler;
> Stormy, husky, brawling,
> City of the Big Shoulders

Such descriptive language made Sandburg instantly popular; both his *Chicago Poems* in 1916 and *Cornhuskers* in 1918 were big hits with a public who loved his conversational style and everyman themes.

And He Could Sing Too!

Sandburg's longtime love of folk songs led him to publish *The American Songbag* in 1927. It included more than 300 songs (picked up during his hobo days) and played a big part in legitimizing folk music in America. Sandburg performed some of these tunes when he was invited to appear publicly, and he continued to play the guitar and sing throughout the '50s and '60s.

Happily, Sandburg enjoyed success throughout his long life—no long-suffering starving artist stuff here. Sandburg is primarily known for his poetry, and he won his first Pulitzer in 1919, for *Cornhuskers*, a collection of his poems. The second installment of his biography of Lincoln earned him another Pulitzer, and he won the prize a third time, in 1950, for *The Complete Poems of Carl Sandburg*. Further proving that he was seriously in touch with the pulse of the times, Sandburg won a Grammy in 1959. The Best Spoken Word award was given for his audio recording of a work about Lincoln backed by the New York Philharmonic.

Sandburg died in 1967, having published dozens of books of poetry, songs, children's stories, biographies, and his own autobiography, all of which reflected his tough-but-lovable, strong-willed midwestern identity. He will long be remembered not just as a quintessential American writer, but as a quintessential Chicagoan too.

- *Carl Sandburg was once asked if there was a word he didn't like. He replied that he never liked the word* exclusive *because it carries the implication that you are shutting people out of your mind and heart.*

- *As a young boy, Sandburg preferred to be called "Charlie" because he thought it sounded more American. He reverted to "Carl" around 1910, with encouragement from his wife.*

Quiz

Chicago is a rough-and-tumble, no-nonsense town. That reputation has been consistently borne out by the city's emissaries to the National Football League, the Bears, and no position on the team better represents the hardcase image of the city than linebacker (especially middle *linebacker). See if you can match the following defensive demons to the descriptions of their careers. Give yourself an extra point for each player whose jersey number you can name.*

Doug Buffone
Brian Urlacher
Dick Butkus
Bill George
Mike Singletary

1. This Hall of Famer spent 14 years in a Bears uniform and helped define the middle linebacker slot. He later joined the team's coaching staff as a defensive assistant.

2. This gifted athlete was one of the most physical players in the history of the sport. He set a team record for career takeaways with 25 fumble recoveries and 22 interceptions.

3. At six feet four and more than 250 pounds, this player is the biggest man ever to hold the middle linebacker slot for the Bears. Combining his immense size with his gift for speed allowed him to redefine the way this defensive position is played.

4. This player was a bright spot in a decade when the Bears struggled greatly. After retirement, he was a local sports announcer and cofounded the Arena Football League.

5. Known for giving his all on every play and at every practice, this middle linebacker spent hours reviewing films before each game. His hallmark intensity allowed him to serve as the anchor of the team's complex "46" defense that led them to a Super Bowl victory.

What Really Caused the Chicago Fire?

✳   ✳   ✳   ✳

Mrs. O'Leary and her cow didn't really start the fire.
So who—or what—did?

The story is a familiar one: Poor old Mrs. O'Leary left a kerosene lantern burning in her barn. A cow kicked the lantern over, and the hay caught fire. The winds blew the flames, and they quickly spread through the wooden city, destroying most of downtown.

The story that Mrs. O'Leary and her cow were the culprits spread around the city before the flames had even stopped smouldering. The cow was butchered and served up as oxtail soup at the Royal Palm, a posh downtown restaurant, on Thanksgiving Day a month after the fire. The O'Learys had to go into hiding because they feared being lynched.

But we now know that the story was total nonsense. While the fire did start in the O'Leary barn, the story that poor Mrs. O'Leary or her cow was responsible was invented by a reporter who thought it made for a colorful story. The local press, much of which was openly anti-Irish, picked up on the story and ran with it; the *Tribune* spoke of Mrs. O'Leary's "typical Irish know-nothingness." Mrs. O'Leary was hounded on the anniversary of the fire for the rest of her life. Not surprisingly, she developed a lifelong hatred for reporters, and she never allowed herself to be photographed.

It Came from Outer Space?

So, if it *wasn't* Mrs. O'Leary, what *did* cause the fire? Lots of stories have gone around over the years. More than one person has sheepishly admitted to family members in their old age that *they* were the cause of the fire, whether by knocking burning ashes from a clay pipe into the hay or by sneaking into the barn to milk the cow on a dare, causing the irate cow to start kicking. They can't *all* have been telling the truth, though.

One even stranger theory alleges that the fire was actually caused by a meteor that crashed down the day of the fire in Peshtigo, Wisconsin. The meteor certainly caused major fires throughout Wisconsin—some of which were actually even bigger than the one that blazed in Chicago. No one is entirely sure whether the fire could possibly have traveled all the way to Chicago (and ended up localized in a barn southwest of the Loop, skipping everything west of Halsted and north of Taylor Street in the process). Still, it seems an awfully funny coincidence that major fires would have broken out in two nearby areas with totally different causes on the same day.

The Mysterious Theory of "Big Jim" O'Leary

Mrs. O'Leary's son had an even wilder story. Young James O'Leary grew up to be "Big Jim" O'Leary, a stockyards saloon-keeper and gambling king. When a statement was made in the *Tribune* that the fire had been started by two young men trying to milk the cow in order to make whiskey punch, he was outraged.

"The true cause of the fire has never been told," he said to a *Tribune* reporter in 1904. "But I'll speak out. That story about the cow kicking over the lamp was the monumental fake of the last century. I know what I'm talking about when I say that the fire was caused by spontaneous combustion!"

That's right. Spontaneous combustion.

According to Big Jim, his father had just purchased some mysterious green hay, which, he said, had spontaneously combusted in the hay loft.

The true origin of the fire will probably never be known, but most scientists agree that there is no type of hay that is known to spontaneously combust. But it's no more likely than the story that Mrs. O'Leary or her cow was the true cause of the fire— in the late 20th century, the city finally issued an apology to poor Mrs. O'Leary.

Pilsen: A Mecca for Immigrants

* * * *

Nestled along a bend in the Chicago River on the Near West Side, Pilsen is a vibrant and spirited community with deep, deep roots.

If you're looking for authentic Mexican cuisine, Pilsen is the place to go. With a Hispanic population of 87 percent—and with more Mexican residents than any other Chicago neighborhood—Pilsen is largely insulated from American influences. It is amazing how much this neighborhood has changed, particularly when you consider its Western European roots.

German and Irish immigrants were drawn to this area in the 1840s after the construction of two railroad lines that—together with the river—formed the boundaries of the neighborhood. The rail lines and the river made the area a key transportation hub, which attracted manufacturing businesses and immigrant workers seeking jobs.

Origin of the Intriguing Name

By the 1870s, the area's economic base was well-established, but the German and Irish residents had been supplanted by Eastern European immigrants. One enterprising immigrant opened a restaurant named At the City of Plzen, after the second-largest metropolis in West Bohemia; before long, the name had been anglicized to Pilsen and applied to the entire neighborhood.

Many of the new residents were sympathetic to the rising socialist movement in the United States, and Pilsen soon became a flashpoint for labor conflicts that drew attention across the city and the nation. Federal troops were sent to the area in 1877 to quell a railroad worker strike, and the ensuing confrontation left 30 dead. A decade later, many Pilsen residents were involved in the labor unrest that culminated in the infamous incident in Haymarket Square in 1886. Though their tactics were controversial, the labor activists of that era did help bring about reforms that raised the standard of living within the community. They also laid the groundwork for the community pride that still defines the neighborhood today.

In the early years of the 20th century, Pilsen became more of a cultural hodgepodge and something of a midwestern gateway to United States. Immigrants from various parts of the globe settled here, drawn by the strong sense of community and the abundance of industrial jobs.

Bring on the Mosaics and Murals

Soon, though, America began to see a huge influx of Hispanic immigrants, and by the 1960s Pilsen had become populated predominantly by Mexican Americans. These new residents maintained the neighborhood's tradition of political activism, and many effective community organizations sprang up to protect the interests of the neighborhood. These new residents also brought a very strong sense of their native culture to the area. Shops and restaurants reflecting their Mexican heritage soon became common. The area is perhaps best known for its many colorful mosaics and murals, which are traditional forms of Mexican public art. These eye-catching pieces depict significant events in the history of the community. Pilsen is also home to the largest Latino arts museum in the country, the National Museum of Mexican Art, which was established in 1982.

Pilsen is the largest Latino community in Chicago, and it is also the city's youngest neighborhood, with a median age of about 18. Many of the manufacturing and industrial jobs have gone away, but the neighborhood has a thriving local retail economy made up of numerous small shops. Instead of large stores or national chains, the streets are lined with countless small grocery stores, clothing shops, cafés, and restaurants owned by neighborhood residents, along with an army of street vendors selling everything from tamales and roasted corn to jewelry and Mexican candies.

Still, Pilsen faces challenges. Many residents live below the poverty line, and longtime residents view gentrification and recent gang activity as threats to community stability. But the area has also seen an influx of college-educated youth who grew up in the neighborhood; these new residents are poised to take up the mantle of community organization and ensure that Pilsen remains the thriving community it has always been.

Chicago Chatter

"Chicago: it's still a frontier town."

—Norman Mark,
Mayors, Madams and Madmen (1979)

"These businessmen in Chicago are reckless, and they fall a lot. But failure doesn't bother them. Catastrophe doesn't bother them. They bounce right back."

—Anthony Trollope

"Chicago's downtown seems to me to constitute, all in all, the best-looking twentieth-century city, the city where contemporary technique has been matched by artistry, intelligence, and comparatively moderated greed. No doubt about it, if style were the one gauge, Chicago would be among the greatest of all the cities of the world."

—Jan Morris, "Boss No More," *Locations,* 1992

"Like the cathedral of the Middle Ages, [the Art Institute] is the one place in the city that should never be closed to the people at any time, even if it took three shifts to keep it open."

—Frank Lloyd Wright

"When friends from abroad come to the United States, I always send them to Chicago, or try to. It is the quintessential American city: muscular, inventive, wonderfully diverse, worldly-wise (if a bit oafish at times), and as unpretentious as its prairie-flat vowels."

—R. W. Apple Jr., "On the Road; Big Shoulders, Buffed for Action,"
The New York Times, March 31, 2000

"Though its people are diverse in race and interests, the city's ethos is remarkably unified. It is—and don't laugh—a reasonably happy place. Not a mindlessly smiley-face kind of place, but a place where people try to be pleasant and get on with it."

—Elizabeth Canning Blackwell, *Irreverent Guide to Chicago*

"I adore Chicago. It is the pulse of America."

—Sarah Bernhardt, *Chicago Tribune Magazine,* 1917

Timeline

(Continued from p. 147)

July–August 1919
Almost 40 Chicagoans die in a week of racial violence, ignited when an African American teenager was drowned after venturing onto a "white" beach. Several hundred are injured before the Illinois militia steps in to restore peace.

October 1, 1919
The Cincinnati Reds beat the Chicago White Sox 9–1 in the first game of the World Series. The Reds will go on to win the Series 5–3. The following year, several members of the White Sox will ignite the "Black Sox Scandal" when they confess to deliberately losing the Series in return for a share in a gambling syndicate's profits.

1920
Chicago voters approve a $2.5 million bond for the construction of Grant Park Stadium. Soon renamed Soldier Field, it will be among the first major city-supported athletic facilities. Overruns will more than triple the construction costs by the end of the decade.

January 16, 1920
The 18th Amendment takes effect, banning alcohol sales and consumption. A large network of alcohol producers and distributors develops, with Chicago becoming the center of this bootlegging activity. The resulting violence and organized crime will become deeply ingrained in Chicago's social fabric.

1922
The American Unity League launches *Tolerance,* a weekly newspaper that prints the names and addresses of Chicago-area Ku Klux Klan members. The exposure will doom the hate group's presence in Chicago.

1922
Brach's Palace of Sweets opens a new factory on the West Side. This facility will make the company founded in 1904 by Emil Brach the largest candy factory in the nation.

October 15, 1922
Pioneering aviator and Chicagoan Bessie Coleman performs in her first local barnstorming exhibition. As an African American woman, Coleman was forced to travel to France for flight training. She will die in a Florida crash in 1926.

1924
Ace Hardware is created by a conglomerate of Chicago-area hardware dealers to serve as a centralizing purchasing entity.

May 21, 1924
Bobby Franks, a 14-year-old Chicagoan, is murdered. Ten days later, the nation is shocked when grad students Richard Loeb and Nathan Leopold confess to the crime.

(Continued on p. 205)

The Trains All Stop at La Salle Street

✳ ✳ ✳ ✳

From its founding, Chicago has been a place where people have come to make money.

While celebrated today for its culture, nightlife, and sports teams, Chicago was founded as a commercial town. From the moment Jean Baptiste Pointe DuSable arrived and set up a trading post, business and the art of making money have been ingrained in Chicago.

Today, the city stands at the crossroads of global finance and is one of the most important business centers in the world. It has the third largest gross metropolitan product in the nation (approximately $520 billion according to 2008 estimates) and was named the fourth most important business center in the world in the MasterCard Worldwide Centers of Commerce Index. In 2008, Chicago placed 16th on the UBS list of the world's richest cities, and it is one of the 10 "financial centers in the world," according to the Global Financial Centers Index.

Beyond the rankings, Chicago has a wealth of high-tech operations, a collection of Fortune 500 companies, and an economic climate that makes it an indispensable part of the world financial system. It also houses one of the 12 Federal Reserve banks, the Chicago Stock Exchange, and the Chicago Mercantile Exchange. They are all centered on La Salle Street, the biggest financial district outside of Wall Street.

Location, Location, Location

How did Chicago become one of the world's most important financial centers? Many arguments can be made, but certainly one of the strongest is the city's centralized location at a time when the nation was still growing. Back when goods and food had to be moved across the country over land, Chicago was well positioned to collect its share of the profits as trains, boats, and airplanes passed through.

Later, when airplanes carrying people replaced railcars carrying cattle, Chicago turned itself into a transportation hub, ensuring the city was a stop on almost every traveler's itinerary.

The reason Chicago emerged as a financial powerhouse may ultimately lie in the city's history as a breeding ground for men and women who simply believed making money was one of the most important of all human endeavors. From the industrial titans of the late 1800s who called Chicago home, such as Cyrus McCormick, inventor of the mechanical reaper, or railroad car magnate George Pullman, the city has nurtured those who found making money their calling. And, as the 19th century became the 20th century, those industrial tycoons simply became financial ones, turning industrial power into financial innovation.

Investments Make the World Go Round

Today, Chicago is known more for its financial and investment wizardry than building machinery, and the list of financial innovations that began in Chicago is impressive. Chicago was one of the first cities to develop an efficient financial exchange for commodities such as corn and hogs, allowing farmers to minimize their risks and financiers to make profits. The modern derivatives market, born in Chicago more than a century ago, allows investors to hedge their bets on everything from interest rates to weather forecasts. In 2008, the Chicago Mercantile Exchange handled 3.3 billion contracts, attesting to the enormously important role that options now play.

Put Your Money Where Your Mouth Is

Chicago is well positioned to remain a key player in the global financial system. The city is currently home to North America's only exchange for greenhouse gas emissions, the Chicago Climate Exchange, a necessary market to help combat global warming. But more importantly, though economic conditions will rise and fall, Chicago will always remember that making money comes first—after that, everything else just falls into place.

A Penny for Your Parking Spot?

* * * *

Chicago streets have historically been lined with parking meters. The same can be said of most other cities, but the Windy City has a unique relationship with these sometimes vexing devices.

Chicagoans have been fuming about parking meters ever since the change-suckers were invented. The intention of the first parking meters, installed in Oklahoma City in 1935, was to circulate shoppers through the parking spots. But the city quickly recognized that they offered another benefit: a welcome source of revenue. It didn't take long for Chicago to get in on this moneymaking racket.

Local Boy Makes a Mint

The following year, Donald Duncan decided he would spread parking meters (like a plague) throughout the world. A resident of the Chicago suburb Oak Park, Duncan had already used his promotional and marketing savvy to build two empires founded on Good Humor ice cream and the Duncan yo-yo. Applying those same skills to the manufacture of parking meters, he convinced local governments around the globe of the benefits of the new technology and helped make meters commonplace. Duncan's meter business changed hands several times and long ago moved its manufacturing operations out of the Midwest, but it remains one of the world's largest providers of parking regulation equipment.

Privatization Comes Calling

The Chicago parker's fantasy—of taking a Louisville Slugger to the nearest meter—has endured for decades. In 2009, parking meters became the center of one of the biggest controversies the city had seen in some time. In February of that year, in the midst of an economic downturn, Mayor Richard Daley announced that he had brokered an arrangement to privatize the city's parking meters. The deal was pushed through the city council in just a few days and went into effect immediately. Chicago received a one-time payment of $1.15 billion in return for allowing a newly formed company, Chicago Parking Meters LLC, an investment fund managed by Morgan Stanley, to manage the city's 36,000 metered parking spots for the next 75 years.

Chicago Parking Meters LLC immediately raised rates, increased the meters' hours of operation, and eliminated free parking on Sundays and holidays. A number of journalists and political organizations lambasted the mayor, saying the negotiations had not been transparent enough and that the new arrangement gave the city a short-term benefit at the expense of Chicago motorists. Some also believed that the city could have at least haggled for significantly more money.

The Future of Parking?

Within just a few months, citizens began complaining about the way street parking was now being handled. With the new higher rates, meters quickly fill up with coins, and broken meters go unrepaired for weeks. The cost for parking was not clearly marked on many meters, and worst of all were the new computerized pay boxes that began replacing individual meters. The suddenly ubiquitous "pay at the box" devices require a driver to walk to the middle of the block, insert coins or a credit card, and then take a time-stamped receipt back to the car to be displayed on the dashboard. Many people find the boxes confusing, and the boxes frequently fail to issue receipts or to accept money, leaving parkers vulnerable to tickets.

At the same time, the company stepped up enforcement efforts; in the first half of 2009, drivers saw a 13 percent increase in the number of parking citations issued. Business owners, on the other hand, are so far happy with the new deal. They believe it has helped speed up spot turnover and increased foot traffic in their establishments. And there are those drivers who appreciate using the credit card option instead of having to fumble around for coins.

Some have called on the mayor to find a way to renegotiate or even cancel the parking meter contract, but so far Daley has stood firmly behind the deal. Thankfully, in this city, there's always the "L" or the bus . . .

The Original Smoke-Filled Room

❋ ❋ ❋ ❋

We all know what the phrase "smoke-filled room" refers to—a place where political bigwigs meet, shielded from the public glare, in order to hammer out the self-serving deals they would prefer to hide from their constituents. This oft-used bit of political shorthand traces its origins to an incident that occurred in a famous Chicago hotel.

With its reputation for hardball politics, Chicago might seem like a natural place for the term "smoke-filled room" to have originated. But this familiar part of the American political lexicon was not coined to describe any actions of local politicians. Rather, it stems from the 1920 Republican Convention that was held at the Chicago Coliseum (1513 S. Wabash).

The race for the Republican presidential nomination was a particularly hard-fought competition that year, and on Friday, June 11, it became clear that the delegates faced an intractable deadlock. That night, a group of Republican senators arranged a private meeting in suites 408 and 410 at Chicago's Blackstone Hotel (636 S. Michigan). Working late into the night, they finally settled on dark-horse candidate Warren G. Harding as the only viable compromise. The first-term senator was called to the room shortly after 2:00 A.M., accepted the deal offered by the power brokers, and took the nomination shortly thereafter.

An Associated Press journalist reported on the secret meeting in a nationally published article, describing the setting as a "smoke-filled room." Ever since, the phrase has been used to describe any private gathering of political figures where deals are struck, but it is particularly meant to indicate a meeting during which party members choose a candidate to put forth for office. The Blackstone, a luxury hotel that first opened in 1910, is still in operation today, and guests can stay in the very rooms where the presidential deal was hashed out—though they can no longer smoke there!

Fast Facts

- For all its reputation, Chicago isn't so windy—a little more so than the U.S. average. However, Chicago has a skyscraper-studded downtown core, the Loop, whose buildings tend to channel the wind. If it's windy, people made it so.

- As of the 2000 census, the ethnic makeup of Chicago was as follows: 36.8 percent African American, 31.3 percent white non-Hispanic, 26 percent Hispanic, 1.1 percent Chinese, and 1 percent Filipino.

- Does the FFA have a presence within the Chicago city limits? Indeed. The Chicago High School for Agricultural Sciences (3857 W. 111th St.), the only institution of its kind in the Midwest, has a 72-acre teaching farm. Oddly enough, their sports teams are called the Cyclones—a weather phenomenon that tends to ruin crops, not help them.

- The Olson Rug & Flooring Company used to maintain a waterfall running through a rock garden and arboretum, next to its facility on Diversey and Pulaski. Unfortunately, Olson sold the property to Marshall Field's in 1965. The water was turned off six years later. Now it's a parking lot.

- Megachurch, Chicago style: The world's tallest church building is the First United Methodist Church, aka Chicago Temple, completed in 1923. It stands 568 feet high. A good percentage of the building is office space—a stroke of fiscal genius, when you think about it.

- **Fact:** In 2004, the New City YMCA was full of transvestites for a Transgender Ball. **Twist:** The Y mistakenly double-booked a youth swimming event at the same time. **Only in Chicago:** Fights broke out when parents arrived and found the locker rooms a real drag.

Graceland Cemetery

* * * *

The place where Chicago's dead elite meet.

Graceland Cemetery was established in 1860, after it was announced that City Cemetery along the lake would be closing because of concerns about sanitation. Thomas B. Bryan purchased 80 acres in the Lakeview community on the North Side and hired landscape architects to turn the land into a magnificent park with rolling hills and a serene lake. Soon, prominent families from all over Chicago were buying up plots at what seemed like a record pace.

After numerous bodies from City Cemetery were reinterred at Graceland, it became clear that Graceland needed more room. Land to the east and northwest was purchased, expanding Graceland to its current size of 119 acres.

A Knight, a Sphinx, and a Figure Deep in Thought

Graceland Cemetery is often referred to as the Cemetery of Architects, and with good reason. The list of individuals buried there reads like a who's who in the history of architecture: Bruce A. Goff, William Holabird, John Wellborn Root, and William Le Baron Jenney, just to name a few. The revered Daniel Burnham's grave lies on an island in Lake Willowmere, and Louis Sullivan's simple grave certainly adheres to the genius's "form follows function" criteria.

Marshall Field is also interred at Graceland. His monument features *Memory,* a sculpture of a seated female figure deep in thought. Daniel Chester French and Henry Bacon, who created the Lincoln Memorial, sculpted this famous statue.

Another eye-catching statue is of a noble knight. This work is entitled

Crusader, and it marks the final resting place of Victor F. Lawson, publisher of the venerable *Daily News.*

Magnificent columns mark Potter Palmer's mausoleum, but the prize for the businessman with the most unusual grave goes to German brewer Peter Schoenhofen. His mausoleum, designed to look like an Egyptian pyramid, has a sphinx and an angel standing guard at the entrance.

Pullman's Coffin Fortress

There is an interesting story surrounding the grave of railroad tycoon George Pullman. For years leading up to his death, Pullman had also worked as a landlord for his railroad employees. Most of these workers despised Pullman after he cut their salaries but kept their rents the same. When Pullman passed away, his family was concerned that some disgruntled workers might dig up his body; to protect against this, the family held a private burial late at night. Then, Pullman's coffin was lowered into a concrete-lined grave, which was covered with tar paper, asphalt, and an extra ton of concrete. After that, railroad ties were placed on top of the grave before it was covered up with dirt. A large column was erected over the grave and flanked with concrete benches.

Another interesting resident of Graceland is Allan Pinkerton, the world's first private detective and founder of the first detective agency, Pinkerton's National Detective Agency. One of Pinkerton's coworkers, Kate Warn, the first female detective, is also interred at Graceland.

A Wandering Girl and a Mysterious Being

No visit to Graceland would be complete without visiting two of the cemetery's most famous statues. The first is of Inez Clarke, a girl who, according to legend, died after being struck by lightning in 1880 at age six. Many people say Inez's statue sometimes comes to life during violent thunderstorms and wanders the cemetery. Visitors swear they have stopped by her grave and found the glass case empty. There is one problem with this legend: According to cemetery records, no one by the name Inez Clarke is buried at Graceland. A boy named Amos Briggs is buried closest to the statue. No one knows why the Inez Clarke statue was made or how it came to be displayed at Graceland, but all agree it is beautiful.

Far and away, the biggest draw at Graceland is the statue sculpted by Lorado Taft for the family of Dexter Graves. The lifesize cloaked statue *Eternal Silence* (commonly called the "Statue of Death") stands in front of the Graves plot looking downward. Over the years, the elements have had their way with the bronze statue, turning it green except for the face, which is partially hidden by a hood. Some have said that no photograph taken of this statue will turn out, but the countless photos posted on the Internet debunk this myth. Others say that to look into the eyes of the statue will bring you luck, allow you to see your own death, or become cursed; consider those odds before you make eye contact with this statue.

No visit to Chicago is complete without a visit to this magnificent urban expanse, which pays tribute to numerous founders of the city in an oasis of serenity beneath the clattering "L."

✳ ✳ ✳ ✳

- *Augustus Dickens, Charles Dickens's youngest brother, is buried in Graceland Cemetery. Charles doted on him when he was young; as Augustus got older, he became an alcoholic and repeatedly got into trouble. Charles bailed him out many times, but when Augustus left his wife and ran off to Chicago with another woman (Bertha Phillips, the daughter of a prominent insurance executive), Charles washed his hands of his brother. When Charles Dickens gave speaking tours in the United States, he never included Chicago on his itinerary. Augustus died in 1866, and Bertha committed suicide in 1868. After her death, their three children were placed in adoptive homes.*

- *William Hulbert, the founder of Major League Baseball's National League, is also buried at Graceland. His gravestone is a large baseball with the names of the first National League teams carved into it.*

Millennium Park

* * * *

*This once-controversial undertaking
is now one of the city's preeminent attractions.*

Chicago's lakefront is its greatest asset. But for decades, miles of
the shore were dominated by industrial infrastructure. Train tracks,
which had been built a few hundred yards offshore during the 19th
century, separated the people of Chicago from the body of water
that made their city one of the fastest growing in history. Its downtown area was a mess of steel and concrete divorced from the
natural beauty and serenity that surrounded it. The eyesores drove
Chicago's wealthiest residents into the northern and western
suburbs, where they had access to the lake or to large swaths of
greenery.

The grandeur of Grant Park, the city's turn-of-the-century Beaux
Arts solution to its malaise, was a wonder for the city. It utilized the
neat patches of grass and complex geometric gardens for concerts,
festivals, and everyday leisure. But the northwest tip of the park still
left a gape of commuter trains, parking spaces, and abandoned
railcars—all owned and maintained by the Illinois Central Railroad
company—that sullied an otherwise idyllic lakeside setting. That all
changed in 1997, when the city won rights to the space above the
tracks. Use of the space was debated for some time before plans
were drawn to build a massive parking structure. In addition, the
parking structure would be covered by about 25 acres of recreational
public space.

The details were vague, and plans for the park quickly fell
behind schedule. The city sought the expertise of superstar architect
Frank Gehry, who had recently won several prestigious awards and
international recognition for a series of magnificent buildings in
locales as varied as Bilbao, Spain, and Cleveland, Ohio. Gehry's
reluctance to sign on to the plan created a major roadblock in
construction of the parking garage and the park itself, which Mayor
Richard M. Daley hoped would be the city's newest artistic play-

ground. What had originally been a $150 million plan had ballooned to more than $200 million—and that was just the beginning.

Finally, exasperated by the city's mismanagement of the site and the funds and its inability to attract Gehry to the project, the Pritzker family came to the rescue. They poneyed up $15 million for what would become the Jay Pritzker Pavilion, home to Frank Gehry's glimmering steel band shell, topped off by enormous frills of stainless steel.

Complete with a Bike Station Worth Millions

Ameritech and Chicago-based Banc One each donated $5 million, and William Daley, former secretary of commerce and the Midwest chair of J.P. Morgan-Chase (and, naturally, the brother of Mayor Richard Daley) arranged for the bank to underwrite the project, allowing for expansions in the city's original plans. The federal government offered an additional $3.1 million in grant money for a bike station under the park. That might sound a little steep for a bike station, but this area—which is complete with showers and a café— was built to encourage motorists to bike downtown instead of drive, and it has been wildly successful.

Soon, the city's large and lofty philanthropic community began giving money to the project, requesting with each donation another large piece of public art, a garden, or a monument commemorating the gift. The results include London-based artist Anish Kapoor's interactive steel sculpture *Cloud Gate*—affectionately dubbed "The Bean" by its legion of fans—which reflects the city's skyline in a panoramic arch; Spanish artist Jaume Plensa's Crown Fountain, two towers of glass bricks with the projected faces of Chicagoans behind a streaming wall of water; and the Lurie Garden, which (at five acres) was the largest rooftop garden in the world at the time of its construction.

When all was said and done, Millennium Park's price tag was about $475 million, but more than half of that was provided through grants and private donations. The city's bill was, in the end, a little large for its britches, but we're willing to bet that will slip your mind as you watch dozens of kids from all over the city splash with delight in Crown Fountain on a hot Chicago summer day.

Millennium Park: Facts and Figures

Year started: 1999
Year opened: 2004
Size: 24.5 acres
Visitors per year: 23 million
Total cost of park: $475 million

The Jay Pritzker Pavillion

Designer: Frank Gehry
Seats: 4,000 people; additional lawn seating for another 11,000

Cloud Gate ("The Bean")

Designer: Anish Kapoor
Weight: 110 tons
Dimensions: 33' high × 42' wide × 66' long with a 12' arch under which viewers can walk
Location: AT&T Plaza

Lurie Garden

Designer: Gustafson Guthrie Nichol Ltd., Piet Oudolf, and Robert Israel
Size: 5 acres
Highlights: 165 species of vegetation; enclosed on two sides by a "shoulder" hedge as a tribute to Carl Sandburg's famous phrase about the city; two interior spaces are planted with trees native to Chicago

Crown Fountain

Designer: Jaume Plensa
Dimensions: 50' high × 23' wide × 16' diameter (each tower)
Features the faces of 1,000 Chicagoans

McDonald's Cycle Center

Dimensions: 16,450 square feet
Accommodates up to 300 bicycles

BP Bridge

Designer: Frank Gehry
Dimensions: 925 feet
5 percent incline

Papa Bear

✳ ✳ ✳ ✳

*George S. Halas was one of Chicago's most enduring sports legends
and a towering figure in the National Football League.
Player, coach, owner, executive, recruiter—he did it all,
on his own terms, and better than just about anybody else.*

Born in Chicago in 1895 to an immigrant family, Halas attended the
University of Illinois, where he studied engineering and excelled at
several sports. After a short stint in the Navy and an even shorter
one on the roster of the New York Yankees, he returned to his
hometown and resigned himself to a career of building bridges.

In 1920, A. E. Staley, the owner of a large starch manufacturer
in Decatur, recruited Halas to coach and manage the company's
football team. Halas jumped at the chance. He led the Decatur
Staleys to a 13–1 season, and then, at a meeting of other teams in
Canton, Ohio, became one of the founders of the American Football
Association, which soon changed its name to today's National
Football League.

Everyone Else
Will Have to Step Aside

Faced with financial difficulties, Staley encouraged Halas to move
the Staleys to Chicago, where the large population would offer
greater support. Chicago already had two professional teams, the
Cardinals and the Tigers, but Halas muscled his way into town
anyway and changed the team's name to the Bears.

These early years were difficult for the
sport, which had a reputation as being a
lowbrow, thuggish game. Even the best-
known teams were hard-pressed to draw
more than a few thousand spectators to a
game. In 1925, Halas helped change all that
by making one of the most brilliant promotional moves of his career. He recruited

college running sensation Harold "Red" Grange during his senior year at the University of Illinois, then took the Bears on a barnstorming tour across the country, playing 17 games in only a few weeks. The contests in New York City and Los Angeles drew in excess of 70,000 fans, unheard of numbers for football in those days. Thanks in part to Halas's stunt, the sport was well on its way to becoming a staple of American entertainment.

Uncompromising Brilliance

While Halas is remembered for his key role in founding professional football, he is revered in the sports world for the amazing record he compiled over his career. During the Bears' first 25 years, Coach Halas took the league championship six times and endured only one losing season. Three different times he turned the coaching reins over to others, then took them back after a restless year or two on the sidelines. He completed a total of 40 seasons as head coach, earning a league-leading 324 wins by the time he hung up his clipboard and whistle for good at age 73.

Halas was also well-known for his temper and bare-knuckle demeanor. Some say that in the early years, when he didn't like the way the referees had called a game, he would pay them by tossing their salary on the ground at their feet—one dollar at a time.

Tough, uncompromising, and talented, he was the perfect personality for this working-class city and its notoriously bruising football crew. In a testament to how well loved he had been by Chicagoans, after his death in 1983, the Bears modified their uniforms by adding the initials GSH to the left sleeve.

- *Halas successfully lobbied to have Bears games broadcast on the radio. He was also the first coach to institute the practice of studying films of opponents' previous games.*

Hints of Earwax and Vomit? Pour Me a Glass!

✴ ✴ ✴ ✴

Chicagoans are known for their flinty wintertime resolve. But what many people don't realize is that the city has a unique secret weapon: they can heat up from the inside out with a bitter—some say vile—swill known as Malört.

Variously compared to nail polish remover and earwax, vomit and formaldehyde, Malört's sharp, stinging taste has given it a reputation for seediness only matched by that of its biggest fans, the bikers and derelicts who inhabit Chicago's many backroom taverns and dive bars. Malört schnapps is named for the Swedish word for its principal ingredient, wormwood, the bitter herb that allegedly gave hallucinogenic properties to absinthe—which, in turn, rotted the brains of a generation of bohemians in 19th-century Montmartre. And, though Malört's only public distributor, Carl Jeppson Liquors, uses a variety of wormwood that doesn't contain any dangerous hallucinatory chemicals, its taste may make you feel like you're having a bad acid trip.

Carl Jeppson, the Swedish immigrant who began selling his concoction after the repeal of Prohibition in the 1930s, may have been a master of understatement in addition to having a taste for the bizarre. He liked to brag that Malört was brewed "for that unique group of drinkers who disdain light flavor or neutral spirit." On the other hand, Jeppson knew that his brew wasn't just another regurgitated variation on a theme, and that there were enough adventurous drinkers in Chicago to make his company a hit.

The grimace-inducing spirit doesn't simply taste, in the words of one bar patron, like drinking bug spray. Oh no—it tastes like drinking bug spray for hours at a time. (Mmm, sign us up!) Which is to say, the flavor isn't simply potent, but long-lasting, as well. But many of the brave souls who consume enough of the vile brew become converts—among the earliest of these were Chicago's North Side

Swedish and Eastern European populations, who became especially fond of Malört and made it, over the years, a staple at many bars in diverse pockets of the city.

But don't expect to find Malört everywhere. Its esoteric following, along with its acquired taste, has also made the drink something of a bottom-shelf novelty. Some bars may boast 30-page liquor menus and keep extra bottles of Blue Label under the counter, but that doesn't mean they'll have Malört. And don't even bother requesting the toxic potion anywhere outside the city; it is only distributed in Chicago.

Today, Jeppson Liquors is still the only known producer of Malört. And, though the distillery traded in Chicago's bitter-cold winters for the sun and warmth of Florida long ago, the brand, operated out of a Chicago apartment, has remained loyal to the city through and through. The label still says "Chicago, U.S.A." in big, bold type, and is emblazoned with a shield bearing the sky-blue stripes and red stars of the Chicago flag.

✳   ✳   ✳   ✳

- *As of 2007, absinthe is again available in the United States. Some scientists still advise against ingesting it, but most believe it is no more dangerous than any other spirit. Some who were supposedly "driven mad" by it (Vincent van Gogh, for instance) had preexisting mental imbalances or were alcoholics. It was banned in most countries after Jean Lanfray, a French farmer, killed his family in a supposed "absinthe rage"; what was overlooked, however, was that he had also injested crème de menthe, a couple cognacs, and at least seven glasses of wine that day. Absinthe does have an extremely high alcohol content, though (50 to 70 percent), so experts advise having no more than a small portion.*

Sandra Cisneros Writes Home

✳ ✳ ✳ ✳

Author Sandra Cisneros built a career out of her experiences on Chicago's Mango Street.

Mexican American writer Sandra Cisneros came of age in Chicago's Humboldt Park neighborhood, a predominantly Puerto Rican section of the city. The area serves as the setting of Cisneros's novella, *The House on Mango Street,* which tells the coming-of-age story of Esperanza Cordero, a Chicana teen struggling to belong in a cramped urban space.

Cisneros wrote the book after graduating from the Iowa Writer's Workshop and moving into an apartment in a 100-year-old building in Bucktown. In an introduction to the 25th anniversary edition, she talks about her "down-at-the-heels" neighborhood in the context of history: "Nelson Algren once wandered those streets. Saul Bellow's turf was over on Division Street, walking distance away. It was a neighborhood that reeked of beer and urine, of sausage and beans." Amid these "distinctive" sights and smells, Cisneros wrote stories that made her a renowned author in her own right.

Like her young protagonist, Cisneros grew up in a crowded house: She was the only daughter in a family of seven children. Her family moved back and forth between Chicago and Mexico City, and Cisneros dreamed of a permanent home. Unlike her protagonist, though, she had a mom who encouraged her to read.

Cisneros went on to publish other books, such as *My Wicked Wicked Ways* (1987) and *Caramelo* (2002). She was the first Chicana author to sign with a major publisher and has won numerous awards. Although she moved to the Southwest United States, her Windy City roots will never cease to influence her writing.

Ludicrous Laws

If we don't say it out loud, we can pretend it doesn't really exist... It is technically illegal to distribute material about venereal disease.

Do you have something to hide?... It is against the law to publicly wear a mask or cowl that conceals your identity.

The Constitution says nothing about freedom of fashion... There is a law on the books against appearing "dressed in the clothes of the opposite sex."

Cows still make us uncomfortable... We've given up on the story that Mrs. O'Leary's cow started the Great Chicago Fire, but it's been illegal to have cows in the Loop since shortly after the fire was put out.

We dug these tunnels so *we* could get through... It was once illegal to drive a horse or vehicle through a tunnel (this was on the books to stop people from clogging the pedestrian tunnels with cattle).

If we sell to minors, we can make more *money*... In 1878, Chicago courts declared that the city ordinance prohibiting the selling of alcohol to minors was illegal.

Pay your bills—your way or *our* way... In the early days of the city, any prisoner who could not pay for his room and board when his sentence ended could be sold into slavery; the released prisoner would have to work for whoever bought him until his debt was worked off. This happened twice—a white vagrant was sold to the town crier (an African American) for a quarter in the late 1830s, and an African American was sold to an abolitionist (also for a quarter) a few years later. Both "slaves" were freed before doing any work.

We take fires seriously... Hotel owners were once required to have a gong on each floor to alert guests in the event of a fire.

Oh, to Be a Fly on the Wall at This Place . . .

✴ ✴ ✴ ✴

While many hotels have legacies, few are as infamous in Chicago's political world as the Hotel Allegro.

Located at 171 West Randolph in the heart of the Loop, this storied site, which some might remember as the Bismarck Hotel (who could forget the Bismarck's seven-story neon sign?), has long been a prime place for wheeling and dealing. The tradition likely started with none other than Richard J. Daley, who held court while serving as Chicago's mayor and chairman of the Democratic Party of Cook County.

The hotel opened in June 1894 and was run by a pair of German brothers, Emil and Karl Eitel, who came to the United States in 1891. In 1924, the Eitels purchased additional property nearby and razed the original Bismarck. In its place they built a four-story restaurant, a new 16-story Bismarck Hotel, the 2,500-seat Palace Theater, and an office building. The new complex opened in 1926. Legend has it that the Bismarck tapped a keg one minute after midnight on December 5, 1933, making the hotel the first establishment in the city to serve alcohol after the end of Prohibition.

But the Bismarck is most known for the antics of Richard J. Daley, who ran Chicago from the 1950s to the '70s. During Daley's tenure, Democratic Party meetings were held at the Bismarck, and politicians could be seen most days lunching in the Walnut Room.

If the Big Boss Tells You to Work, Are You Going to Just Sit There?

In the 1970s, the Palace Theater closed, and the space became the Pavilion Room, which Daley used for rallies. He would rouse his precinct captains by pounding out the words, "Work, work, work!" Off they would go, into every corner of the city to campaign for the biggest boss of them all.

"Richard J. Daley was the most powerful politician in the history of Illinois politics," says Bob Crawford, who covered Chicago politics for local radio station WBBM-AM 780 for more than 40 years. "He ran the political life of Chicago with an iron hand. . . . the old man's power was so great that no one dare defy him.

"Whenever the party had a meeting, we would know about it, but it was held in secret. Then a door would open, and . . . Daley and everyone else would come out. But they didn't want anyone to hear the knockdown, drag out discussions they had inside.

"I remember standing in the hallway waiting outside to be allowed in, wondering what was going on in the meetings," Crawford says. "Some of us would put our ears up to the wall to hear what was going on. Some people even brought paper cups to listen better.

"They got wise to us," Crawford says. "Because they would see us quoting things they thought had been said in private behind closed doors. So then Mayor Daley sent his bodyguards to make all the media wait out in the ballroom. They brought us coffee and tried to soften us up but we couldn't hear anything but raised voices and applause. When they would finally open the door, the old man would give a rebel-rousing speech."

The tradition continues today. The former Bismarck opened as the four-star Hotel Allegro in 1998, and in 2001, when Paul Vallas announced his bid for governor to succeed Rod Blagojevich, he chose the Allegro as the site for the announcement. When Todd Stroger was slated to replace his father for Cook County Board president after his father died in 2006, Democratic committeemen crammed into a small room at the Allegro for the vote.

If you want to stay current on Chicago politics, it's best to keep one eye on the Allegro.

✳ ✳ ✳ ✳

- *During World War I, anti-German sentiment in the United States caused the owners of the Bismarck to change the hotel's name to the Randolph Hotel. The Bismarck name was restored in 1918.*

- *In 1956, the Bismarck became the first hotel in the Midwest to offer phones in every room.*

Weekend Warriors

✳ ✳ ✳ ✳

*Like many American communities, Chicago has numerous
public parks dotted with ball fields where weekend warriors gather
for league softball games in the summer. But Chicagoans play
their own unique version of the game.*

Though softball is a popular recreational sport all over the nation, its home is Chicago. The first softball was made here in 1887 by George Hancock, who fashioned it from (naturally enough) an old boxing glove and used it to create an indoor version of baseball. By the early 1900s, the sport was being played outdoors and had begun to spread across the Midwest. Several variations of the game developed, with the key difference being the size of the ball. The first national championships—held in Chicago in 1933 during the Century of Progress Exposition and won by a Chicago team—used a 14-inch ball.

The American Softball Association was formed that same year, and the sport took off nationwide. Most other areas quickly moved to a version often called kitten ball, which uses a 12-inch ball and allows the fielders to wear mitts. Wimps! This remains the most well known version today, having been popularized through college teams. Chicagoans, however, stayed fiercely loyal to the original game and embraced the 16-inch mush ball and bare-handed fielding. After all, with a glove, where's the challenge?. The sport's heyday during the 1930s and 1940s centered around the professional Windy City League, which regularly garnered coverage in the local sports sections and sometimes drew higher attendance than the city's two major-league baseball teams. Though the Windy City League folded decades ago, their game remains the most popular bat-and-ball sport in the city today. According to DeBeer and Sons, the company that manufactures the 16-inch ball under the name Clincher, 85 percent of their product is sold in the Chicago area.

You Want Me to Play Where? Short Center?

Year after year, the city is able to support dozens of leagues with hundreds of teams that draw thousands of players from all walks of life. Teams are usually coed, and many players remain active in the game until their 50s—two advantages of the larger ball, which travels slowly no matter how hard you hit it, allowing a wider array of people to participate. The large ball also means that offensively it's a game of precision rather than power. Home runs do happen but not that often; runs are scored primarily by advancing the runners through well-placed singles and doubles. The rules make that harder by calling for a ten-player lineup for each team rather than the traditional nine. The extra fielder—called the short center—is stationed in between second base and center field to catch the all-too-common short fly ball.

These Players Will Never Be Hand Models

The absence of mitts requires a higher level of skill among the fielders, who must be adept at handling the unwieldy ball. On the downside, mush ball aficionados perpetually suffer from jammed and broken fingers that are proudly earned and stoically shrugged off while playing defense.

For many of the thousands of Chicagoans who take to the fields every summer, the game is a way to get some exercise, enjoy the outdoors, and relax with friends. But a great many players are lifelong devotees of the sport. Some belong to several teams and play three or four games a week—sometimes even two in a night on opposite ends of the city, which is no small feat in this sprawling metropolis. And there is no doubt the city as a whole takes its homegrown game seriously. The public school system has accepted it as a lettered sport in high schools, and there is even a Chicago Softball Hall of Fame that honors local legends of the game, such as Lewa Yacilla, the beloved Windy City League pitcher who earned more than 3,000 career wins and threw the only no-hitter in the league's history. There is no physical site for the Hall of Fame as of yet, but board members are soliciting funds to build one in suburban Forest Park.

The Butcher Was a Wienie

* * * *

So, the mugger is dead, your wife is dead, but you made it out unscathed? Something doesn't quite add up . . .

In 1920, butcher Carl Wanderer—a veteran of World War I—approached a drifter in a bar and offered him the princely sum of $10 to pretend to rob him. Wanderer explained that he was in the doghouse with his wife, but that if he punched a mugger in front of her, he'd look like a hero. The drifter agreed to the deal.

The next day, as Wanderer and his wife (who was due to deliver the couple's first child the following month) returned home from the movies, the drifter attacked them in the entryway of their apartment building. Wanderer pulled out a gun, shot the drifter to death, then turned and shot his wife to death too. Wanderer told police that his wife had tragically been killed during the ruckus. For a couple of days, Wanderer was hailed as a hero. But the police—and, more importantly, the newspaper reporters—had an uneasy feeling about Wanderer's story. They were especially suspicious of the fact that he and the drifter had exactly the same model of pistol.

Reporters soon discovered that Wanderer had a girlfriend—a 16-year-old who worked across the street from Wanderer's butcher shop. Within weeks, Wanderer's story had fallen apart, and he broke down and confessed to the murders.

Initially put on trial only for the murder of his wife, Wanderer was sentenced to 25 years in prison. The newspapers were outraged that he hadn't been sentenced to hang and published the names and addresses of the jurors so that people could harass them. Eventually, Wanderer was rushed back into court to stand trial for the death of the drifter. This time, he was sentenced to death.

At his hanging, he entertained the reporters by singing a popular song of the day, "Old Pal Why Don't You Answer Me," just before his execution. One reporter said, "He shoulda been a song plugger." Another, however, said, "He should have been hanged just for his voice!" All were thankful Wanderer would sing no more.

Fast Facts

- The first known mention of Chicago as a "windy city" was in 1876, in reference to a local tornado. That suggests that the story about the moniker stemming from Chicagoans' boastful efforts to get the 1893 world's fair—while amusing—is baloney.

- As late as 1894, there was a Massacre Tree with bullet holes from the 1812 Fort Dearborn attack by the Potawatomi standing in the South Loop. When a storm took the tree down in August of that year, no removal was needed—the crowds carved it up for souvenirs.

- On September 20, 1926, Al Capone was the target of what must surely be the sorriest display of gang marksmanship in Chicago history. Nine carloads of thugs uncorked more than 1,000 rounds of pistol and submachine-gun fire on Al's hotel—without killing anyone.

- On December 29, 1942, FBI Director J. Edgar Hoover himself joined in the recapture of Roger "The Terrible" Touhy, an old Al Capone enemy who had broken out of prison. One of Touhy's cronies said to Hoover, "You're a lot fatter in person than on the radio."

- Chicago kept its old gallows down in a basement for many years just in case it caught killer "Terrible Tommy" O'Connor, convicted in 1921 and escaped from confinement pending hanging. Only in 1977 did they presume O'Connor dead and auctioned off the old gallows.

- **Fact:** In 1937, there was a big gambling operation at 139 N. Wabash, near city hall and across the street from Field's in the Loop. **Twist:** The police raided it on September 16, and actually arrested people. **Only in Chicago:** Two-thirds of the 600 gamblers were women: grannies, softball moms, stenographers, and such.

 Chicago Cuisine

While other cities such as New York, St. Louis, and Vienna may bicker over who invented the hot dog by first serving an all-beef sausage on a bun, Chicagoans stay above the fray, content in the knowledge that they *perfected* the familiar culinary treat.

Chicago is most definitely a hot dog town. The metropolitan area supports some 2,000 hot dog stands—that's more than all of the city's McDonald's, Burger King, Wendy's, and Subway franchises combined—which means hot dog lovers are usually never more than a half mile from a fix. What makes them so popular here? That's hard to say, but it may well have to do with the unique array of condiments that are served up on a true Chicago dog.

Nuclear-Green Peppers Just Taste Better

The recipe calls for an all-beef hot dog (preferably from the area's top supplier, the Vienna Beef Company) on a poppy seed bun (again, purists say this should be from the local S. Rosen's bakery). The dog should be heated in water that's warmed to just below boiling, and the poppy seed bun should be lightly steamed. Then come the toppings—chopped onions, tomato slices, a quartered dill pickle, sweet relish (dyed a bright nuclear green), sport peppers, and a dash of celery salt. Some call it a hot dog that's been "dragged through the garden."

The one thing *never* served on a Chicago dog is ketchup, however, and Chicagoans are adamant about this point. Many stand owners will refuse to add ketchup, even at a customer's request. Others are more accommodating to ketchup lovers but still refuse to participate in the desecration of their hot dogs. As Maurie Berman, who owns the famous Superdawg drive-in on the Northwest Side, put it, "Yes we provide ketchup, but we have the customer defile it himself."

A Taste for Ketchup Could Cost You Your Job, Your Friends—Your Place in the World

The no-ketchup rule has even become a political issue. In 1995, Chicago's representative in the U.S. Senate, Carol Moseley Braun, contributed a recipe for the Chicago-style dog to a cookbook that was distributed by an industry association, but she got the recipe all wrong, omitting the onions, tomatoes, and celery salt, but worst of all, calling for ketchup! Famed political writer Mike Royko devoted an entire column to chastising Moseley Braun for the embarrassing error. While he was willing to overlook the missing items, he claimed the ketchup gaffe was intolerable, even going so far as to call for the senator's ouster from office over the matter.

The origins of the Chicago recipe are uncertain, with several venerable stands claiming authorship. Fluky's, for example, holds that its founder originated the recipe while selling hot dogs for a nickel from a pushcart during the Depression. Wherever the recipe came from, though, it's now the standard at virtually every hot dog joint in the city.

Chicago's Top Dogs

Superdawg: At this old-school drive-in at the corner of Milwaukee and Devon, customers order through a speaker in the parking lot, and a waitress serves meals on trays hooked over car windows.

Portillo's: This revered Chicago establishment has locations throughout the Chicagoland area; dogs are served Chicago style and diners can top off their meal with a slice of Portillo's signature, decadent, to-die-for chocolate cake.

Jrs.'s: This small chain doesn't offer many seats at their various suburban locations, but this doesn't stop Chicagoans from crowding the joints. South-Siders swear Jrs.'s serves up the best dog in the city.

Hot Doug's: This unique Roscoe Village restaurant serves various mouth-watering sausages, from standard Chicago-style hot dogs to andouille sausage to veggie dogs.

Fluky's: This chain used to be ubiquitous and revered around Chicago, but—in one of the saddest signs of the times—the lone Fluky's outlet resides inside the Wal-Mart on Touhy Avenue. Could this be the secret to this particular Wal-Mart's success? We'd like to think so.

Significant Streets

✴ ✴ ✴ ✴

*Chicagoans revere the city's logical, efficient grid system.
The city boasts numerous "major" streets,
but here is a list of some that stand out.*

- **Astor:** North/south street; named after John Jacob Astor, this is arguably Chicago's most prestigious address
- **Columbus:** North/south street; this street loves a parade
- **Devon:** East/west street; this street is a brilliant mix of cultures, from Orthodox to Indian American to Pakistani American
- **Elston:** Diagonal street; Chicagoans treasure Elston as an alternative to the Kennedy expressway during rush hour
- **Halsted:** North/south street; one of the city's most diverse streets, Halsted extends through Boys Town, Greek Town, UIC, Pilsen, Bridgeport, and Englewood
- **Lake Shore Drive:** North/south street; even newcomers and tourists know this is Chicago's most scenic route
- **La Salle:** North/south street; where the money goes 'round and 'round
- **Madison:** East/west street; Madison divides the North and South sides of the city
- **Michigan:** North/south street; this mile is simply magnificent
- **Milwaukee:** Diagonal street; Milwaukee Avenue was the trail Native Americans used to herd their buffalo to the river
- **Oak:** East/west street known for its high-end shopping; think twice about turning down this street if you don't have at least a million dollars to your name
- **Ogden:** Diagonal street; Ogden used to run all the way into Lincoln Park but now ends at Chicago and Halsted
- **Ravenswood:** This thoroughfare looks suspiciously like an alley—and can be confusing for newcomers—but natives adore it

- **Rush:** North/south street; known for its singles scene, but don't let the area's "Viagra Triangle" nickname scare you away; classy restaurants have been encroaching on this area in recent years, so others now feel right at home here too

- **Southport:** North/south street; this North Side street is known for its boutiques, restaurants, and live-music venues

- **State:** North/south street; divides the West and East sides; also the major Loop retail strip

- **Wells:** North/south street; this street is the main commercial strip in Old Town, boasting many shops, pubs, restaurants, and—of course—Second City

- **Western:** North/south street; at 23.67 miles, Western is the longest continuous street in Chicago

✳ ✳ ✳ ✳

- *Wacker runs in each direction at one point or another. One of Chicago's most notorious streets, it has been the scene of high-speed chases in numerous movies, from* The Blues Brothers *to* The Dark Knight. *Wacker was named for brewer and businessman Charles H. Wacker. After serving as director of the World's Columbian Exposition in 1893, Wacker helped implement the Plan of Chicago. Wacker hated traffic congestion so much, he proposed relocating the South Water Street Market and renovating South Water Street into a double-deck drive. Hence the street was renamed Wacker Drive.*

- *If newcomers end up on a diagonal street, they often find themselves confused and cursing. Before long, however, they will appreciate these routes as the natives do, because they are often the most efficient route between two points.*

- *Elston Avenue begins and ends at intersections with the same street (Milwaukee Avenue).*

A Tale of Two Chinatowns

* * * *

If Chicago needed more proof that it's a truly international city, it need look no farther than its Chinatown—or its other Chinatown.

Chinese immigrants were attracted to jobs in Chicago in the 1880s and '90s, when the city was gearing up for the 1893 world's fair. In the next two decades, the population of Chinese in Chicago doubled, and they began leaving an indelible mark on the city.

The Chinese lived and worked in small enclaves, one in what is now the South Loop—its storefronts razed in the 1970s to make room for the Metropolitan Correctional Center—and another, larger one by the corner of Cermak Road and Wentworth Avenue.

The Chinese characters on storefronts attracted Chicagoans with international interests to the block around Cermak and Wentworth. With parades and celebrations, which were organized and funded by Chinatown's many active civic organizations, the area became a tourist destination and a point of great pride for city leaders.

They Come to See the Gate, but They Come Back for the Mai-Tais

Even today, few neighborhoods in the city are imbued with the sense of playful novelty embodied by every inch of Chinatown's pagodas, lanterns, flowers, sculptures, and banners, which have accumulated over time as symbols of the community and nostalgia for China. Tourists and Chicagoans from other parts of the city flock to Chinatown to see the magnificent Chinatown Gate and the replica of Beijing's Nine Dragon Wall. Visitors usually make return trips for the area's mesmerizing selection of bulk teas and herbs, intricate robes and slippers, fantastic dim sum, and volcano-style Mai-Tais.

North Side Pride

During the 1970s, when the United States opened relations with China, more and more immigrants began to move to Chicago en masse. These new arrivals established New Chinatown on the North

Side, in Uptown, where storefronts and apartments were affordable and plentiful. Many Indochinese immigrants came to the area as well, giving the neighborhood the alternative monikers Little Vietnam and Little Saigon.

The origins of Chicago's two Chinatowns do have some similarities: New Chinatown, which had been one of the city's most decadent areas in the 1920s, had fallen into disrepair by the 1970s as people began to turn away from urban life. The first and second waves of immigration from Southeast Asia flanked a century of growth and decline in one of America's most manic cities.

Still, it's easy to tell these places apart. There's something reticent about New Chinatown, its modest storefronts mostly restaurants and grocery stores, their signs bright but not as chaotic or grandiose as those on the South Side. There is no parade route here and, though the top of the Argyle Street "L" station is graced with a rusty pagoda, the streets lack the crowded, frenetic luster so often associated with the South Side Chinatown.

The North Side restaurants are unadorned, trading intricate woodwork and hanging lanterns for Formica tabletops and big bottles of hot sauce, but they're filled with Vietnamese and Chinese patrons and their children, along with Chicagoans searching for something off the beaten path. And New Chinatown's ecumenical spirit has made it a civic fixture unlike any other. Its proximity to a host of other ethnic neighborhoods—and its hodgepodge of Thai-, Vietnamese-, and Chinese-owned businesses and restaurants—give the neighborhood a particularly worldly sensibility not unlike that of the city it calls home.

* * * *

- *If the firehouse at 212 South Cermak Road in Chinatown looks familiar, it probably is: It was used for numerous scenes in the 1991 movie* Backdraft.

A Bygone Ride

* * * *

When Chicagoans get the itch to ride a coaster or nosh on corn dogs and funnel cakes, they're likely to head to Six Flags or any number of corporate-owned parks in nearby Wisconsin or Indiana. But if you were a theme park fan who lived in Chicago between 1904 and 1967, you could just hop the bus to Belmont and Western and visit locally owned and operated Riverview Park.

The area on which Riverview would eventually stand was formerly a 22-acre expanse used primarily as a picnic grounds. The owners of the land were William Schmidt and George Goldman, who purchased it toward the end of the 1800s. When William Schmidt's son George came home from vacationing in Europe, he told his dad that he ought to build an amusement park similar to those he'd seen overseas (most notably Tivoli Gardens in Copenhagen). William gathered the financing and broke ground for Riverview Sharpshooters Park in 1904.

At that time in America, amusement parks were gaining in popularity. In 1893, the World's Columbian Exposition was held in Chicago. This world's fair was the first to have a Ferris wheel and an arcade midway, as well as concessions. This heady conglomeration of attractions was the template used for amusement parks for the next half-century.

Carnival for the Senses

Within three short years of opening the gates, Riverview was a mammoth success. The public came in droves to ride the rides, eat the food, and experience all the visual delights offered by the park's owners, which now included financiers Nicholas Valerius and Paul Cooper.

Riverview offered its first roller coaster during this time, a ride called "The Top" for its resemblance to the child's toy. "The Velvet Coaster" (named for its subtle dips and turns) was also added.

"Shoot-the-Chutes," a ramp ride that splashed into a lagoon, was soon a featured attraction, along with a ballroom, a giant swing, the "Tunnel of Love" ride, and "The Derby," a racing coaster.

More and more rides (including four more roller coasters) were added throughout the early 1900s, as Riverview experienced steady growth. The 1920s brought five more coasters and more crowds. A thrill ride called "The Bobs," which was built in 1924 and featured an 85-foot drop, was the most popular ride at Riverview for decades.

Weathering the Storms

Surprisingly, attendance at the park was decent even through the Great Depression, as well as both World Wars. Promotions such as "Two-Cent Day" helped keep people moving through the park in the

early '30s, though additions and improvements to the park weren't possible for some time.

By the time World War II had arrived, small additions and changes had been made to the park, but once again officials found themselves short on money and materials; one water ride that used rubber inner tubes faced extinction because rubber was a precious commodity during wartime. Still, Riverview brought in

patrons, largely because traveling wasn't an option for many people at the time. Rather than spending the money and resources to go on a long trip, those looking to get away could immerse themselves in the wonders of Riverview, wandering through the maze inside Aladdin's Castle, floating 186 feet above the city on the popular Pair-O-Chutes, or taking a spin around the roller rink. Plus, it was the time of the baby boom, and families now comprised more members—which meant more tickets sold.

Sorry, We're Closed

Though a few rides were added to the park in the '50s and early '60s (notably the thrill ride "The Wild Mouse") and Chicagoans still heeded the establishment's advice to come to Riverview to "laugh your troubles away," the announcement came in 1967 that Riverview would not open the following season. It was reported that Riverview was still bringing in around $65,000 on a good day, so many theories flew about why the park would close.

Some believe that racial unrest brought about the end of Riverview. While it's true that racial discord was alive and well in Chicago in the 1960s (along with the rest of America) and Riverview was the site of numerous fights sparked by the issue, it wasn't the main reason the park decided to close its doors. Nor can Chicago politics be blamed for the closing, though the costs of union labor and paying the private police force that guarded the park were getting to be too much for the owners.

No, as it turns out, the land on which the park sat turned out to be worth much more than the money the park could make. Real estate prices in the area were rising rapidly, and the money needed to repair aging rides was increasing. The owners had installed an ornate ride in the early '60s that cost more than a quarter-million dollars, and it was reportedly hemorrhaging money. A Chicago investment firm purchased the park on October 3, 1967, for an estimated $6.5 million—and it was immediately demolished.

Those who wish to see an artifact from Riverview can head to Six Flags over Georgia, where a Merry-Go-Round from the park now resides. Otherwise, not much is left of the magical Riverview; the area at the crossroads of Belmont, Clybourn, and Western now offers a college, a shopping center, a police station, and a parking lot—and maybe a few memories for those who visited the place where you could laugh your cares away.

* * * *

- *The popular Riverview ride "Flying Turns" came from Chicago's 1933 Century of Progress Exposition.*

Timeline

(Continued from p. 171)

November 10, 1924
Dean O'Banion is gunned down by some of Capone's men as he clips chrysanthemums in his North State Street flower shop.

1925
A. Philip Randolph spearheads efforts to organize employees of the Chicago-based Pullman Company. The International Brotherhood of Sleeping Car Porters and Maids will become the American Federation of Labor's first African American labor union.

1926
The radio show *Amos 'n' Andy* premieres on Chicago radio station WGN. Initially known as *Sam 'n' Henry,* the title characters' names were changed in 1928. As southern transplants relocated to Chicago, the stereotyped African American characters entertained some listeners but offended others.

1927
The United Biscuit Company (forerunner to Keebler) is created in Chicago by a merger of several small cracker bakeries.

February 14, 1929
Four members of the Capone crime syndicate raid a liquor warehouse belonging to rival gangster George "Bugs" Moran and open fire. The St. Valentine's Day Massacre claims seven lives and becomes a touchstone of Chicago gangster lore.

1930
The Adler Planetarium & Astronomy Museum opens in a unique 12-sided building designed by noted architect Ernst Grunsfeld. The centerpiece of the museum is a newly invented Zeiss projector donated by Max Adler, a retired Sears, Roebuck & Co. executive.

July 6, 1933
Comiskey Park hosts the first All-Star Game.

July 1, 1934
Brookfield Zoo officially opens its gates to the public. It will become America's first zoo without bars.

July 22, 1934
John Dillinger is ambushed and killed by federal agents outside Chicago's Biograph Theater.

1936
Richard Loeb, the confessed killer of Bobby Franks, is killed in a razor attack by a fellow inmate at the Stateville Correctional Facility.

1936
Louis Skidmore and Nathaniel Owings establish the Skidmore & Owings architecture firm. They will join forces with John Merrill in 1939. As Skidmore, Owings & Merrill they will design many important edifices around Chicago, including the Sears Tower, the John Hancock Center, and the University of Chicago and Northwestern University libraries.

(Continued on p. 225)

A Celebration of Education

✳ ✳ ✳ ✳

*Chicagoans gather in Bronzeville every August to enjoy
the Bud Billiken Parade, one of the largest celebrations of its kind.*

Robert Abbot began publishing the *Chicago Defender* newspaper in the early 1900s, and it quickly became one of the most important African American news outlets in the country. Concerned with the plight of African American youth, in 1923, Abbot added a children's page to the paper and introduced the Bud Billiken Club. The organization sought to instill both individual pride and a sense of community responsibility in its young members and became widely popular almost overnight. In 1929, Abbott decided to create a communal activity for all of the club's members and organized a parade and picnic in historic Bronzeville. The Bud Billiken Parade celebrates education and the start of the school year and has been held every year since on the second Saturday of August.

The marchers include school bands, cheerleading teams, youth clubs, performance groups, and (of course) local businesses and elected officials. But the event has also drawn many national figures over the years, including Duke Ellington, Joe Louis, Muhammad Ali, Michael Jordan, Oprah Winfrey, Spike Lee, Queen Latifah, Brandy, L. L. Cool J., and Presidents Harry Truman, John F. Kennedy, and Lyndon Johnson. The masters of ceremonies for the very first Bud Billiken parade in 1929 were Frank Gosden and Charles Correll—the radio stars who became famous as the radio characters Amos 'n' Andy.

In its early days, the parade was a relatively small event, but it has grown into one of the largest annual parades in the United States, typically drawing well in excess of one million spectators. The route still runs through Bronzeville, down the main thoroughfare of Martin Luther King Jr. Memorial Drive, stretching a mile and a half from 39th Street to 51st Street. The parade ends at the neighborhood's sprawling Washington Park, where a barbecue with free food and souvenirs—along with the inevitable speeches by local politicians—await all of the attendees.

An Opportunity to Earn a Little Cash

For many, the festive day also offers an opportunity to earn a significant amount of extra money. Vendors pass through the massive crowds hawking T-shirts, novelties, and bottled water. Residents who live along the parade route set up their grills on their lawns and sell hamburgers, hot dogs, and grilled chicken over their front yard fences. Though most of these operations are unlicensed and therefore technically illegal, the city looks the other way, acknowledging the well-intentioned spirit of the day.

The parade is first and foremost a family affair, with parents and children dominating the crowd. Many residents have been attending regularly for decades, and it's not uncommon to see three or even four generations of a family enjoying the beloved event. The spirit of the parade as envisioned by founder Robert Abbott has not been lost over time. Those speeches by the local politicians focus on matters of community involvement and political awareness, and many activist organizations use the event to convey their message to the crowds and recruit new members. Though founded in a different era in a very different society, the Bud Billiken Parade remains a powerfully unifying event, as its founder intended.

* * * *

- *Bud Billiken is not an actual person but a name created by the* Chicago Defender *staff. The origins are unclear, but some sources say Bud was the nickname of the paper's publisher, Robert Abbott, and a Billiken is a mythical protector of children.*

A Tower
Formerly Known as Sears

* * * *

On May 3, 1973—just one year after the United States claimed the title of world's tallest building with the World Trade Center in New York—the Sears Tower was "topped out" and stole the title.

Named for Sears, Roebuck & Co., who sought to have the "largest headquarters in the world," this immense structure reaches 1,454 feet into the Chicago sky. With a footprint of three acres in downtown Chicago, the building contains 3.8 million square feet of rentable space. At full capacity, nearly 16,500 people work inside it each day. From its observation deck on the 103rd floor, on a clear day, one can see four different states: Illinois, Indiana, Wisconsin, and Michigan. The tower now features an area called the Ledge, where visitors can stand in retractable enclosed glass boxes that jut out four feet from the tower. If you look down at your feet, the view is either thrilling or vertigo-inducing.

Sears, Roebuck & Co. moved their offices to suburban Hoffman Estates in 1992. In 2009, the building was renamed Willis Tower for its new majority tenant, Willis Group Holdings, a London-based insurance broker. Chicagoans have resisted the change, continuing to use the tower's original name.

The owners of the tower announced ambitious green renovation plans in 2009. The project is expected to take five years and involves roof gardens, wind turbines, solar panels, a new lighting control system, and restroom renovations. The project will reduce the building's electricity use by 80 percent and will save 24 million gallons of water each year.

Though the tower has not been considered the world's tallest building since 1996, it still looms the highest in the hearts and minds of Chicagoans, who are always thrilled to spot it in the distance on return trips home.

Quiz

Chicago is riddled with memories of infamous crimes.
Take the following quiz to test your criminal knowledge.

1. What was Al Capone's cause of death?

a) Cardiac arrest
b) Syphilis
c) Pancreatic cancer
d) Kidney failure

2. Defense lawyers argued Chicagoan Jack Ruby was suffering from what affliction when he shot Oswald?

a) A blackout related to epilepsy
b) Alzheimer's
c) Bipolar disorder
d) Low blood sugar

3. Which Chicagoan directed *Public Enemies* (2009)?

a) Jonathan Demme
b) Michael Mann
c) Quentin Tarantino
d) Cameron Crowe

4. Who coined the term "Public Enemy"?

a) The FBI
b) The Chicago Crime Commission
c) Elliot Ness
d) J. Edgar Hoover

5. A 2009 FBI study came up with a list of the 25 most dangerous areas in America. How many Chicago locations made this infamous list?

a) 4
b) 1
c) 8
d) 3

6. Chicago-born Ted Kaczynski (aka "the Unabomber") held a Ph.D. in mathematics from the University of Michigan. At which Ivy League school did he obtain his undergrad degree?

a) Cornell
b) Harvard
c) Columbia
d) Dartmouth

Answers: 1. b, 2. a, 3. b, 4. b, 5. a (State & Garfield, Wallace & 58th, Winchester & 60th, and Yale & 66th), 6. b

Warning: Disco Can Provoke Intense Anger

* * * *

When most people hear disco, they want to get up and dance, right?
Not everyone.

Late in 1978, Chicago radio station WDAI made some changes.
They decided to switch to an all-disco format in keeping with the
taste of the times. Folks everywhere were electric-boogalooing to
Donna Summer, KC and the Sunshine Band, and the BeeGees. One
employee, rock 'n' roll deejay Steve Dahl, got canned when the
change took place.

Dahl was less than pleased with the pink slip, but he was able to
snag a job at rock station WLUP, aka "The Loop." Dahl's morning
radio show was soon a big hit. Still smarting from the disco fiasco—
or maybe interested in drumming up publicity for his show—Dahl
pitched the idea of a "Disco Demolition Night" for the July 12, 1979,
Sox doubleheader against the Detroit Tigers. The price of admission
would be 98 cents (for 97.9, the Loop's place on the FM dial) and a
disco record. Between games, the records would be piled inside a
giant box in the outfield, and the box would be ceremoniously blown
up. Sounds relatively innocuous, correct?

How It All Went Awry

Mike Veeck, the White Sox marketing
director who helped organize the event,
expected about 35,000 people to show
up. When it came time to let people into
Comiskey Park, there were 60,000
waiting for 52,000 seats. Those who
couldn't get in through the gate tried to
climb the fences.

In a 2009 *New York Times* interview, Tigers
shortstop Alan Trammell commented, "I remember from the get-go,

it wasn't a normal crowd. The outfielders were definitely scared, and Ronnie [Tigers center fielder Ron LeFlore, a former convict] wasn't usually afraid of anything."

After the first game was over, an army fatigue- and helmet-wearing Dahl, along with his entourage, drove onto the field where the huge crate full of disco records had been positioned. The DJ led the crowd in chants of "Disco sucks!" and detonated the explosives that had been rigged inside the crate. The explosion ripped a hole in the outfield grass and kept burning as the ringleaders of the spectacle drove off. As they did, people from every side of the stands rushed the field.

People burned banners, fights broke out, and many thousands wandered aimlessly, looking for a piece of the action. The Chicago Police were called in after failed attempts by sportscaster Harry Caray and Sox owner Bill Veeck to get fans back in their seats. When the smoke cleared, six people were injured, 39 had been arrested for disorderly conduct, and the second game was forfeited to the Tigers, on the grounds that the Sox had failed to provide a suitable playing field.

When asked about the incident in 2009, Mike Veeck claimed that though the crowd did get out of hand, the attendees were not actually violent. He chalked this up to the fact that most of the revelers seemed to be high rather than drunk: "Had we had drunks to deal with, then we would have had some trouble." Hmm . . .

What Did Disco Ever Do to You?

Many culture and music critics have examined what happened that night. Some say that the entire event was like a book burning, a hateful act born out of fear and rage at the minority and gay culture that had infiltrated America via disco music. Most others thought it was just a joke that got out of hand. Dahl supporters argued that they never intended to hurt anyone. They simply resented disco because it seemed to be taking over, and in their view, it was superficial and empty, while rock 'n' roll had real artistic merit.

Whatever your view, disco did start to lose its power in the coming years, but it was probably just the natural order of things.

A Mysterious Submarine

* * * *

*Someone took a homemade submarine for a test run in the river,
and the sub failed miserably.*

In 1915, a diver named "Frenchy" Deneau was digging a trench in
the river near the Wells Street Bridge when he came across a chunk
of metal. At first, he thought he'd found a piece of the *Eastland,* a
ship that had capsized a few months earlier around the same spot.
To Frenchy's surprise, he had found the wreck of a homemade
submarine that had been buried under three feet of river muck.

Frenchy had the vessel raised for exhibition purposes. It was
found to contain the remains of a dead guy and his dog. Frenchy put
it on display on South State Street in February 1916. For a dime,
visitors could see the submarine *and* the dead guy—and even the
dead dog! Groups of ten or more children got in half-off on Saturday
mornings. Oh, what pleasant family outings those must have been!

The Aptly Named Fool Killer

The press put forth various theories about how long the sub had
been down there, who the guy on board was, and what could possibly have possessed him to test out a homemade submarine without
asking someone to stay nearby to help in case things took an ominous turn. None of their theories hold up, but the name they gave it
has stuck: the Fool Killer. It was most likely sold for scrap by 1918,
but who knows? It could still be rotting away in someone's garage
someplace.

The press claimed the sub had been in the river since the 1870s
or 1890s, but historians now believe that the sub may have been
down there even longer! The best evidence suggests that it was built
by a man named Lodner Philips, who built several experimental
submarines; he seems to have sunk a model matching the Fool
Killer's description in the late 1840s. But (assuming the skulls were
real and not a publicity stunt), the name of the man onboard has
never been determined.

Bragging Rights

- The Chicago River has an amazing 36 movable bridges.
- The Art Institute's Impressionist and Post-Impressionist collections are the largest in the United States and the largest outside the Musée d'Orsay in Paris. The massive collection includes works by Renoir, Monet, Degas, Seurat, and Gauguin.
- Chicago has some of the country's most elaborate theaters and movie palaces, including the Chicago Theatre, the Aragon Ballroom, and the Riviera—all of which are still functioning. Chicago's Uptown neighborhood is home to the largest of them all, the palatial Uptown Theater, which—though closed to the public while under perpetual renovation—remains a hidden architectural and cultural gem.
- Merchandise Mart, the sprawling Art Deco behemoth, is the world's largest commercial building. With a plethora of shops, offices, service centers, and special-event venues, Merchandise Mart spans two city blocks and rises 25 stories high.
- Chicago is known for its architectural achievements, and it is home to works by some of the world's most celebrated contemporary architects, from Frank Gehry, who designed the iridescent Pritzker Pavilion in 2004, to Renzo Piano, who gave the Art Institute its Modern Wing in 2009.
- One of the nation's most eminent institutions of higher education, the University of Chicago is associated with more Nobel Laureates—81, at the time of this printing—than any other college or university in the world.
- Chicago is at the center of the culinary world's latest revolution—molecular gastronomy. Many of the city's most famous chefs, including Homaro Cantu, the proprietor of Chicago's popular restaurant Moto, are surprising the taste buds by utilizing specific chemical properties to change the texture, shape, and culinary form of many foods. Try Moto's edible paper with savory inks or breads dusted with "Goat Cheese Snow." The biggest surprise may be that you'll actually go back for seconds.

Green River

✳ ✳ ✳ ✳

There are many secrets in an old city like Chicago, but one that fascinates the public every spring is exactly how 40 pounds of orange powder dyes the Chicago River a startling shade of green.

In 1961, one widely spread story goes, a plumber walked into the Chicago Plumber's Union office with bright green stains on his overalls. He'd been checking pipes for leaks, trying to determine sources of pollution in the river. His supervisor, Stephen Bailey, was a boyhood friend of Mayor Richard J. Daley and brought the idea of a new St. Patrick's Day tradition to the Mayor's Office. In 1962, the city started dyeing the river to add to their already exuberant St. Patrick's Day parades.

Other than the men in the boats on the river, the only thing that's changed over the years is the actual dye itself. In 1962, the team used an oil-based dye that was so potent it kept the river green for nearly a week. Organizers then substituted a vegetable dye, and officials say it's harmless to the river's ecology (a claim that leaves many environmentalists skeptical).

The exact dye recipe is a closely guarded secret. The public knows that it's delivered to the river as an orange powder that is slung into the water by the scoopful. Once there, it clumps and then awaits "stirring" by the propellers of a single small boat piloted by a favored crew of plumbers. The resulting emerald green hue is so startling, many think there just *has* to be something harmful in it. But organizers swear that—while they won't give out the secret formula— the dye only adds harmless fun in a city strong with Irish spirit.

Fast Facts

- Mayor Buckner S. Morris (served 1855–56) took his Know-Nothing Party's hatred of immigrants to new levels. He enforced the law against Sunday saloonkeeping—but only against beer halls, beloved of the North Side's German newcomers. Nein! *The resulting Lager Beer Riot led to 60 arrests on April 21, 1855.*

- From about 1914 to 1971, Anderson Punch (aka "The Chicken Man") sang and street-performed with trained chickens, mostly on the South Side. He seemed to make a basic living on tips.

- Chicago political rhetoric: Ed Litsinger, a fierce "Big Bill" Thompson political rival, in 1928 had this to say about Big Bill, "this man, with the carcass of a rhinoceros and the brains of a baboon." Ed wasn't done: He called Thompson and two of his cronies "The Three Must-Get-Theirs."

- Captain Bill Drury—one of the best cops in the city's history—joined the force in 1924 and took on organized crime. There is reason to believe that criminal interests engineered his 1947 dismissal. As a crime reporter, he kept after his targets. In 1950, Drury was assassinated in his garage. No one was ever charged with the murder, but many suspected that mob boss Anthony Accardo had ordered the hit.

- Remarkable: Prohibition era mob leader Johnny Torrio never carried a firearm. Evidently he felt it best to trust in his well-armed bodyguards. It might not be as insane as it sounds; since no guarded figure is safe from those who guard him, one might as well trust them all the way.

- Hugh Hefner opened the original Playboy Club on Walton Street in the Gold Coast neighborhood in 1960. It seems too coincidental that the Playboy Bunnies started bunnying on Leap Day, but they did: Opening day was February 29, 1960.

Chicago Books

* * * *

Chicago has been the inspiration and setting for many great novels. Here are seven classics.

- **The Cliffdwellers:** Author Henry Blake Fuller was born and raised in Chicago, and his feelings for the city were a mixture of nostalgia for its old ways and mistrust of the industrialism that overtook it in the late 19th century. His 1893 novel *The Cliffdwellers,* set in the fictitious Clifton Building, followed a large cast of characters as they attempted to adapt to the modern way of life. The book's protagonist, George Ogden, is a transplant from Boston who finds himself disillusioned by his experience in the Chicago business world.

- **The Jungle:** The socialist newspaper *The Appeal to Reason* sent journalist Upton Sinclair to investigate corruption, specifically in the meatpacking industry. What emerged was *The Jungle,* a 1906 novel that would have not just a huge intellectual influence but immeasurable practical influence all across America. Though Sinclair intended the novel to be a sweeping indictment of capitalism and industrialism, he was disappointed when the public took a narrower view, demanding food safety but not any real systemic change.

- **Sister Carrie:** Theodore Dreiser's debut novel, this work was considered shocking in its day for its frankness in regard to sexuality. Young Caroline "Sister Carrie" Meeber, bored with her life in rural Wisconsin, goes to Chicago to find adventure and excitement. Intent on leaving poverty behind and attaining the finer things in life, Carrie ends up abandoning her morals and using one man after another.

- **Native Son:** One of the great naturalist novels of the 20th century, Richard Wright's *Native Son* (1940) is the story of Bigger Thomas, an ignorant, brutal product of a South Side slum. Thomas kills two women and is defended by a crusading Communist lawyer named

Boris Max. Max tries to save the life of his client by arguing that the murders were an inevitability of the environment in which he was raised.

- ***Maud Martha:*** The first African American to win a Pulitzer Prize, Gwendolyn Brooks was raised in and lived much of her life in Chicago. Best known as a poet, her only novel was *Maud Martha*, published in 1953. A character study, *Maud Martha* is the beautiful story of a girl coming of age as she struggles with issues of domestic strife, racism, sexism, and classism.

Gwendolyn Brooks

- ***Young Lonigan:*** The first in James T. Farrell's Studs Lonigan trilogy, *Young Lonigan* (1932) drew on Farrell's own experiences coming of age in a large, Irish American Catholic family. Unlike Farrell himself, however, 15-year-old Studs is a troubled lad who can't seem to escape the darker forces of Chicago's crime-ridden slums. Lonigan's fatal flaw is his complete and utter lack of imagination. The Lonigan novels implicitly argued that capitalism was to blame for corruption and moral decay, and—though Farrell's subsequent series were more hopeful than the Lonigan series—Farrell clung to his radical beliefs until his death in 1979. His writing has gone in and out of fashion many times, reflecting political changes in both academia and the United States at large.

- ***Endless Love:*** Often forgotten or misjudged after Franco Zeffirelli's dreadful film adaptation, at the time of its publication in 1979, Scott Spencer's *Endless Love* was hailed by critics as an insightful, heartbreaking depiction of the desperation of young love. When Chicago teen David Axelrod is forbidden to see his girlfriend, Jade, he sets her family's house on fire, intending to put it out and "rescue" them. Needless to say, things don't quite go as planned . . .

The Green Mill

* * * *

A little bar on Chicago's North Side
holds a century's worth of history and lore.

Today Chicago is one of a few American cities where bars serve liquor until 5:00 A.M., but in the 1920s, Prohibition reigned supreme—well, sort of. Chicago has plenty of stories from this era, but there are few landmarks that recall Chicago's mob heyday like the Green Mill jazz club.

In 1910, Tom Chamales turned the Green Mill into one of Chicago's swankiest establishments. During Prohibition, Chamales leased the bar to the mob. One of Capone's mobster cronies, "Machine Gun" Jack McGurn, became a manager. One of the most infamous incidents associated with the Green Mill occurred when McGurn exacted revenge after singer Joe E. Lewis left the Green Mill for a gig at a competing establishment. Several days into Lewis's new gig, he was brutally attacked in his apartment. He was unable to speak for an entire year, but after his recovery he (surprise!) resumed his gig at the Green Mill, this time as a comedian.

Throughout the decades, the club has drawn a diverse crowd of music lovers, mob aficionados, and locals. Everyone from Charlie Chaplin to Frank Sinatra has partied here. They might even have sat at the famed table where Al Capone once watched both entrances, lest he needed to make a quick getaway.

Crowds come and go, but good music remains the same. To this day the Green Mill is the go-to spot for jazz on Chicago's North Side. Harry Connick Jr., Branford Marsalis, and Paulinho Garcia have all graced its stage. In the 1980s, the Green Mill started one of the first poetry-slam nights in the country, the Uptown Poetry Slam. The slam is still popular at the Green Mill today, along with, of course, a full calendar of jazz.

Airing Old Wounds

* * * *

An Albany Park museum brings back painful memories for Cambodians, but founders hope making peace with the past will help survivors move forward into the future.

Chicago is home to the only Cambodian museum in the United States. A small contingent of approximately 2,500 Cambodian refugees settled in Chicago, beginning in the 1970s and continuing through the early 1990s. The refugees formed the Cambodian Association of Illinois and founded the 3,500-square-foot Cambodian American Heritage Museum and Killing Fields Memorial.

The memorial honors the more than 2 million victims of Pol Pot's Communist Khmer Rouge genocidal regime, which ruled Cambodia from 1975 to '79. The leaders tried to turn Cambodia into an agricultural utopia but succeeded only in killing its citizens through malnutrition and overwork. The memorial begins with the words "We continue our journey with compassion, understanding, and wisdom," and that is certainly the lesson of the memorial— continuing the journey with the wisdom that has been learned from past experience. The names of those who died during the Khmer Rouge regime are etched into the glass memorial. Surviving relatives see the etchings and sense their loved ones present among them.

Museum exhibits showcase what life is like in Cambodia today. Childhood games made of wooden sticks and seed pods, beautiful silk scarves, and three-dimensional stone and wood bas-relief depict a rich culture. Artists in residence (many of whom are themselves genocide survivors) offer classes most Saturdays on such subjects as Traditional Khmer language, dance, and music. One artist in residence—fifth-generation sculptor Chhoeut Tuy—handcrafted a cement four-faced deity known as Brahma and a 10-foot celestial Apsara. These figures stand at the front of the museum and serve as symbols of a new beginning for a weary but hopeful people.

Gems Along the Shore

✳ ✳ ✳ ✳

Chicago boasts one of the longest stretches of freshwater shoreline of any city in the world, and, despite its potential real estate value, much of it is has been set aside as public space.
The list below highlights some notable spots.

- **South Shore Cultural Center:** Formerly a private lakefront country club, the South Shore Cultural Center at 70th and South Shore Drive is now a part of the city's massive public parks system. The 58-acre site hosts a nine-hole golf course, tennis courts, stables, an art gallery, and a lavish 100-year-old clubhouse that is often rented for private parties—including Barack and Michelle Obama's 1992 wedding reception.

- **Promontory Point:** Jutting out into Lake Michigan at South 55th Street, Promontory Point is a park first conceived as part of Burnham and Bennett's 1909 Plan of Chicago. The artificial structure, which was built in the 1920s and 1930s using innovative landfill techniques, allows visitors to stroll some 6,000 feet out onto the lake itself.

- **Northerly Island:** This manmade island just south of downtown was used as a main exhibition area for the 1933 Century of Progress exposition. Though it once housed the Meigs Field landing strip for small planes, much of the island is now set aside as a nature reserve, though it does include one of the city's major concert venues as well.

- **Chicago Harbor Light:** The Chicago Harbor Lighthouse dramatically marks the entrance to the city's main marine port. Built in 1893, it is one of the oldest existing lighthouses in Illinois. The structure has become a symbol of Chicago's role as a maritime shipping hub connecting the East Coast to the South via the Great Lakes and the Mississippi River. Its bright white tower and red-roofed outbuildings can easily be seen from the shore.

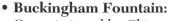

- **Buckingham Fountain:**
  Commissioned by Chicago philan-
  thropist Kate Buckingham,
  Buckingham Fountain was
  donated to the city in
  1927. One of the largest
  outdoor fountains in the
  world, the massive
  structure on Congress Avenue and Columbus Drive holds
  1.5 million gallons of water and shoots geysers bathed in colored
  light as high as 150 feet.

- **Navy Pier:** This mile-and-a-half-long pier was opened in 1916 at
  the point where the Chicago River flows into Lake Michigan.
  Originally conceived as both a commercial marine facility and an
  entertainment venue, the pier was renovated in the mid-1990s and
  has become a center for public life in the city. The site offers boat
  tour excursions, various restaurants and shops, a towering Ferris
  wheel, live theater, an IMAX theater, and a children's museum.

- **Oak Street Beach:** Located off Lake Shore Drive just north of
  the Magnificent Mile, Oak Street beach is *the* place for Chicago's
  young and beautiful sun worshippers to gather during the swelter-
  ing summer months. The beach was created in the 1890s as part of
  a massive breakwater project designed to protect Lake Shore
  Drive from erosion.

- **Theater on the Lake:** Situated in sprawling Lincoln Park, the
  Theater on the Lake is housed in a simple brick building that
  offers views of Lake Michigan as well as low-priced live theater.
  Operated by the Chicago Park District, the theater has been in
  continuous operation since the 1940s. It offers various productions
  every summer, from family friendly performances to Shakespeare.

- **Montrose Point Bird Sanctuary:** Located near Montrose Beach,
  one of the city's favorite family beaches, the bird sanctuary provides food, water, and shelter to the more than 300 species of
  migratory birds that pass through the Chicago area. The 15-acre
  site was created in the 1950s as a buffer around an army installa-
  tion. It became so popular with the feathered crowd that it was
  designated a protected nature area after the army left in the 1970s.

Lights, Camera, Chicago

✳ ✳ ✳ ✳

*Hundreds of films have been shot in Chicago;
here is a sampling of the most well known and representative.*

- **North By Northwest:** Alfred Hitchcock chose several spots to film this 1959 movie, which many consider to be his masterpiece. Chicago played a part providing a backdrop for scenes at the Ambassador East Hotel (1301 N. State Pkwy.) and at Midway Airport.

- **The Sting:** Paul Newman and Robert Redford filmed several scenes for this classic 1973 crime-comedy in Chicago. Look for them at La Salle Street Station, at freight yards on the West Side, and at Union Station.

- **Ordinary People:** This highly acclaimed 1980 drama was all over the northern suburbs. The restaurant scene was filmed at a pan-cake house in Wilmette, the school shots took place at Lake Forest High School, and various interior scenes were shot at Fort Sheridan.

- **The Blues Brothers:** A Chicago movie legend, *The Blues Brothers* (1980) defined the Chicago attitude for millions who saw the film. The brothers jump the 95th Street Bridge, run down lower Wacker Drive, and join in a street dance on 47th Street, right near the "L."

- **Sixteen Candles:** Skokie, Glencoe, Northbrook, Niles, and Evanston are just some of the suburbs John Hughes and his production team visited while making this 1983 teen favorite.

- **Ferris Beuller's Day Off:** When Chicagoland teenager Ferris ditches school, he's ditching the very real Glenbrook North High School; when he and his friends hang out in the city, you can see Wrigley Field, the Art Institute, Lake Shore Drive, and several other city landmarks, all of which make *Ferris Beuller's Day Off* (1986) a jewel in the crown of Chicago movies.

- **The Color of Money:** This 1986 Paul Newman/Tom Cruise/ Martin Scorsese juggernaut was almost entirely shot around the Windy City. The pool hall where Vincent first grabs Fast Eddie's attention is Fitzgerald's in Berwyn, a suburb west of the city. Some scenes were also filmed at Chris's Billiards in Jefferson Park and the Gingerman Tavern on Clark Street.

- **The Untouchables:** Where else could this 1987 movie about Chicago gangsters be filmed? Watch for various shots of city landmarks, including Union Station and the Daley Center, where a few of the "untouchables" throw a certain guy off the roof...

- **Home Alone:** If you find yourself cruising along in Winnetka, check out house number 671 on Lincoln Avenue—it's the *Home Alone* house. The majority of interiors in this 1990 blockbuster were filmed on the North Shore.

- **Rudy:** This 1993 film about a special Notre Dame footballer was filmed partly in South Bend, Indiana. It was a hop, skip, and a pass over to Chicago from there, however, so the production unit split its time between the college and the city.

- **The Fugitive:** In this 1993 TV-inspired thriller, lead Harrison Ford makes a phone call near Michigan Avenue, gets shot at coming out of the Daley Center, and walks in a parade on Dearborn Street. The Hilton on South Michigan Avenue and Cook County Hospital were used in the nail-biting conclusion.

- **High Fidelity:** Filmed in multiple Chicago neighborhoods including Wicker Park, Logan Square, and Uptown, Local boy John Cusack stars in this 2000 Chicago-based love story. Watch for shots from across the city—Double Door, Green Mill, and the Kinzie Street Bridge, to name just a few.

- **Barbershop:** The lights, camera, and action took it to the South Side in this 2002 movie starring Ice Cube and Cedric the Entertainer. Several scenes were shot at the intersection of East 79th and Exchange.

- **The Dark Knight:** The most memorable scenes in this 2008 action flick were shot on Lower Wacker Drive and at the old Chicago Post Office. "Gotham City Police" cars and paddy wagons could often be seen parked in filming areas.

Chicago Chatter

"[Chicago is] Perhaps the most typically American place in America."

—James Bryce,
The American Commonwealth (1888)

"He saw again in his mind's eye . . . a picture of the map on the wall of the railway station—the map with a picture of iron roads from all over the Middle West centering in a dark blotch in the corner. . . .

"'Chicago!' he said to himself . . . the rhythm of [the] word . . . said itself over and over in his mind: 'Chicago! Chicago!'"

—Floyd Dell, *Moon-Calf* (1921)

"Going to Chicago was like going out of the world."

—Muddy Waters

"Chicago is a seat-of-the-pants kind of town. If you have troubles, they're your troubles, not Chicago's."

—Elizabeth Canning Blackwell,
Irreverent Guide to Chicago

"People who don't fit in anywhere else fit in here. It's a collection of square pegs."

—Tony Fitzpatrick

"Chicago . . . fairly smokes and roars with business."

—Henry Ward Beecher

"There is no place anywhere like Chicago."

—Clarence A. Andrews,
Chicago in Story, a Literary History

"This is Chicago! An audacious city that set herself up in a swamp: but the swamp long ago was obliterated and only the audacity remains."

—Robert Shackleton

(Continued from p. 205)

May 30, 1937
In an event that has come to be known as the Memorial Day Massacre, Chicago police gun down a group of striking Republic Steel workers, killing 10 and wounding 90.

1942
James Farmer and George Houser found the Chicago Committee of Racial Equality. It will be the first chapter of CORE, the Christian civil rights advocacy organization that pioneered the use of nonviolent civil disobedience.

1942
Construction of the massive public housing complex that will come to be known as Cabrini-Green begins with the completion of the Frances Cabrini Rowhouses.

1943
Chicago Cubs owner Philip Wrigley founds the All-American Girls Baseball League in an effort to keep baseball fans interested while the male ballplayers are engaged in the war effort.

1945
The "Curse of the Billy Goat" is placed on the Chicago Cubs after Billy Goat tavern owner William Sianis and his pet goat are denied entrance to Wrigley Field.

1946
Civil rights activists with the Chicago chapter of CORE success-fully campaign to desegregate the White City Roller Rink at 63rd and Parkway (now King Drive).

February 1948
Chicago's morning and evening papers, the *Sun* and the *Times*, merge to form the *Chicago Sun-Times*.

May 25, 1950
A speeding Chicago Transit Authority Green Hornet trolley fails to heed a flagman's signal and slams into a truck carrying 8,000 gallons of fuel. The resulting explosion will engulf several buildings in the area (62nd and State), claim 33 lives, and send dozens more to the hospital with severe burns.

July 1951
In an appalling incident that focused international attention on Chicago, thousands of residents of the all-white suburb of Cicero repeatedly attack an apartment building in which a black family is attempting to settle.

1953
Chicagoan Hugh Hefner founds his iconic *Playboy* magazine. Marilyn Monroe graces the first cover, and all 50,000 copies quickly sell out.

September 6, 1955
WTTW-TV launches on Chicago's channel 11 in an effort spear-headed by community leader Edward Ryerson. The new station will be Chicago's first to offer educational programming.

(Continued on p. 235)

Baseball's Darkest Hour

* * * *

*Baseball's Golden Age was preceded by its darkest hour:
the 1919 World Series–fixing scandal.*

The *Chicago Herald and Examiner* described him as "a little
urchin," the young lad who emerged from the crowd outside a
Chicago courthouse on that September day in 1920 and was said to
have grabbed Joe Jackson by the coat sleeve. The newspaper's report
of the exchange went like this:

"It ain't true, is it?" the lad said.

"Yes, kid, I'm afraid it is," Jackson replied.

"Well, I'd never have thought it," the boy exclaimed.

Nowhere did the newspaper report that the boy demanded, "Say
it ain't so, Joe," although this version of the story was passed down
through the generations. A few years before his 1951 death, Jackson
told *Sport Magazine* that the story was made up by a sportswriter.
He said the only words exchanged on the way out of the courthouse
that day were between him and a law enforcement officer.

What *is* so is this: Members of the 1919 Chicago White Sox
committed baseball's cardinal sin, deliberately losing the World
Series to the Cincinnati Reds for pay.

Ripe for a Fix

Two years after their 1917 world championship, the White Sox took
the American League pennant. The White Sox were favored to
defeat Cincinnati in the World Series—heavily favored, in some
gambling circles. By all accounts, Sox infielder Chick Gandil made
contact with gamblers and indicated that the Series could be thrown.
He immediately involved 29-game-winner Eddie Cicotte, and others
followed: Jackson, pitcher Claude Williams, infielders Buck Weaver
and "Swede" Risberg, outfielder Oscar "Happy" Felsch, and utility
man Fred McMullin. Some of the players would play lead parts in
the fixing of games. Others, notably Weaver and some say Jackson,
knew about the plan but were not active participants.

When the Series began, the players were promised a total of $100,000 to throw the games. By the time the Reds won the Series in eight games, the payout was considerably less, and whispers about what had taken place began swelling to a roar. Sportswriters speculated about a possible fix even before Cincinnati wrapped up the Series, but nobody wanted to believe it could be true.

Conspiracy to Defraud the Public

The 1920 season began with rumors about gambling in other big-league dugouts. In September a grand jury convened to examine instances of gambling in the game, and the jury soon looked at the 1919 World Series. Eight White Sox players were called to testify, and several admitted knowledge of the fix. All eight were indicted for conspiracy to defraud the public and injure "the business of Charles Comiskey and the American League." Although the group was acquitted due to lack of evidence, the damage had been done.

Bring in the Judge

The Black Sox were not as fortunate on the scales of baseball justice, as Judge Kenesaw Mountain Landis, baseball's first commissioner, suspended all eight players for life. It was a crushing blow for Chicago, and for Weaver and Jackson in particular. While Gandil had received $35,000 and Cicotte $10,000 for the fix, Weaver received nothing. Actually, it was proven that he had *turned down* an invitation to participate in the scam. And Jackson, considered one of the greatest outfielders and hitters in the history of the game, hit .375 with six RBI in the 1919 Series while playing errorless defense.

Many still clamor for Shoeless Joe to be enshrined in the Hall of Fame, arguing that his numbers support the claim that he did nothing to contribute to the fixing of the 1919 World Series. However, the $5,000 he accepted from the gamblers sealed his fate as a tragic figure in baseball's most infamous 20th-century scandal.

Say it ain't so, Joe.
Too bad it is.

This City Loves a Parade

* * * *

Chicago is in every sense a global city, influenced by both world events and the contributions of its diverse inhabitants. Its spirit of multiculturalism is ever present on its busy streets, but it is never more salient than during one of Chicago's vibrant parades.

- **Chinatown Parade:** At the beginning of February, when the doldrums of winter get Chicagoans down, they head to the city's vibrant Chinatown neighborhood on the South Side to ring in the Chinese New Year. Dancers, musicians, paper dragons, and floats glide through the streets draped in red and yellow—traditional colors for the celebration—wishing residents, visitors, and local businesses a prosperous and joyful new year.

- **South Side Irish Parade:** For decades, the official St. Patrick's Day parade, which takes place downtown, was in competition with the South Side Irish Parade, which took place in the Beverly neighborhood on the city's Southwest Side. But due in part to the growth of its uproarious—sometimes uncontrollable—crowds, the parade's planning committee announced in 2009 that the parade would cease to exist in its current incarnation, leaving its future hanging precariously in the balance.

- **Greek Independence Day Parade:** Commemorating Greece's 1821 independence from the Ottoman Empire, this spring parade draws together thousands of members of Chicago's large Greek community, including leaders from the Greek Orthodox Church and civic and commercial leadership from the city's bustling Greektown neighborhood.

- **Polish Constitution Day Parade:** One of the oldest parades in the city, the Polish Constitution Day Parade has drawn countless revelers to the lakefront each May for a hundred years and counting. Commemorating the ratification of the Polish Constitution in 1781, the parade has also come to celebrate the culture and history of Chicago's immense and influential Polish population.

- **Puerto Rican Day Parade:** One of the city's most dazzling public events, Chicago's Puerto Rican Day Parade has bounced through Grant Park every June for decades. Lavish floats, honorary marshals, and local political bigwigs make up the scene, which is celebrated by countless Chicagoans and visitors from throughout the Midwest.

- **Gay Pride Parade:** Chicago's Boys Town neighborhood salutes Gay Pride Month each June with this colorful, spirited parade. The parade is the final of many celebratory events, including the Halsted Food Sampling and the Pride Run and Walk.

- **Indian and Pakistani Independence Day Parades:** Every summer, thousands of people gather along the sidewalks of West Devon Avenue in Rogers Park, the city's most diverse neighborhood, to celebrate the anniversary of the subcontinent's independence from British Colonial rule—which officially occurred on August 15, 1947. The city's Indian and Pakistani populations hold their respective parades on different days, but do so in a spirit of camaraderie and multiculturalism.

- **General Von Steuben Parade:** Marching along Lincoln Avenue through Chicago's old German and Austrian enclave each September, the Von Steuben Day Parade celebrates the life of Baron Friedric Von Steuben, the German American Revolutionary War hero who came to the United States to enlist under George Washington.

- **Pilsen Mexican Independence Day Parade:** One of four Mexican Independence Day parades around the city—the other three are downtown, on 26th Street, and in the South Chicago neighborhood—the 18th Street parade boasts more than 150 floats, along with the requisite music, dancing, food, and drink that make September 16 one of Chicago's most exciting and celebrated holidays.

The Capture of U-505

* * * *

During World War II's Battle of the Atlantic, German U-boats sank more than 2,800 Allied ships, and the German Navy lost almost 800 submarines. One German sub escaped a watery grave and now rests, not under hundreds of feet of water rusting away, but in a treasured gallery beneath the streets of Chicago.

As German U-boats plied the waters off the coasts of America and Europe, sinking Allied ships at will, Allied leaders scrambled to find a solution to the problem of marauding U-boats. While the development of convoys reduced the number of merchant ships lost, the Allies were not satisfied with this defensive tactic. A convoy's escort could protect a group of cargo ships, but in many cases enemy submarines were able to escape after launching an initial attack.

In 1943 the Allies developed a new strategy to confront the U-boat menace—hunter-killer groups composed of one escort aircraft carrier and several destroyer escorts began proactively searching for German prey. Captain Daniel V. Gallery, USN, was commanding officer of one such hunter-killer force, Task Group 22.3, which was comprised of the escort carrier USS *Guadalcanal* and five destroyer escorts: USS *Pillsbury*, USS *Jenks*, USS *Pope*, USS *Flaherty*, and USS *Chatelain*.

Target: U-505

The year 1944 had been a successful one for Captain Gallery. Under his leadership, the *Guadalcanal* participated in actions that destroyed the *U-544*, *U-515*, and *U-68*.

The *U-505*, a Type IX-C German submarine, was responsible for sinking eight Allied ships totaling 47,000 tons. The U-boat patrolled the coast of West Africa, the Panama Canal, and Trinidad. In June 1944, the sub left her pen in Lorient, France, for an 80-day patrol in the Gulf of Guinea.

On May 15, 1944, TG 22.3 set sail from Norfolk, Virginia, to the Canary Islands. After two weeks of fruitless searching, the task force headed to Casablanca for refueling. Minutes after setting course for port, *Chatelain's* commander reported "possible sound contact." After a brief battle, *U-505* was on the surface, and most of its crew was in the water.

While men from the *Chatelain* and *Jenks* rescued survivors, a nine-man boarding party led by Lieutenant Albert David from the *Pillsbury* took control of the stricken sub. German sailors had attempted to scuttle their boat by opening a pipe; Motor Machinist Mate 1st Class Zenon Lukosius searched for, recovered, and resecured the pipe cover, preventing further flooding.

Priceless Pickings

The capture of *U-505* resulted in the acquiring of two complete M4 Enigma encoding machines, codebooks, notebooks containing decrypted messages, and several acoustic torpedoes. The captured material gave Allies insight into the German Navy's code, which indicated the precise locations of German subs. The breaking of this code afforded Allied commanders the opportunity to send sub hunter groups to specific areas. Convoys could also now be rerouted from areas where German subs were known to be operating.

A Most Unlikely Resting Spot

U-505 was eventually towed to Bermuda, where it was scrutinized by experts from the Office of Naval Intelligence. The sub's crew was transferred to a POW camp in Louisiana, where they were kept in isolation to keep news of the submarine's capture secret. Because the crewmen were not allowed to send letters home, some families assumed their men were dead.

Captain Gallery successfully campaigned to have *U-505* donated to the Museum of Science and Technology (now known as the Museum of Science and Industry) in his hometown of Chicago, and in September 1954, the sub was relocated from the Navy Yard in Portsmouth, Virginia, to the Chicago museum. In April 2004, the submarine was refurbished and relocated to an underground, climate-controlled, 35,000-square-foot exhibit. Countless visitors to the museum are forever grateful for the opportunity to meander through this magnificent World War II relic.

The City of Bridges

* * * *

Chicago boasts more movable bridges than any other city in the world.

The Chicago River System is 156 miles long and includes the North Shore Channel, the Sanitary and Ship Canal, and the Cal-Sag Channel. The city's 36 movable bridges must be raised and lowered by a complex system that is carefully administered by a select crew of specially trained bridge tenders.

The Chicago River was once a highway that never slept. Tenders had to stay close to their charges in order to lift or lower the bridge at all hours of the day. This led to the building of bridge tender houses, and in areas of the river downtown, these houses are quite architecturally elaborate. Because the bridge tender needed an unobstructed view of the waterway, the bridge tender houses have windows on all sides. Needless to say, the views through these windows are magnificent. Do not run scrambling to visit the houses, however—nearly all the houses are closed to the public. The only one with public access is the southwest tower of the double-decker Michigan Avenue Bridge, which houses the Bridgehouse & Chicago River Museum.

Today, the Chicago River System may be quieter, but the city's bridges are still opened nearly 30,000 times a year by 70 tenders. Bridge tenders often drive in sequence in packs of three to allow boats through the river system, and the houses are merely workstations, instead of permanent living quarters. This is likely a relief to the bridge tenders. As noted in one bridge tender's obituary, that of Gustav Massman, who died in 1985 at the age of 100: "For the first 18 years, he worked 7 days a week straight without a single vacation."

* * * *

- *Chicago's Cortland Street Bridge is the oldest trunnion bascule bridge in the country. This type of bridge is revered in engineering circles because it achieves nearly perfect balance and uses minimal electricity.*

Fast Facts

- Captain Frank Pape (1909–2000) of the Chicago Police Department had a reputation as America's toughest police officer. "I represent the city of Chicago, and Chicago stopped taking orders from gangsters a long time ago," Pape once said.

- "Machine Gun" Jack McGurn, who came to Chicago with Al Capone, attempted a second career as a pro golfer when the police heat grew too warm. He was arrested while playing in the 1933 Western Open at Olympia Fields. Worse yet, he didn't make the cut.

- Chicagoan Oscar S. DePriest, the child of freedmen, made a fortune through business and investing savvy. In 1928, DePriest became the 20th century's first African American congressman.

- Chicago's mayors have come from eight political parties: the Whig, Democratic, Independent Democrat, Republican, Know-Nothing, Citizens, Fireproof, and People's parties. Only one mayor has come from each of the latter four, which may be just as well.

- CPD officer Frederico Andaverde was decorated for a 2004 gun battle in which he was hit but not wounded. A suspect's 9mm slug went through the squad car door and hit Andaverde in the butt—right in the wallet. The thick billfold full of various plastic cards stopped the bullet cold. Andaverde walked away with a bruise.

- The Bears used to be the Decatur Staleys, after their sponsor: food company A. E. Staley. Less well known: A. E. Staley Manufacturing Company is still operating in Decatur. The company is now owned by Tate & Lyle and makes cornstarch and pretty much anything corn-related except Lifetime movies.

The Lawn Chairs of Winter

* * * *

While driving in a brutal Chicago winter can be difficult, the real challenge most Chicagoans face is parking on streets piled high with snow. The unwritten rule of the city is that if you shovel out a parking space, you're entitled to save it, and woe unto the driver who dares to violate your claim—or rather, woe unto his car.

The mean streets of Chicago get just a little meaner during the city's notoriously harsh winters, as residents vie for precious parking spots amid the mounds of frozen snow. The city has an unwritten rule, often referred to as the "dibs" system, under which anyone who shovels out a parking space in front of their house can reserve it with milk crates, sawhorses, weight benches, or—most commonly—lawn chairs. Of course nothing prevents another driver from removing the placeholder and taking the spot—nothing, that is, except the retribution that's almost certain to come from the spot's "owner."

Many drivers have reported having their side mirrors broken or their tires deflated when they've taken "someone else's" spot. Truly dedicated vengeance seekers have gone so far as to get out their shovels, bury the offending vehicle in a mound of snow, and then pour buckets of water over it, leaving it encased in an icy tomb until the weather makes its way back up above freezing.

Saving spots is a violation of the city ordinance that prevents obstruction of the public way; many residents oppose the practice,

but Chicago officials seem inclined to sympathize with the shovelers. When Alderman Tom Allen was asked why city leaders don't clamp down on the parking space squatters, he responded, saying residents "might string us up." Even Mayor Daley has publicly come out in defense of the system: "If someone spends all that time digging their car out, do not drive in that spot. This is Chicago—fair warning."

Timeline

(Continued from p. 225)

March 1958
Nathan Leopold is paroled after spending 33 years behind bars for the murder of Bobby Franks.

December 1, 1958
Ninety-two students and three nuns die when a fire consumes Our Lady of the Angels grade school.

December 16, 1959
Chicago's Second City theater opens on North Wells Street.

1962
Chicagoans Gordon and Carole Segal open a home furnishings store in Old Town. Five years later the company will begin issuing its ubiquitous Crate & Barrel catalogs. Annual sales will reach $300 million by the mid-1990s.

1966
The Chicago Bulls franchise is born as an expansion team, with Johnny "Red" Kerr as head coach.

July 13, 1966
Richard Speck breaks into a Chicago town house late at night and herds nine young women into one of the bedrooms. Eight of the women are murdered one by one during the early morning hours of July 14th. The ninth escapes by hiding under a bed.

April 4, 1968
Martin Luther King Jr. is assassinated, touching off race riots throughout Chicago's West Side.

Eleven are killed and hundreds are injured as violence consumes nearly 30 blocks of the city.

August 29, 1968
The Democratic National Convention closes at Chicago's International Amphitheater after three days of rioting, violence, and charges of police brutality.

December 4, 1969
Chicago Black Panthers Fred Hampton and Mark Clark are killed on the West Side as police and federal agents raid their apartment, looking for weapons and fugitives. Police officers claimed the two were killed in a firefight, but an investigation into the incident concluded that while police fired off nearly 100 rounds, Hampton and Clark fired only one.

1971
Murderer Nathan Leopold dies in San Juan, Puerto Rico.

August 1, 1971
The Union Stock Yards close after more than a century in the meat processing and packing business. The closure was mostly due to the development of refrigerated trucks, which allowed packinghouses to be located in less-expensive, rural areas.

1973
Construction is completed on Chicago's Sears Tower, the tallest building in the world at 1,450 feet.

(Continued on p. 263)

Small Screen, Big City

* * * *

*A great many television shows have been set in Chicago,
some forgettable and some groundbreaking. While many of
the series could well have been set in any industrial urban area,
they all took advantage of the city's unique look and personality
to add to the tone of the show.*

- **The Untouchables:** This crime drama, which aired from 1959 to 1963, chronicled the exploits of Chicago's most famous G-man, Elliot Ness, during Prohibition. Though the series offered a highly fictionalized version of Ness's career (it often had him arresting real-life criminals that Ness was never involved with), it enjoyed a loyal following and survived for decades in reruns, helping to perpetuate Chicago's image as the crime capital of America.

- **The Bob Newhart Show:** Bob Newhart starred in this 1970s sitcom as a Chicago psychiatrist who encountered as many strange characters in his personal life as in his professional practice. The cast included an array of quirky, mostly unattached professional adults who regularly engaged in witty, sophisticated, and often sarcastic banter at each other's expense.

- **Good Times:** A popular sitcom with a five-year run, *Good Times* followed the ups and downs of an African American family living in Chicago's public housing system. The show, which starred Esther Rolle, John Amos, and Jimmie Walker, was groundbreaking for its realistic handling of the violence, bigotry, and domestic tensions that characterize life below the poverty line.

- **ER:** Debuting in 1994, *ER* was an innovative medical drama set in the chaotic emergency room of a Chicago teaching hospital. The show, which was created by Michael Crichton, earned more Emmy nominations than any other drama in history and made stars of several cast members, including George Clooney, Anthony Edwards, Juliana Margulies, and Noah Wyle.

- **Chicago Hope:** This series was a medical drama set in a fictional Chicago hospital. The show benefited from two big-name stars, Mandy Patinkin and Adam Arkin. When Patinkin and creator David E. Kelley left the show after its second season, *Chicago Hope* progressively lost ground to *ER* and was canceled in 2000.

- **Hill Street Blues:** This series reinvented the television drama when it first aired in 1981. Each episode, which followed a single day in the lives of the police in a tough urban precinct, included humor, violence, drama, and ongoing storylines featuring more than a dozen regular characters. Though the show was careful never to name the city it took place in, stock exterior scenes captured the distinctive grittiness of Chicago, and the cops' uniforms and squad cars were clearly modeled after those of the Chicago Police Department.

- **Perfect Strangers:** This buddy sitcom enjoyed a seven-year run on ABC in the late 1980s and early 1990s. Using a fish-out-of-water premise, it followed the misadventures of a good-hearted but naive immigrant from a small Mediterranean island who lives in Chicago with his neurotic cousin, a photographer and writer for a fictional Chicago newspaper.

- **Married with Children:** This early sitcom from the FOX network focused on the dysfunctional Bundy family. The show drew criticism for its vulgar, sexual humor and bankrupt notions of family values; however, it proved to be a substantial hit for the struggling young network and became one of the longest-running sitcoms of its era. Set in Chicago, the show made frequent reference to parts of the city and included landmarks such as Buckingham Fountain in its opening credits.

- **My Boys:** This sitcom follows the life of a 30-something female sportswriter in Chicago who can't get over her tomboy tendencies. Her circle of friends is almost exclusively male, and though she feels she is a kindred spirit to the boys, she perennially finds herself paying a price for her unconventional life.

Local Legends

Most big cities have ghost stories, and Chicago is no different. But beyond the tales of haunted houses and spirit-infested graveyards, one Chicago legend stands out. It's the story of a beautiful phantom that nearly everyone in the Windy City has heard of. Her name is "Resurrection Mary," and she is Chicago's most famous ghost.

The story of Resurrection Mary begins in the mid-1930s and centers around the Oh Henry Ballroom (known today as Willowbrook Ballroom), located in the southwestern suburbs on Archer Avenue. Several young men began relating similar stories of meeting a girl at a dance, spending the evening with her, and then offering her a ride home at closing time. Her vague directions always led to the gates of Resurrection Cemetery—where the girl would inexplicably vanish!

A short time later, numerous drivers began reporting a ghostly young woman on the road near the gates of Resurrection Cemetery. Some drivers claimed that she was looking for a ride, but others reported that she attempted to jump onto the running boards of their automobiles as they drove past. Some drivers even claimed to have accidentally run over the girl outside the cemetery, but when they went to her aid, her body was gone. Others said that their automobiles actually passed through the young woman before she disappeared through the cemetery gates.

Police and local newspapers began hearing similar stories from frazzled drivers who had encountered the mysterious young woman. These firsthand accounts created the legend of Resurrection Mary.

One Last Dance

One of the prime candidates for Mary's real-life identity was a young Polish girl named Mary Bregovy. Mary loved to dance, especially at the Oh Henry Ballroom, and was killed one night in March 1934 after spending the evening at the ballroom and then downtown at some of the late-night clubs. She was killed along Wacker Drive in Chicago when the car she was riding in crashed into an elevated train support. Her parents buried her in Resurrection Cemetery, and a short time later, a caretaker spotted her ghost walking through the graveyard. Stranger still, passing motorists on Archer Avenue soon began telling stories of her apparition trying to hitch rides as they passed by the cemetery's front gates. For this reason, many believe that the ghost stories of Mary Bregovy may have given birth to the legend of Resurrection Mary. Many believe she is continually returning to her eternal resting place after one last dance.

Will the Real Resurrection Mary Please Stand Up?

However, there may be more than one Resurrection Mary haunting Archer Avenue. Descriptions of the phantom have varied. Mary Bregovy had bobbed, light-brown hair, but some reports describe Resurrection Mary as having long blonde hair. Who could this ghost be?

It's possible that this may be a young woman named Mary Miskowski, who was killed along Archer Avenue in October 1930. According to sources, she also loved to dance at the Oh Henry Ballroom and at some of the local nightspots. Many people who knew her believed that she might be the ghostly hitchhiker.

We may never know Resurrection Mary's true identity. But there's no denying that sightings of her have been backed up with credible eyewitness accounts. Witnesses have given specific places, dates, and times of their encounters with Mary—encounters that remain unexplained. Besides that, Mary is one of the few ghosts to ever leave physical evidence behind!

She Left Her Mark on the Cemetery Gates

On August 10, 1976, around 10:30 P.M., a man driving past Resurrection Cemetery noticed a young girl wearing a white dress standing inside the cemetery gates. She was holding on to the bars of the gate, looking out toward the road. Thinking that she was locked in the cemetery, the man stopped at a nearby police station and alerted an officer to the young woman's predicament. An officer responded to the call, but when he arrived at the cemetery, the girl was gone. He called out with his loudspeaker and looked for her with his spotlight, but nobody was there. However, when he walked up to the gates for a closer inspection, he saw something very unusual. It looked as though someone had gripped the oxidized bronze bars with such intensity that handprints were seared into the metal. The bars were blackened and burned at precisely the spot where a small woman's hands would have been.

When word got out about the handprints, people from all over came to see them. Cemetery officials denied that anything supernatural had occurred, and they later claimed that the marks were created when a truck accidentally backed into the gates and a worker tried to heat them up and bend them back. It  was a convenient explanation, but most people still had their suspicions.

Cemetery officials were disturbed by this new publicity. In an attempt to dispel the crowds of curiosity seekers, they tried to remove the marks with a blowtorch. This made them even more noticeable, so they cut out the bars, with plans to straighten or replace them. Removing the bars only made things worse, as people wondered what the cemetery had to hide. Local officials were so embarrassed that the bars were put back into place, straightened, and then left alone so that the burned areas would oxidize and eventually match the other bars. However, the black-ened areas of the bars did not oxidize, and the twisted handprints remained obvious until the late 1990s, when the bars were finally removed. At great expense, Resurrection Cemetery replaced the entire front gates, and the notorious bars were gone for good.

A Broken Spirit Lingers

Sightings of Resurrection Mary aren't as frequent as in years past, but they do continue. Even though a good portion of the encounters can be explained by the fact that Mary has become such a part of Chicago lore that nearly everyone has heard of her, some of the sightings seem to be authentic. So whether you believe in her or not, Mary is still seen walking along Archer Avenue, people still claim to pick her up during the cold winter months, and she continues to be the Windy City's most famous ghost.

The Ultimate Reversal

* * * *

Chicago is known for its engineering marvels.
The City of the Big Shoulders has been flexing its industrial muscle
since the 1870s, when rapid growth—and a famous fire—forced the
city upward and outward. But the city's greatest engineering feat
was forcing the Chicago River to reverse its flow.

When the city was founded in the 1830s, the Chicago River—then
called "Chicagou," a Native American word for "bitter onions"—
flowed directly into Lake Michigan, bringing with it both industrial
pollution and bodily waste. By the 1860s and '70s, population and
industry had grown so rapidly that pollution in the river and along
Lake Michigan, the city's source of drinking water, was beginning to
reach dangerous levels. When a major storm flushed thousands of
gallons of waste into the lake in 1885, contaminating the city's water
with bacteria, thousands of people died of typhoid and cholera. City
officials were forced to act.

The city dredged and deepened the river and extended it inland.
Combined with a series of enormous canal locks finished in 1900,
the river's extension forced the water in the river to run backward
from the lake and south through a network of waterways before
spilling into the Mississippi.

At the beginning of the 20th century, with the lake and river
sparkling clean, the city saw a boom in commercial and residential
building that helped turn it from a gritty, industrial port into
the business, travel, and cultural hub its residents enjoy today.
Apartments and office buildings line the river, which, running
under the world's largest network of drawbridges and splashing
sidewalks and pavilions as it flows, remains one of the city's most
treasured gems.

It's the only river in the world to run away from its mouth, and a
little Chicago ingenuity has kept the city's greatest recreational
spot—and its source of water—clean ever since.

Bitter Onions or Striped Skunk?

✳ ✳ ✳ ✳

Many know Chicago's name derives from an indigenous name for the Chicago River. Chicaga, Chicagou, Checagwa—something like that. And it has something, they might add, to do with "bitter onions." But few modern Chicagoans know that the origins of their beloved town's famous name may be lost in the notebook of a 17th-century explorer, that the word is as French as it is Native American, and, most important, that the great debate over its origin is far from over.

Records of the language of the Illinois and Miami Native Americans, who inhabited the area and presumably named many landmarks in the region, only date back to the end of the 17th century, when beleaguered Jesuits and French explorers recorded thousands of words and suggested certain overly practical origins.

It's true that many place names in the Midwest were based on descriptions of the terrain and that the stinky onions that peppered the riverbanks may have been the region's most salient botanical novelty. But it's also true that many explorers were translating the language into a kind of crude French, and their methods were often rooted in trial, error, and complacency.

It appears that the name of the river was first recorded by René-Robert Cavelier, Sieur de La Salle, whose own exhausting moniker suggests a predilection for complicated language. In his notes, La Salle used "8," the Arabic numeral, as a kind of shorthand to stand in for the last syllable of the word that would become "Chicago." Historians have argued that the "8" stands in for an "a," an "ou," a "wa," though they insist it couldn't be an "o," as it is now.

More recently, scholars have noted that the locals' supposed fixation on onions is as apocryphal as it sounds, the error based on a mistranslation of La Salle's hastily written notes. Now it seems likely that the word Chicago is most closely linked to *sikaakwa* or *sikaa-konki*, which relate not to "bitter onions," but "striped skunk"— perhaps a sign that, linguistics aside, Chicago has never been known for pleasant aromas.

Colorful Printers Row

* * * *

From brothels to book publishing to residential lofts and restaurants,
Printers Row has always been a hub of activity.

Printers Row is a two-block area in the South Loop. In the early 20th century, an overlapping section of the neighborhood—along South Dearborn, South Federal, and South Plymouth streets—was known as the Printing House Row District. Now a designated landmark, Printing House Row was Chicago's hub of—you guessed it—printing and publishing.

Before 1880, printers set type by hand, but in 1884, Ottmar Mergenthaler designed the Linotype, a machine that quickly produced lines of type. This mechanized form of typesetting greatly increased productivity. The Mergenthaler Linotype Building was erected in 1886 on Plymouth Court. Other companies—such as Rand McNally, M. A. Donohue, and Lakeside Press—moved into the area. Their respective presses endlessly whirred, producing trade publications, magazines, and catalogs. The towering buildings that housed these presses, such as the Donohue Building (1883), the Duplicator Building (1886), and the Pontiac Building (1891), serve as classic examples of the First School of Chicago Architecture.

Before it became the printing district, this area was the Custom House Levee, Chicago's vice district, home to gaming houses and bordellos. Eventually, an escalation in crime—or more likely, an increase in arrests—shut down business in the Levee District. In 1886, printers and publishers began moving in and held court until the 1970s, when many of the buildings in Printers Row were converted into residential lofts. The area is now known for its trendy restaurants and for the Printers Row Book Fair, which takes over the area for one weekend every summer.

Quiz

*Test your Windy City knowledge
with the following collection of questions.*

1. Which of the following John Cusack films was set in Chicago?
a) *1408*
b) *Being John Malkovich*
c) *Eight Men Out*
d) *The Grifters*

2. The Beatles first came to Chicago in 1964. Where did they perform?
a) Chicago Stadium
b) International Amphitheater
c) Soldier Field
d) Comiskey Park

3. The daughter of this senatorial candidate was brutally murdered in the family's Kenilworth home weeks before his election. Her murderer was never apprehended.
a) Paul Douglas
b) Paul Simon
c) Chuck Percy
d) Peter Fitzgerald

4. Which of the following Chicago streets was part of U.S. Route 66?
a) Ogden
b) Madison
c) State
d) Elston

5. This animal escaped from its Lincoln Park Zoo enclosure in 1982 and wandered around the zoo for a while before it was captured.
a) Jerome the giraffe
b) Otto the gorilla
c) Cleopatra the camel
d) Tatiana the lioness

6. This gifted writer was born in Chicago in 1930.
a) Saul Bellow
b) Shel Silverstein
c) Nelson Algren
d) Studs Terkel

1. c, 2. b, 3. c, 4. a, 5. b, 6. b

Fast Facts

- In the 1894 Pullman strike, workers refused to handle trains containing a Pullman car. It was illegal, however, to refuse to handle a train carrying U.S. mail. Bosses broke the strike by adding Pullman cars to all trains hauling mail, bringing federal intervention against the strikers.

- On July 23, 2009, White Sox pitcher Mark Buehrle pitched a perfect game—only the 18th perfect game in the history of the major leagues. Buehrle followed up his masterpiece with a telephone chat with First Fan President Obama.

- Chicago's German community was quite visible in its heyday (1850–1914). Unfortunately, the World War I Teutonophobia that swept the nation caused most German Americans to lower their cultural profile. The war would end, but the community's identity never quite recovered.

- Hawks goalie Sam LoPresti, one of the few U.S. nationals playing in the pre-World War II NHL, was off West Africa with the Navy in 1942 when a German U-boat torpedoed his ship. He endured a 42-day ordeal in a lifeboat, losing 55 pounds before rescue.

- In 1964, the Cubs' trade of outfielder Lou Brock for pitcher Ernie Broglio seemed like the stupidest move ever—for St. Louis. What fool would swap a proven winner like Broglio (70–55, 3.43 ERA) for a strikeout-prone lifetime .257 hitter with a questionable glove?

- The Chicago Blackhawks have six retired jerseys: #1 (goalie Glenn Hall), #3 (defensemen Pierre Pilote and Keith Magnuson), #9 (left wing Bobby Hull), #18 (center Denis Savard), #21 (center Stan Mikita), and #35 (goalie Tony Esposito).

"Let's Play Two!"

* * * *

During the 1950s and '60s, Ernie Banks was one of the most
feared hitters and skilled fielders in Major League Baseball.
But it was his sunny disposition and abiding love of the game
that earned him the undying respect of Chicagoans on both
the North and South sides.

Ernie Banks is without a doubt the most beloved player ever to
appear on the Chicago Cubs roster. Known as Mr. Cub, this hard-
hitting shortstop and first baseman was one of the league's dominant
power hitters during the 1950s and 1960s, often racking up more
dingers than the better-known hitting legends of the era such as
Mickey Mantle, Willie Mays, and Hank Aaron.

Banks became the Chicago team's first African American player
in 1953 after spending a few years on a Negro League barnstorming
club. He quickly earned the starting shortstop position in Chicago as
well as the begrudging respect of pitchers around the nation. In
1955, he led the league in home runs and smacked a first-time-ever
five grand slams—a single-season record that would stand for
30 years.

Over the next five seasons, he banged out
more round-trippers than any player in the
majors. Lean and wiry, he did not have the
typical physique of a power hitter, but like
Hank Aaron, he had remarkably strong and
quick wrists, which allowed him to wield
his bat like a whip and make mince-
meat of such legendary pitchers as
Sandy Koufax and Don Drysdale.

Though his fielding was erratic
in his first few seasons, the young
slugger worked tirelessly to hone
his glove skills. He eventually
became one of the most proficient

infielders in the game, winning the Gold Glove Award in 1960. A few years earlier, he had won back-to-back Most Valuable Player (MVP) awards, as well. The MVP honors are particularly notable because he was playing for a perennially losing team. During the '50s, the Cubs never finished better than fifth place, and it was unheard of for the MVP to go to a player on a team that wasn't at least contending for the pennant.

Banks played his entire career from 1953 to 1971 in a Cubs uniform. His affiliation with the most lovable losers in baseball history also granted him another ignominious record in the baseball annals—most games played (2,528) without a single post-season appearance. Most of us would find it unbearable to be trapped in such a paradox—to be one of the league's best players shackled to one of the league's worst teams. But Banks never bellyached, never lamented, and never uttered a word of frustration. Rather, he always displayed a remarkably cheery, grateful, and humble persona and took the field each day as if he were a rookie reporting for his first big-league game. On perfect Chicago summer days, Banks would often use his famous pregame slogan "Let's play two!" For long-suffering Cub's fans, his combination of unquestionable prowess and unmatched passion for the game made him a beacon of hope during long, dark years.

Banks hung up his spikes after the 1971 season, but he remained with the club as a coach. In the second month of Banks's second season after retirement, Cubs manager Whitey Lockman was ejected from a game after an argument with an umpire, and Banks helmed the club for the remaining inning and a half of play in the Cubs' victory, making him the first African American to manage a Major League Baseball team during a game. Banks was elected to the Baseball Hall of Fame in 1977, his jersey number was retired in 1982 (the first Cubs jersey to be so honored), and he has been, and will always remain, a defining figure in the history of the Chicago Cubs.

✳ ✳ ✳ ✳

- *The Wrigley Field nickname "the Friendly Confines" is closely associated with Ernie Banks. Some believe he coined the phrase; all agree he popularized it.*

Chicago's Elite

✳ ✳ ✳ ✳

*Chicago's blue-collar sensibilities aren't for everybody.
Here are a handful of the city's most wealthy industrialists, media
moguls, and old money heirs.*

- **The Pritzkers (net worth estimated at $15 billion):** Heirs of Nicholas Pritzker, who founded the Hyatt Hotel chain and the Marmon Group with his sons Jay and Robert, the Pritzkers are among the city's most respected economic minds and most generous philanthropists. Feuding over inheritance—which ended in the fortune being split 11 ways—has marked much of their legacy, though the family name remains a symbol of great power and influence throughout the corporate world.

- **Ty Warner ($4.4 billion):** He may not exactly be a titan of industry, but Warner's shrewd business savvy helped launch one of the most profitable consumer crazes in history—Beanie Babies, the collectable plush toys that at one time raked in thousands of dollars at auction houses around the world. He also, reportedly, bought the penthouse in Santiago Calatrava's troubled, yet-to-be-built Chicago Spire.

- **Sam Zell ($5 billion):** This real estate mogul bought the Chicago-based Tribune Company for $8.2 billion in 2007, just before it fell into a downward spiral. Zell was forced to begin selling its assets—including *Newsday,* the Chicago Cubs, and office space in the company's famous Michigan Avenue headquarters—before the Tribune Company filed for bankruptcy protection in 2009.

- **Joseph Mansueto ($1.1 billion):** He founded investment research company Morningstar in his Chicago apartment with just

$80,000 dollars in 1984 and quickly made his company into one of the country's most profitable—and most respected—financial groups.

- **Oprah Winfrey ($2.7 billion):** Perhaps the most influential figure on the list, Winfrey—known to her army of loyal fans simply as Oprah—sits atop one of the largest media empires in the country. Her famous talk show, along with her magazine and films, have made her a household name and catapulted her into the world of the super rich. Chicagoans will treasure Oprah's last segments—in 2009 the talk show queen announced that 2010 (the 25th season) would be the last year for *The Oprah Winfrey Show.*

- **Matthew Bucksbaum ($2.2 billion):** The son of a Chicago grocer, Bucksbaum opened a shopping center in Cedar Rapids, Iowa, in 1954 and went on to become a pioneer in the world of consumer culture, founding General Growth Properties, which owns more than 200 shopping malls around the country.

- **Neil Bluhm ($1.5 billion):** This lawyer and real estate mogul currently owns the Four Seasons hotel in Chicago, the MGM Tower in Los Angeles, and a slew of casinos throughout the United States and Canada. An art collector and philanthropist, Bluhm has made donations to Northwestern Memorial Hospital and New York's Whitney Museum.

- **Kenneth Griffin ($1.5 billion):** Poised to become one of the youngest billionaires in the country, Griffin began making his fortune when he was an undergraduate at Harvard before moving to Chicago and founding Citadel Investments. A noted art collector and philanthropist, Griffin also made headlines in 2006 when he bought a Jasper Johns painting for $80 million.

To Market We Went

$*$ $*$ $*$ $*$

Maxwell Street has been minimized, but its legacy remains.

No other area in Chicago better represents the toughness, the grit, and the passion of this city's immigrant strivers than Maxwell Street. Sadly, the market is little more than a memory now, and what a bittersweet memory it is for those old enough to have experienced both its vibrant heyday and its slow, heartbreaking demise.

The Birth of a Bazaar

Maxwell Street was located on the Near West Side, running east and west and intersecting with Halsted Street. In the late 19th century, large numbers of Ashkenazi Jews from Eastern Europe and Russia began to settle in the area. Most of these immigrants were extremely poor and needed all the help they could get from local settlement houses such as Jane Addams's famous altruistic project, Hull House. Charity could only go so far, however, and the immigrants began to model a work ethic for their children that would change the neighborhood forever and eventually spell the end of an era.

Many Maxwell Street merchants started out on the very lowest rung of retail, peddling scrap metal or used clothing out of dilapidated pushcarts or even out of knapsacks on their backs. Saving every penny they could, some were able to eventually rent or buy store space and run more comfortable, attractive businesses. By the time the second generations of many of these families were old enough to take over, life had changed dramatically for the better through their hard work and perseverance.

Little Shops, Big Money

Some vendors on Maxwell Street never escaped the world of grinding poverty and pushcarts, but many others made small fortunes out of stores that sold appliances, clothing, sporting goods, and food. Often, this led to these merchants and their families keeping their businesses in the Maxwell Street area, but establishing new resi-

dences in "better" Chicago neighborhoods or suburbs. They wanted their
children to have all the advantages in life
that they had not, including college
educations, and very few of these
college graduates would take an interest
in continuing the family businesses on
Maxwell Street.

While these changes were occurring
in Chicago, changes were occurring all across the country for African
Americans. By the early 20th century, many southern African
Americans were discouraged by their status. They began migrating
north, many of them to Chicago and other urban areas where
manufacturing jobs were plentiful. As Jews moved out of the
Maxwell Street neighborhood, these southern blacks moved in. By
the 1920s, the area was predominantly African American.

Birth of the Blues, Death of the Market

The southern blacks who settled in the Maxwell Street neighborhood brought their music with them, and that music evolved into
what we now call the Chicago blues. The Maxwell Street musicians
played their music outdoors, and they began to use electric guitars
and amplifiers so that they could be heard by as many passersby as
possible. This created the distinctive Chicago blues sound and
eventually led to rock 'n' roll as well.

The demise of the Maxwell Street neighborhood was slow and
painful. The 1957 construction of the Dan Ryan Expressway and the
1065 relocation of the University of Illinois at Chicago contributed
to the area's decline. The deathblow to Maxwell Street came at the
turn of the 21st century, when Mayor Daley and the State of Illinois
allowed the university to exercise eminent domain for an expansion
and tear down the last remaining vestiges of this once-thriving
community. Attempts by residents, business owners, and historical
activists to have Maxwell Street designated a National Historical
District failed, and what remained of the market moved to Canal
and Roosevelt. Visitors can still listen to blues and sample Mexican
street food, but anyone who treasured the old market is sure to come
away disappointed.

Shelter or Inspiration?

* * * *

Most people wander into a tavern to relax or blow off steam,
but several Chicago writers took inspiration from
the city's watering holes.

Nelson Algren's realm was the Polish District, particularly its back alleys and seedy nightclubs. The Polonia Triangle, where Milwaukee and Ashland avenues meet Division Street, is home to a fountain dedicated in Algren's name. He is said to have frequented the Rainbo Club, a speakeasy featuring burlesque dancers; the Gold Star, a bar on Division; and Lottie's Pub (which was called Zagorski's Tavern in Algren's day), a debaucherous Bucktown hangout. All establishments still exist, though most agree Algren would not recognize today's Rainbo Club.

Studs Terkel also spent time on Division Street, between Western and California avenues. In fact, it served as the title of his groundbreaking book, *Division Street: America.* He featured Lawry's Tavern on Diversey in his book *The Great Divide.*

Saul Bellow was partial to Hyde Park's Woodlawn Tap, then known as Jimmy's, after Jimmy Wilson, the former owner. It's located within walking distance of the University of Chicago, where Bellow studied and taught. Its clientele remains an interesting cross section of artists, booksellers, tradesmen, construction workers, and students and Nobel Prize winners from the university.

Mike Royko, meanwhile, showed up after work, on most days, at the now-legendary Billy Goat Tavern, located under Michigan Avenue near the Chicago River. Chicago journalist Rick Kogan wrote of the tavern, "People come to the Goat for a variety of reasons, not the least of which is to find shelter from whatever storms are raging in their personal or professional lives, or may be afflicting the city, the planet, or any number of sports teams."

Cheers to Chicago taverns, for "sheltering" these literary greats!

The Chicago Imagists

* * * *

One of the most exciting movements in the art world since World War II, Chicago Imagism looked at the world through eyes seasoned by the sweeping colors of advertisements and consumer culture.

- **Roger Brown** (1941–97): Beloved in Chicago for donating his massive collection of primitive and outsider art to the Art Institute, Brown worked in several media, using rich color and simple form to comment on contemporary society. The brilliance and spirituality of his paintings have made them lasting favorites.

- **Gladys Nilsson** (b. 1940): Nilsson's highly detailed watercolors brought her wide acclaim during the 1960s. Her distorted images of daily life are playful and spirited, celebrating life's unpredictability.

- **Jim Nutt** (b. 1938): Influenced by everything from renaissance portraiture to 1950s comic books, Nutt's images are characterized by their flat, sometimes childish forms and their humorous combination of the old and new: His work gives the sense of Mona Lisa listening to bebop or Henry VIII just back from Venice beach.

- **Ed Paschke** (1939–2004): Perhaps the most famous of the lot, Paschke, with his vibrant colors and witty details, has been a beloved figure in the art world for decades. His lithographs of such famous figures as George Washington and Hunter S. Thompson are particularly famous.

- **Barbara Rossi** (b. 1940): Known for her meticulously drawn images of the body, Rossi's work has been greatly discussed in academic circles for its subtle feminism. Her forms appear grotesque and, wedged together, are reminiscent of scenes of poverty in the developing world.

- **Karl Wirsum** (b. 1939): Wirsum's works, with their severe neon lines and black backgrounds, suggest a nocturnal cityscape and the bold, carnival-like advertisements that blanketed Chicago in the 1960s and '70s. He used the kinds of intricate patterns and zigzags usually seen in African batiks.

Studs Terkel: Lending an Ear to America

* * * *

This Chicago oral historian never tired of his work.

Few Chicago personalities so captured the energy and pulse of the city as Studs Terkel. In his long career, the writer, actor, and broadcaster focused his attention on the lives of ordinary citizens. Tape recorder in hand, he initiated conversations with all sorts of people—from farm workers and folksingers to switchboard operators and valets—and ultimately popularized the oral history form.

Louis Terkel was born in the Bronx in 1912. He later took the name "Studs" after the protagonist of novelist James T. Farrell's Studs Lonigan trilogy. In 1923, the Terkel family moved to Chicago, where his parents managed hotels, including a rooming house on Grand Avenue and Wells Street, aptly named the Wells-Grand. Here, and at Bughouse Square—a legendary gathering place for speakers, "soapboxers," and poets—the energetic and ever-curious Terkel absorbed the stories of working-class Chicagoans.

After studying law at the University of Chicago, marrying social worker Ida Goldberg, and completing a year of civil service in Washington, D.C., Terkel returned to Chicago and honed his communication skills. Along with other now-famous writers (including the Chicago-based Nelson Algren, Richard Wright, and Saul Bellow), he participated in the WPA Writers' Project, a Depression-era initiative to keep writers busy and well funded. Terkel worked in the radio division, which led to gigs on radio soap operas, news shows, and eventually the stage. In 1945, he disc jockeyed his own WENR program called *The Wax Museum,* playing a mishmash of jazz, gospel, folk, country, and opera. He then went on to star in an unscripted TV drama called *Studs' Place,* in which he played himself as the owner of a local barbecue joint. NBC axed the show in 1952 (under pressure from the House Committee on Un-American Activities) due to Terkel's left-leaning politics.

Though his television contract was canceled, this action did little to silence Terkel. In fact, he began to make a career out of conversation—asking people questions and encouraging them to voice their opinions and experiences. His most successful radio project was *The Studs Terkel Program*, which broadcast daily from 1952 to 1997 on Chicago's fine arts station, WFMT. On the show, Terkel spoke with a wide variety of guests—labor organizers, performing artists, architects, historians—Chicagoans and non-Chicagoans alike. In 1980, his journalistic work earned him the prestigious Peabody Award.

In 1956, he published his first book, *Giants of Jazz*, followed by many important volumes of oral history. *Division Street: America* (1967) featured interviews with people who had lived in and around the Windy City. "I was on the prowl for a cross section of urban thought, using no one method or technique," Terkel said of this work. "I was aware it would take me to suburbs, upper, lower, and middle income, as well as to the inner city itself and its outlying sections. It finally came down to individuals, no matter where they lived." He followed this best seller with *Hard Times: An Oral History of the Great Depression* (1970) and *Working: People Talk About What They Do All Day and How They Feel About What They Do* (1974). In 1985, he won the Pulitzer Prize for *The Good War*, which collected citizens' memories and perspectives of World War II. In 2001, he published his last book of oral history, *Will the Circle Be Unbroken? Reflections on Death, Rebirth, and Hunger for a Faith*.

In Terkel's later years, he maintained a jam-packed schedule of writing, interviewing, and community appearances. He published the memoirs *Touch and Go* (2007) and *P.S.: Further Thoughts From a Lifetime of Listening* (2008). In archiving the hopes and daily lives of Americans, he never lost a close connection to Chicago, the city he called "America's dream, writ large. And flamboyantly." The lifelong listener passed away on October 31, 2008, at age 96.

Bragging Rights

- Chicago's River North area boasts the greatest concentration of art galleries in the United States, outside of Manhattan (confound New York!).
- Chicago houses the nexus of the American rail system, and everyone knows Warren Buffett is banking on the railroads as the future of transportation.
- Chicagoans were ecstatic when the Joffrey Ballet moved from New York to Chicago in 1995, but the Joffrey is not the only show in town. Lively performances can be found at Hubbard Street Dance, the Dance Chicago festival, the Dance Center of Columbia College, and the Museum of Contemporary Art.
- Sue, at the Field Museum, is the largest intact Tyrannosaurus Rex skeleton. Unveiled in 2000, Sue's skeleton is 42 feet long from head to tail and 13 feet tall at the hips.
- Wrigley Field is the second oldest major-league baseball stadium (after Fenway Park in Boston).
- Lincoln Park Zoo is one of the few remaining free major wildlife attractions in the United States.
- Uptown's Green Mill is the world's oldest jazz club.
- Chicago boasts more Poles than any city outside Poland and more Swedes than any city outside Sweden.
- Chicagoans revere their lake. Lake Michigan—the fifth largest freshwater lake in the world—is 307 miles long and 118 miles wide. It is only a little smaller than West Virginia. It has an average depth of 279 feet and a maximum depth of 925 feet. It is also the only Great Lake that the United States can claim solely as its own (all the others share borders with Canada). Chicago's 33 beaches are a majestic sight in the summer. When the lake churns and roars late in the fall (even flooding onto Lake Shore Drive at times), Chicagoans do not curse their lake—they just turn and take a different route. Chicago is currently taking drastic measures to protect its lake from the invasive Asian carp.

Fast Facts

- In 2008, a cougar from North Dakota found its way to Chicago's Roscoe Village neighborhood. Chicago police were called to the scene, and when officers came upon the animal, they shot it dead. Animal rights activists were troubled by the way police handled the situation, but responding officers pleaded insufficient experience in dealing with big cats.

- In the 1938 Stanley Cup finals, the Chicago Blackhawks found themselves in Toronto without a healthy goalie. They found career minor-leaguer Alfie Moore getting drunk in a local bar and signed him. Whatever he was drinking, we'd like some: Alfie and the Hawks beat the Leafs 3–1.

- Like contemporary hippies, all the 1968–75 Bulls needed was Love. They started to become a competitive team with the 1968 acquisition of forward Bob Love from Milwaukee. Until the arrival of Jordan, Love held many of the Bulls' scoring records.

- Whatever became of feared Blackhawks enforcer and scorer Al Secord? At the time of this writing, he is currently a commercial pilot for American Airlines—and we doubt anyone dares bump him on the runway.

- Leo Durocher (Cubs manager 1966–72) seemed perfect for Chicago: He was aggressive and colorful and had a history of winning. Why wasn't it a match made in heaven? Those Cubs teams had two major Chicago heroes, Ernie Banks and Ron Santo, and Durocher didn't get along with either. Guess who got fired?

- Boston Celtics NBA great Bob Cousy could well have become a Chicago hoop legend. The Chicago Stags (1946–50) obtained draft rights to Cousy but folded before he could wear their blue and red. Instead, his retired green #14 jersey hangs in Boston's TD Garden.

The Chicago Blues

* * * *

When music aficionados think Chicago, they think of the blues, and for good reason. During the first half of the 20th century, Chicago became the center of American blues music and brought this distinctive African American art form into the mainstream.

In the first few decades of the 20th century, the United States witnessed the Great Migration—the movement of southern African Americans to the northern industrial centers. Drawn by the prospects of jobs and entrepreneurial opportunity and seeking relief from the overt racism of their hometowns, blacks migrated in droves to the urban centers of New York, St. Louis, and Chicago. Along with hope, these migrants brought with them the unique culture and heritage of their people, and Chicago was forever changed.

The city was a bustling, vibrant community full of opportunity, and it accepted a great many of these American transplants. Among them were gifted musicians such as Big Bill Broonzy, Blind Lemon Jefferson, Tampa Red (Hudson Walker), Memphis Slim (Peter Chatman), Memphis Minnie Douglas, Howlin' Wolf, and Sonny Boy Williamson. These individuals knew hard times and hard work and sought to share those experiences through their distinctive blues music. They played in dingy urban clubs, at neighborhood rent parties, and, when they could, in the studios of major and minor record labels. Pursuing every outlet they could find, these performers started a revolution in American popular music by bringing the sound of the Mississippi Delta to a welcoming audience.

A Delta Sharecropper Comes to Town

By the 1940s, Chicago was enjoying a vibrant blues scene, defined by popular clubs on the South and West sides such as Silvio's, 708, the Flame Club, and Gatewood's Tavern, as well as the weekend open-air market on Maxwell Street, where aspiring artists performed regularly. Then in 1943, a Mississippi sharecropper named McKinley Morganfield came to town to join Chicago's thriving music scene. He made connections with Broonzy and other leading figures of the Chicago blues world, adopting their techniques and playing to their audiences. He changed his traditional acoustic style of guitar playing in favor of the amplified, electric sound that allowed the Chicago blues bands to be heard over the streetcars and raucous crowds of the rough urban setting. He also made a deal with the newly founded Chess Records, an upstart company run by Polish immigrants Phil and Leonard Chess that would become one of the most successful independent record labels of the era. Morganfield, better known by his stage name of Muddy Waters, helped create a whole new visceral sound that expressed the pathos of Delta blues through the driving rhythm of urban electric instrumentation. Chicago blues was born.

The country went mad for the new, riveting sounds out of Chicago, and Muddy Waters became one of the most popular and successful performers of the day. He gathered around him some of the most talented musicians of the Chicago blues style—Little Walter Jacobs, Willie Dixon, Jimmy Rogers, and Memphis Slim—and then leveraged his success to mentor such blues greats as Pinetop Perkins, Buddy Guy, and Koko Taylor, all of whom came out of the new blues capital of the world.

Rock 'n' Roll Moves In

The 1960s saw a decline in the popularity of this innovative music as the youth culture moved on to the next best thing—rock 'n' roll. What these mainstream audiences didn't realize, however, was that what they saw as the fresh, innovative sound of rock was directly derived from the electrified blues of southern African Americans. Broonzy, Waters, and their many, many Chicago colleagues had created a musical foundation on which the likes of Elvis Presley, The Beatles, The Rolling Stones, Led Zeppelin, and Eric Clapton would build the house of rock 'n' roll.

Andersonville: Sweeping Changes, Cherished History

✳ ✳ ✳ ✳

A mix of old and new makes Andersonville one of Chicago's most colorful neighborhoods

By 1890, there were 43,000 Swedish-born immigrants living in Chicago. Many of them were living in Andersonville, a part of Edgewater (population 62,000), one of Chicago's 77 official community areas. What was once an outlying village is now a vibrant city neighborhood in much demand by residents and business owners. In fact, perhaps no other community in Chicago has been as successful as Andersonville in retaining an old-world charm while at the same time integrating new ideas of multiculturalism and diversity.

Born of Necessity

Like many communities, Andersonville was born of economic hardship. Wooden homes had been outlawed in Chicago after the Great Fire of 1871, but most Swedish immigrants were impoverished and couldn't possibly afford to build brick homes. Moving outside the city limits was their only option, and they continued to settle in Andersonville, where they could build their wooden homes and practice the various trades they had learned in the old country.

The first businesses to spring up in Andersonville reflected the immigrants' heritage and immediate needs: pastry making, blacksmithing, sausage production, and construction. The commercial district centered on North Clark Street, a bustling hive of activity that was then (as it is now) best known for its mouthwatering delis, bakeries, and restaurants. Realty companies also thrived, as Swedish American families persisted in their exodus from the city proper.

Early Signs of Diversity

The Swedish tradition of tolerance has deep roots. Sweden has not actively participated in a war since 1814, and its brand of socialism has been largely praised by the rest of the world. The immigrants in Andersonville carried these ideals with them from their old country and strove to make their neighborhood a place of collective respect.

Nowhere was that tolerance more in evidence than in the variance of religious groups within the Swedish American community. Episcopalians, Catholics, and Lutherans lived side by side in Andersonville with virtually no religious tension. Other citizens of the neighborhood embraced such alternative philosophies as free thought or humanism, both of which teach that ethics should be based on science and logic rather than dogma. Acceptance of new ideas about psychology, sociology, and education was widespread in the Swedish American community, as it was in other Northern European immigrant groups in the United States.

Unique Traditions

A number of quaint, unique traditions developed in Andersonville over the decades. One of the most charming was the ritualistic emergence of the merchants of Clark Street at precisely 10:00 every morning to sweep the sidewalks en masse. This custom was so beloved by the area's residents that the business owners would proudly march with their brooms over their shoulders every year in the Midsommarfest parade.

Andersonville's Midsommarfest was—and is—a street festival that grew out of the Swedish tradition of celebrating the summer solstice. Midsommarfest is a time of merrymaking with music, dancing, and delicious food. Vendors sell clothing, jewelry, and handcrafted Swedish gift items. The fest is currently held annually over a June weekend and attracts approximately 40,000 revelers.

In late November, St. Morten's Gos Day heralds the coming of the holiday season, and bell-ringers—joined by St. Nicholas and Sven the Viking—make their annual march down Clark Street. A few weeks later the same street hosts the parade of St. Lucia, in which white-robed girls lead torchbearers to the Swedish American Museum.

A New Multiculturalism

After World War II, many Swedish American families began to move to Chicago's suburbs, but the Andersonville Chamber of Commerce worked with those who stayed in the neighborhood to preserve their unique heritage and encourage their entrepreneurialism. Indeed, the Swedes and their small, local businesses provided a blueprint of sorts for the other ethnic groups that would come to share their space. Today, Clark Street is home to not only Swedish American establishments such as Swedish Bakery and Ann Sather Restaurant but also restaurants and stores owned by Italian, Mexican, Lebanese, Korean, Ethiopian, and Thai newcomers.

The gay and lesbian community is now also an integral part of Andersonville, finding it to be a welcoming area for both singles and gay families. In 2000, the U.S. Census estimated the national average of single-sex couple households to be at 1.1 percent, but in Andersonville and the surrounding area, it ranged from 6.6 to 8.0 percent. Local businesses like the Women & Children First bookstore, the Cheetah Gym, the Atmosphere nightclub, and many others cater to a largely gay clientele. Churches such as Ebenezer Lutheran Church and religious groups such as the Gay & Lesbian Outreach Center for Youth and Dignity Chicago are active in the Andersonville neighborhood, providing support and affirmation to all members, regardless of sexual orientation.

The Best of Old and New

Though many changes have come to Andersonville, there is no indication that its history will be forgotten anytime soon. The Swedish American Museum on Clark Street stands as a symbol of the citizens' commitment to their heritage while embracing the diversity of the future. People of all races, religions, income levels, and orientations continue to add unique characteristics to this now "hot" neighborhood. Andersonville is truly the best of old and new.

✳ ✳ ✳ ✳

- *Famous Swedish American Chicagoans include Charles Walgreen and Carl Sandburg.*

- *In 1976, King Carl XVI Gustaf of Sweden attended the opening of the Swedish American Museum in Andersonville.*

Timeline

(Continued from p. 235)

May 25, 1979
An American Airlines DC-10 crashes during takeoff from O'Hare Airport. All 271 people on board are killed, as are two on the ground.

1983
A court order enforces the "Shakman decrees," a series of rulings prohibiting politically motivated punishments of city and state employees.

1985
Oprah Winfrey launches her eponymous talk show, which will soon become wildly popular from coast to coast.

1986
Geraldo Rivera opens "Al Capone's vault" in Chicago's abandoned Lexington Hotel (2135 S. Michigan Ave.) in front of a live, national television audience. It is empty.

April 18, 1991
The Chicago White Sox play their first game at the new Comiskey Park. It will retain the name of the team's first owner until 2003, when financial pressures compel the organization to accept sponsorship and rename the park U.S. Cellular Field.

October 6, 1993
Chicago Bulls superstar Michael Jordan "retires" to launch an unremarkable baseball career. He will return to the court, and the Bulls will return to their winning ways, less than two years later.

May 10, 1994
Chicago serial killer John Wayne Gacy is executed for the murder of more than 30 boys and young men between the ages of 14 and 21.

July 12, 1995
A deadly heat wave hits Chicago, claiming the lives of several hundred Chicagoans. The fact that the victims were predominately poor and elderly raised national awareness of the dangers of aging in social isolation.

September 26, 2006
Iva Toguri D'Aquino, the Japanese propaganda mouthpiece known as "Tokyo Rose," dies in Chicago after spending her later years working in her family's unassuming retail shop.

November 7, 2006
Twelve United Airlines employees report a sighting of an unidentified flying object over O'Hare Airport's gate C-17.

November 4, 2008
Illinois senator Barack Obama, a former Chicago community organizer, is elected the first African American president of the United States.

November 20, 2009
Oprah Winfrey announces that her talk show's run will end in 2011, after it completes its 25th season.

Serenading the Windy City

* * *

*Over the years, dozens and dozens of songs have been
written that feature or mention Chicago,
and many have become national or even international hits.
Some simply use Chicago as a big city backdrop, while others
glorify a unique aspect of the city's character or capture
a significant moment in its turbulent history.*

- **"Chicago (That Toddling Town)":** Composer Fred Fisher got
  his start in the music business in Chicago and went on to become a
  major figure in New York City's Tin Pan Alley. His Midwestern
  roots showed through, however, in "Chicago (That Toddling
  Town)," his most enduring song. The swinging tune, which paints
  Chicago as a raucous, nonstop party town, became a hit in the
  1920s and has been recorded by the likes of Tony Bennett, Frank
  Sinatra, Duke Ellington, and Benny Goodman.

- **"My Kind of Town":** In the 1964 film *Robin and the Seven
  Hoods,* Frank Sinatra and his Rat Pack buddies played Prohibition-
  era gangsters, and Frank debuted "My Kind of Town." Written by
  Jimmy Van Heusen and Sammy Cahn, the Oscar-nominated song,
  which mentions such landmarks as the Wrigley Building and the
  Stockyards, became a staple of Sinatra's repertoire.

- **"Chicago":** Written by Graham Nash in 1970 and popularized
  by the group Crosby, Stills, Nash, and Young, "Chicago" is a
  moving plea that calls on its audience to take political action.
  The song brings attention to the plight of the Chicago Seven,
  the young political activists who were tried for inciting a riot at
  the 1968 Democratic National Convention.

- **"Lake Shore Drive":** Aliotta, Haynes, and Jeremiah are a little-
  known folk group from the hinterlands of Wisconsin who likely
  would not be remembered if it weren't for their fondness for the
  distinctive Chicago thoroughfare called Lake Shore Drive. The
  trio wrote and recorded a raggy piano number that perfectly

conveys the experience of driving down the eight-lane concrete ribbon that follows almost the entire length of the city's shoreline.

- **"The Lincoln Park Pirates"**: Singer-songwriter Steve Goodman was considered by many to be the Windy City's unofficial court composer for such songs as "Daley's Gone," his heartfelt homage to the city's best-known mayor, and the witty and tender "A Dying Cub Fan's Last Request." In "Lincoln Park Pirates," he sends a blistering shot across the bow of the Lincoln Towing Company, Chicago's most notorious enforcer of private parking lot restrictions. Reminiscent of a sea shanty, the tune blasts the reviled auto impounders for their exorbitant fees and well-known habit of damaging the cars in their custody.

- **"Bad, Bad Leroy Brown"**: Jim Croce was a radio sensation in the early 1970s who was known for his distinctive pop tunes and evocative love songs. One of his most enduring numbers is "Bad, Bad Leroy Brown," a streetwise boogie number about a tough guy from Chicago's South Side who gets his comeuppance when he tries to move in on another man's wife.

- **"The Night Chicago Died"**: Paper Lace was a forgettable British pop band from the 1970s that scored a major hit in the States with "The Night Chicago Died." The insipid tune tells the fictional story of a shoot-out between Chicago police and the henchmen of bootlegger Al Capone. It is often cited as one of the worst songs of the 1970s.

- **"Sweet Home Chicago"**: One of a handful of songs written and recorded by legendary bluesman Robert Johnson, "Sweet Home Chicago" has become a staple in the blues canon and was given a huge boost in popularity when it was featured in the 1980 film *The Blues Brothers*.

You Can Thank Chicago

McDonald's

In 1940, two brothers opened a barbecue restaurant in San Bernardino, California. Within a few years, they were offering their busy patrons quick service and a pared down menu, including an unusual thin-cut version of French fries. In 1954, restaurant appliance salesman Ray Kroc visited the operation and struck a deal with the brothers to franchise their operation nationwide. Within a year, Kroc had opened the first McDonald's fast-food restaurant in the Chicago area (specifically, in the suburb of Des Plaines), and by 1956 the company had more than 700 stores nationwide. McDonald's is now one of the largest restaurant operations in the world, with outlets in more than 100 countries.

Remote Control

Headquartered in Chicago, the Zenith Corporation offered Americans one of the most well known brands of television sets in the 1950s. The company's popularity skyrocketed, however, when Zenith engineer Robert Adler developed the first practical wireless remote control. The company had previously offered a wired remote, the Lazy Bones, which had a cumbersome 20-foot cable. Adler's Space Command remote, introduced by Zenith in 1956, used ultrasonic sound to send signals to the set without wires.

Modem

In the 1970s, USRobotics was an electronics company operated by five University of Chicago graduates out of a single office on Chicago's North Side. A short while later, the company introduced the world's first commercially available computer modem, setting the foundation for the explosion of the World Wide Web and helping make the Internet a presence in almost every home in the country. By the mid-1990s, the company had become the largest provider of modems in the world, employing more than 5,000 people and earning revenues in excess of $800 million a year.

Fast Facts

- When new owners remodeled the 22-story La Salle Hotel in 1936, they paid scant attention to fire safety improvements. On June 5, 1946, someone tossed a cigarette down an elevator shaft. Sixty-one people died. Now we know why cities make contractors bring old buildings up to code.

- Quick: Who's the only Bull to hang 50 points on the opposition besides M. J.? Chet Walker, with 56 against the Cincinnati Royals on February 6, 1972. To put things in perspective, Jordan bucketed half-a-hundred 39 times.

- Bosses Michael "Hinky Dink" Kenna and "Bathhouse" John Coughlin operated the First Ward as their private graft fiefdom from 1897 to 1938. There was one simple rule: Those who paid the most got the most. Coughlin, a wannabe poet, often had his doggerel oeuvres published in the papers.

- If your NBA roots go back to the early 1960s, you remember Chicago's team before the Bulls: the Packers (1961–62; of all the names to use in Chicago!) and Zephyrs (1962–63). The latter team became the Baltimore Bullets, Capital Bullets, Washington Bullets, and Washington Wizards in sequence.

- Noteworthy antagonist and pugilist Reggie Fleming got 145 penalty minutes in his first Blackhawk season (1960–61), a high number for the day. Less well known: 37 came in a single game. A minor, three fighting majors, a misconduct, and a game misconduct. Anyone for anger management?

- Pisa has theirs, we have ours. In 1933, Niles built a 1:2 scale replica of the famous Leaning Tower. It first served as a water tower designed to supply two swimming pools at a company park, but it is now part of a branch of the YMCA.

Bachelor's Grove

✳ ✳ ✳ ✳

Hidden away inside the Rubio Woods Forest Preserve near Midlothian, Illinois, lies Bachelor's Grove Cemetery, widely reported to be one of the most haunted cemeteries in the United States. Haunted or not, the cemetery certainly has an intriguing history that raises many questions but provides few answers.

Like almost everything associated with the cemetery, the origin of the cemetery's name is shrouded in mystery. Some claim that the cemetery got its name in the early 1800s when several unmarried men built homes nearby, causing locals to nickname the area Bachelor's Grove. Others, however, believe the name was originally Batchelder's Grove, named after a family that lived in the area.

Abandoned and Vandalized

Despite its small size (about an acre), the cemetery became a popular site over the years because of its convenient location right off the Midlothian Turnpike. The quaint pond at the rear of the cemetery added to the allure, and as a result, about 200 individuals made Bachelor's Grove their final resting place.

All that changed during the 1960s when the branch of the Midlothian Turnpike that ran past the cemetery was closed, cutting it off from traffic. With the road essentially abandoned, people stopped coming to the cemetery altogether. The last burial at Bachelor's Grove took place in 1965, although there was an interment of ashes in 1989.

Without a proper road to get to the cemetery, Bachelor's Grove fell into a state of disrepair. Along with the cover of the Rubio Woods, this made the cemetery an attractive location for late-night parties, vandalism, and senseless desecration. Today, of the nearly 200 graves, only 20 or so still have tombstones. The rest have been broken or gone missing. This, combined with rumors that some graves were dug up, is why many believe that the inhabitants of Bachelor's Grove do not rest in peace.

Resident Ghosts

Who haunts Bachelor's Grove? For starters, the ghost of a woman dressed in white has been spotted late at night walking among the tombstones or sitting on top of them. So many people have seen her throughout the years that she is commonly known as the Madonna of Bachelor's Grove.

There are also reports of strange, flashing lights moving around the cemetery, especially near the algae-covered pond in the back. Some believe that the pond was used as an impromptu "burial ground" for Chicago-area gangsters and that the lights are the spirits of their victims. Others believe the ghost lights are related to the legend that, many years ago, a man plowing the nearby fields died when his horse became spooked and ran into the pond, drowning both man and horse.

A Disappearing House

Probably the most fascinating paranormal activity reported at Bachelor's Grove is that of the ghost house. On certain nights, a spectral house is said to appear in the distance along the abandoned road leading to the cemetery. Those who have witnessed this strange apparition say that the house slowly fades away until it disappears without a trace. Similarly, others have spotted a ghostly car barreling down the road, complete with glowing headlights.

Should you wish to visit Bachelor's Grove in the hopes of encountering some of these spirits, it is open every day but only during daylight hours. The abandoned road now serves as a well-worn path through the woods up to the cemetery. Just remember that you are visiting hallowed ground and the final resting places of men, women, and children.

Support Your Local Street Gang

* * * *

*Like any major urban area, Chicago has had to contend with
the problem of violent street gangs that become a dangerous blight
on low-income neighborhoods. But one innovative attempt
at reforming the city's most wayward citizens
led to a bizarre and convoluted chain of events.*

Chicago has always had its share of youthful thugs who turn to a life
of crime, from individual delinquents perpetrating petty theft to
well-organized gang enterprises that engage in robbery, drug traf-
ficking, and even murder.

In the late 1950s and early 1960s, two youth gangs on the South
and West sides grew to an unprecedented level of prominence using
similar tactics. Jeff Fort, de facto leader of a small street gang in the
Woodlawn neighborhood at the tender age of 14, used a combination of charisma, organizational skills, and violence to consolidate
dozens of neighboring gangs into the Blackstone Rangers. Edward
Perry pulled off a similar feat with his Vice Lords in the Lawndale
community around the same time. By the early 1960s, both gangs
claimed thousands of members and firmly controlled the streets in
their respective areas. Robbery, extortion, and shootings were
common, and police began to see the two groups as among the
greatest threats to public safety in the city.

When the 1960s counterculture movement took off, youth
organizations of another kind began to get significant attention from
the public and the media. Groups such as Students for a Democratic
Society brought the voice of a youthful generation into politics,
supporting liberal positions on the Vietnam War as well as on domestic issues such as race relations, sex education, and economic
inequality. While some mainstream Americans saw this political
activism of the younger generation as a positive sign, many felt
threatened by their radical beliefs and extreme, often disruptive

tactics. At the same time, the Black Panthers created even greater fear among those in the establishment; though they espoused principles of self-help, personal responsibility, and community service for young blacks, they also engaged in militant rhetoric about their right to defend themselves from oppression.

Endorsements from Jackson and Farrakhan, Funding from Merrill and Rockefeller

Fort and Perry were drawn to the positive examples of these other youth organizations and began to turn the resources at their disposal toward helping their communities. The gangs participated in civil rights marches and worked for equal housing and improved economic opportunity for their neighbors. They got involved in political campaigns and get-out-the-vote efforts aimed at breaking the grip of Chicago's Democratic machine politics. Their work in these areas drew endorsements from community leaders Jesse Jackson and Louis Farrakhan and funding from prominent businessmen such as insurance magnate W. Clement Stone and Charles Merrill Jr., son of the founder of Merrill-Lynch. The Rangers even got a federal grant to set up and run a job-training program in Woodlawn, while the Vice Lords received a grant from the Rockefeller Foundation.

The gangs were still engaging in serious criminal behavior, though, and it's unclear whether the Rangers and the Vice Lords were using political activism as a cover to draw attention away from their illicit enterprises, or if there was simply a split within the gangs over whether or not to give up their criminal ways. The Chicago Police certainly weren't buying the story and added significant resources to the gang units, stepping up arrests and targeting the gang's leadership. Some Chicago insiders believe the police effort was really a backlash instigated by Mayor Richard J. Daley out of fear of the political power the gangs were helping muster. Whatever the case, the law-enforcement blitz proved effective in dismantling the Blackstone Rangers; Fort was sentenced to federal prison for an alleged domestic terrorism plot involving rocket launchers purchased from Libya. Perry wound up dead, and the Vice Lords new leadership returned their focus to strictly criminal activities. They remain a menace in Chicago and several other cities.

Bittersweetness

* * * *

The Bears' first-round draft pick in 1975 would become one of the most accomplished runners the NFL would ever see.

In the first four decades after the National Football League was founded in the 1920s, Chicagoans enjoyed bragging rights, as the Bears fielded some of the best athletes and most innovative tactics in the league. As the 1970s arrived, however, the team found itself in a rapid spiral toward the cellar, and it seemed the Monsters of the Midway might never regain their former glory.

A Man of Many and Varied Talents

In 1975, general manager Jim Finks drafted Walter Payton, a little-known running back from Jackson State. Payton led the league in kick returns his rookie season, and the next year he began to show true brilliance as a running back, earning the first of nine trips to the Pro Bowl. When he left the field for the last time in 1987, he took with him an unprecedented slew of league records: 3,838 rushing attempts for 16,726 yards, 110 touchdowns, and 77 games with 100 yards gained. He also had 492 pass receptions netting 4,538 yards and 15 more touchdowns. As if that weren't enough, he threw 11 completed passes, eight of which yielded touchdowns, and he was also the team's backup punter. Payton stood five feet ten and weighed 200 pounds, a remarkably small stature for a power runner. He relied on rigorous conditioning to bring his body to its peak of power and stamina every season. Payton reintroduced the stiff-arm to the game, and defensive players feared him for it. In addition to his ball-carrying prowess, he was also generally recognized as one of the best blocking backs in the game.

Sweetness

Despite that physical toughness and love of competition, Payton was well known for his offbeat humor, warm heart, and gentle demeanor, which in part accounts for his nickname of "Sweetness" (though his brilliance on the field also contributed to this moniker). He was even-tempered on and off the field and always seemed to have a word of encouragement for other players. After being tackled, he would jump to his feet and hold out a hand to help up the defender who had just taken him down. While other ball handlers developed elaborate celebration routines to perform after a touchdown, when Payton reached the end zone, he typically handed the ball over to one of his offensive lineman and gave him the opportunity to spike it.

The Passing of a Legend

After retiring in 1987, Payton devoted the same discipline and energy he had shown on the field to an array of successful business and charitable endeavors. Tragically, however, he was diagnosed with a rare liver disorder that soon led to cancer. Payton handled even this tragic circumstance with his signature grace. In a 1999 *Sports Illustrated* interview shortly before his death, Payton reflected on his illness and his legacy: "The love that people, the fans, have shown through letters and phone calls makes me cry when I think about it. Those letters keep me going. It's not often that you find out how many people you've touched. . . . I wouldn't wish this situation on anyone, but I've found real peace and understand the impact athletes have on people. Those athletes who say they're not role models and that they don't care never want to have that discussion with me."

Payton passed away in 1999 at age 45. The city held a public memorial ceremony at Soldier Field attended by tens of thousands of fans. An enduring figure in the NFL record books, Payton's name also lives on through the Walter Payton Cancer Fund, the Walter Payton Liver Center at the University of Illinois Medical Center, the Walter and Connie Payton Foundation, and Chicago's Walter Payton College Preparatory High School.

Index

* * * *

Lurie Garden, 182, 183
Lutnia restaurant, 15

M

Madonna of Bachelor's Grove, 269
Magnuson, Keith, 245
Mailer, Norman, 119
Mail order companies, 56, 123, 153
Malamud, Bernard, 77
Malnati, Adolpho "Rudy," 79
Malört schnapps, 186–87
Manhattan building, 123
Manhattan Project, 136–37
Mansueto, Joseph, 248–49
Man With the Golden Arm, The
    (Algren), 124
Marquette, Jacques, 11
Married with Children, 237
Marshall, Benjamin, 77
Marshall Field & Co., 56, 153
Maud Martha (Brooks), 217
Maxwell Street, 250–51
Mayors. *See also specific names.*
    assassinated, 19, 110
    Daleys, 61–63
    Harold Washington, 32–33
    political parties, 233
    quiz, 95
McCaskey, Ed, 77
McCormick, Cyrus, 11
McDonalds Cycle Center, 182–83
McDonald's restaurant, 266
McGovern, George, 97
McGurn, "Machine Gun" Jack, 28, 218,
    233
McMullin, Fred, 226
McNally, Andrew, 16–17
Meatpacking industry, 39, 138–39, 153,
    216, 235
Medill, Joseph, 26
Medinah Temple, 64
Memorial Day Massacre, 157, 225
Memory (French, Bacon sculpture), 178
Mencken, H. L., 75
Meng, George, 43
Merchandise Mart, 213
Mergenthaler Linotype Building, 243
Merrill, John, 205
Mexican Americans, 169, 177, 229

Mexican Independence Day parades, 229
Midsommarfest (Andersonville), 261
Midway Plaisance, 129
Mies van der Rohe, Ludwig, 117, 129
Mikita, Stan, 245
Millennium Park, 35, 181–83
Milwaukee Avenue, 198, 199
Miro, Joan, 35
Miskowski, Mary, 239
Missile bases, 146
Molecular gastronomy, 213
Monroe, Marilyn, 225
Montgomery Ward, 56, 123, 153
Montrose Point Bird Sanctuary, 221
Moore, Alfie, 257
Moore, Henry, 137
Moran, George "Bugs," 27–28
Morganfield, McKinley (Muddy
    Waters), 259
Morningstar, 248–49
Morris, Buckner S., 215
Morris, Jan, 26, 170
Moseley Braun, Carol, 196–97
Mother Jones (Mary Harris), 90
Moto restaurant, 213
Motorola company, 65, 161
Mount Carmel Cemetery, 85
Movies, 88–89, 201, 222–23
Movie stars, 99, 140
Muddy Waters (McKinley Morganfield),
    259
Mudgett, Herman Webster (H. H.
    Holmes), 44–46
Muller, Jack, 19
Mulqueen, Jack and Elaine, 106–7
Mulqueens, The, 106
Mundelein, George Cardinal, 73
Murders and murderers. *See also*
    Gangsters and criminals; *and*
    specific names.
    mayor assassinations, 19, 110
    notorious, 44–46, 130–35, 156, 194
    number of, 85
Museum of Contemporary Art, 256
Museum of Science and Industry, 113,
    129, 231
Museums
    Adler Planetarium & Astronomy
        Museum, 148, 205

Contributing Writers

✳ ✳ ✳ ✳

Mark W. Anderson is an independent writer and journalist with a long history of writing about Chicago and its people. An avid listener of jazz and big band sounds, the lifelong Chicagoan lives with his wife and small dog in a Northwest Side bungalow stacked with books and records.

Anthony G. Craine is a freelance writer living in Chicago.

Mary Fons-Misetic is a full-time freelance writer, nationally ranked slampoet, Neo-Futurist, and proud Chicagoan by choice. Read her popular blog, PaperGirl, at www.maryfons.com.

NM Gamso is a freelance writer living in Brooklyn, New York, and pursuing a Ph.D. in English literature. He grew up in the Midwest and still dreams about his beloved Chicago, which he called home for several years. In his free time, he enjoys reading, playing music, riding his bike, and reminiscing about hours blissfully wasted in Chicago's 24-hour taquerías.

Anne Holub arrived in Chicago in 2003 thinking it would be one long John Hughes movie. There have been high jinks, crazy parties, and heart-to-hearts in libraries, but very few Ferraris sent backward into trees. This is probably for the best.

J.K. Kelley has a B.A. in history from the University of Washington in Seattle. He has contributed to numerous Armchair Reader books. He resides in the desiccated sagebrush of eastern Washington with his wife, Deb, his parrot, Alex, Fabius the Labrador retriever, and Leonidas the miniature schnauzer.

David Morrow is an accomplished writer and editor who has worked in the publishing industry for more than 20 years. His recent work includes coauthoring *Florida on Film* and contributing to the reference guide *Disasters, Accidents, and Crises in American History*.

Laura Pearson lives in the Windy City, where she writes about arts and culture for a variety of publications. She also works as a literary researcher for the Chicago Artists Resource, a program of the Chicago Department of Cultural Affairs.

Dawn Reiss is a writer, reporter, and editor. A former *St. Petersburg Times* staff writer and Chicago Headline Club president, her work has been published by *Travel + Leisure*, *Chicago* magazine, *Chicago Tribune*, CNN.com, and *American Way*. She blogs at "A Quirk in the Road" for True/Slant.com.

Adam Selzer writes books for young readers by day and serves as a historian/guide for Weird Chicago Tours by night. If you can find two cooler jobs, take them! His nonfiction books include *The Smart Aleck's Guide to American History* and *Your Neighborhood Gives Me the Creeps: True Tales of an Accidental Ghost Hunter*. Check him out at http://www.adamselzer.com

Troy Taylor is the author of more than 50 books on ghosts and crime and is the founder of the American Ghost Society. He resides in central Illinois.

Kelly Wittmann is the author or coauthor of seven educational, humor, and reference books. She lives in Chicago.